At Tate Modern, the 2020 and 2024 exhibitions were the joint curatorial effort of Carine Harmand, The John Ellerman Foundation Curator, and Yasufumi Nakamori, former Senior Curator of Photography, with Amrita Dhallu, Assistant Curator, International Art, Sarah Allen, former Assistant Curator, International Art, and Kerryn Greenberg, former Head of International Collection Exhibitions. Administrative support was provided in the first phase by Amy Emmerson Martin, Assistant Curator, and later by Lynn Rothwell, Exhibitions Assistant, and Stephanie Hadfield, Exhibitions Assistant. Hayley McConnell, Exhibitions Registrar, and later Rita Machado, Registrar, and Sean Crawford, Assistant Registrar, served as registrars.

The exhibition traveled to our partnering institutions: Maison Européenne de la Photographie in Paris, Gropius Bau in Berlin, Bildmuseet at Umeå University in Sweden, IVAM in Valencia, GL Strand in Copenhagen, National Gallery of Iceland in Reykjavik, and Kunstmuseum Luzern in Switzerland. Our sincere thanks go to the teams of each one of these galleries. These collaborations remain meaningful and vital to the generation and success of this exhibition.

For their unerring support we thank Maria Balshaw, Director, Tate; Catherine Wood, Director of Programme, Tate Modern; Achim Borchardt-Hume, former Director of Exhibitions and Programmes, Tate Modern; and Neil Casey, Associate Director, Business and Operations, Amy Dillmann, Head of Programme Management, Tate Modern; Helen Sainsbury, former Head of Exhibitions and Programme Management, Tate Modern, along with Rachel Kent, former Head of International Touring Exhibitions, Tate Modern. We express heartfelt thanks to the teams in Research and Interpretation, Press, Marketing, Public Programmes, Design, Installation, Development, Uniqlo Tate Lates and Tate Exchange, who have all worked diligently and with passion to realise the exhibition. Special thanks are due to members of our LGTBQIA+ and BAME networks, including Alex Pilcher, James Brandon, Tram Nguyen, Fiontán Moran, La Kingsbeer, Rudi Minto de Wijs, Nick Virk and Tamsin Hong, and those who generously offered their time, expertise and advice in the early planning of the show. Thanks are also due to colleagues in Conservation, Library and Archive, Front of House and Security. We thank our colleagues in Tate Publishing: Bill Jones, Roz Hill, and in particular Alice Chasey, whose patience and advice throughout has been hugely appreciated. We are grateful to Jenny Wilson for copy-editing and proofreading the catalogue texts. Thanks are due also to Lewis Chaplin and Sarah Piegay Espenon of Loose Joints Publishing for designing a beautiful book.

We are grateful to the Zanele Muholi Exhibition Supporters Circle, including Wendy Fisher and The Kirsh Foundation, Tate Patrons and Tate Members for supporting the exhibition.

Muholi is an artist who understood, early in their career as an artist, the power of the photographic image to represent marginalised individuals and identities. At the point of their retrospective in 2024, the proliferation of photographic images in our social landscape, and as social currency, makes the singular style and activist reach of Muholi's body of work all the more recognizable as highly significant, and pioneering. We are grateful to the artist, and thrilled to be able to share this exhibition with our audiences at last.

Karin Hindsbo
Director, Tate Modern

Glossary

Sinazo Chiya, Genevieve Louw,
Bongani Matabane, Maggie Matich

Glossary

Sinazo Chiya, Genevieve Louw,
Bongani Matabane, Maggie Matich

ALLY

An individual who actively supports the social movements and rights of LGBTQIA+ and other marginalised identities, but who does not identify as LGBTQIA+ or as a member of said marginalised groups.

APARTHEID

A former policy/oppressive system that was officially implemented in South Africa from 1948 until 1994, to enforce racial segregation and political, economic and social discrimination against people of colour or anyone who was not classified as white. The word 'apartheid' is an Afrikaans word meaning 'apartness'. The term has also been used to refer to global forms of institutionalised/systemic racial and socio-economic oppression that is still prevalent in societies across the world.

ASEXUAL

An umbrella term used to describe those with a variation of romantic and/or sexual attraction, including a lack of attraction. The term can also describe people who are emotionally, psychologically and intellectually attracted to people, or where their attraction is not limited to physical sexual expression.

ASSIGNMENT

Within the dominant culture informed by Western scientific models that classify gender and sex as binary, gender and sex are commonly assigned at birth based on external biological sex characteristics (genitalia) and reproductive functions. A vulva-bearing child is typically assigned female at birth (commonly shortened to 'AFAB'), while a penis-bearing child is typically assigned male at birth (commonly shortened to 'AMAB'). AFAB and AMAB are terms commonly used by transgender, gender-non-conforming and non-binary people to demonstrate that the sex and/or gender one was assigned at birth may not necessarily match one's true gender identity.

BISEXUAL

An umbrella term used to describe a romantic and/or sexual orientation towards more than one gender. Bisexual people may describe themselves using one or more of a variety of terms, including (but not limited to) pansexual and queer.

BLACK LESBIAN FEMINISM

A political identity, movement and school of thought that incorporates perspectives, experiences and politics around race, gender, class and sexual orientation, and surfaces the inextricable links between them.

BUTCH

A term used in queer culture to describe someone who often (but not always) expresses themselves in a typically masculine way. This term should not be used to describe someone unless they expressly identify as such.

CIS/CISGENDER	A term used to describe someone whose gender identity matches the sex and gender they were assigned at birth.
CIVIL UNION	Also known as a civil partnership, a civil union is a legally recognised arrangement which grants most or all of the rights, responsibilities and legal consequences of a marriage except the title itself. Civil unions were created primarily to provide recognition in law for same-sex couples and partnerships.
'CORRECTIVE RAPE'	A term used to describe a hate crime in which a person is raped because of their perceived sexual orientation or gender identity. The intended consequence of such acts is to enforce heterosexuality and gender conformity.
FAMILY	A term widely used by queer and trans people to identify other queer and trans people. Also known as 'chosen family'.
FEMME	A term used in LGBTQIA+ culture to describe someone who often (but not always) expresses themselves in a typically feminine way. This term should not be used to describe someone unless they expressly identify as such.
GAY	A term used to refer to a man, trans person or non-binary person who tends to have a romantic and/or sexual orientation towards men. The term can also be used more broadly and colloquially to describe a same-sex or queer orientation.
GENDER	Often expressed in terms of masculinity and femininity, gender is culturally determined and is assumed from the sex assigned at birth. One's gender is made up of one's gender identity (a person's innate sense of their own gender) and gender expression (how a person outwardly expresses their gender).
GENDER BINARY	The system of dividing gender into two distinct categories – man and woman – thus excluding non-binary and gender-non-conforming individuals.
GENDER DYSPHORIA	Used to describe a person's discomfort or distress because there is a mismatch between their sex assigned at birth and their gender identity.
GENDER NON-CONFORMING/ NON-CONFORMITY	A person who does not conform to the binary gender categories that society prescribes (man and woman) through their gender identity/expression.
HATE CRIME	Any incident that may or may not constitute a criminal offence, perceived as being motivated by prejudice or hate. The perpetrators seek to demean and dehumanise their victims, whom they consider different from them based on actual or perceived race, ethnicity, gender, age, sexual orientation, disability, health status, nationality, social origin, religious convictions, culture, language or other characteristics.

HETERONORMATIVITY — A socio-political system that, predicated on the gender binary, upholds heterosexuality as the norm or default sexual orientation. Heteronormativity encompasses a belief that people fall into distinct and 'complementary' genders (men and women) with natural roles in life. It assumes that sexual, romantic and marital relations are most fitting between a cisgender man and a cisgender woman, positioning all other sexual orientations as 'deviations'.

HOMONATIONALISM — A form of LGBTQIA+ advocacy that frames LGBTQIA+ rights in nationalistic terms that privilege North American and European expressions over those of the Middle East and the Global South, particularly Africa. Homonationalism sees the conceptual realignment of LGBTQIA+ activism to fit the goals and ideologies of both neoliberalism and the far right in order to justify racist, classist, Islamophobic and xenophobic perspectives. This framing is based on prejudices that migrant people are supposedly homophobic, and that Western society is egalitarian.

HOMOPHOBIA — The fear or dislike of someone based on prejudice or negative attitudes, beliefs or views about LGBTQIA+ people.

HOMOSEXUAL — A person who has a romantic and/or sexual orientation towards someone of the same gender. 'Homosexual' is often considered a more medical term. The terms 'lesbian' and 'gay' are now more generally used.

INTERSECTIONALITY — Emerging from the traditions of critical race theory, womanism and Black feminist thought, intersectionality encompasses the study of overlapping or intersecting social identities and related systems of oppression, domination or discrimination. The term was formalised by legal scholar Kimberlé Crenshaw in 1989 in a discussion around Black women's employment in the US. Intersectionality rejects the notion of universal experiences of womanhood in favour of a more holistic assessment of how one's race, class, ethnicity, age, ability, sexuality, nationality and religion can impact one's experience of womanhood or gender, but also how these social inequalities intertwine with and shape one another.

INTERSEX — A term used to describe a person who may have biological attributes that do not fit with societal assumptions about what constitutes 'male' or 'female'. These biological variations may manifest in different ways and at different stages throughout an individual's life. Being intersex relates to biological sex characteristics and is distinct from a person's sexual orientation or gender identity.

ISINGQUMO — A type of language used amongst the LGBTQIA+ community in South Africa, mostly among the Nguni people.

ISISTABANE/ STABANE	A slur or derogatory isiZulu term used in vernacular language to refer to a person who is from the LGBTQIA+ community in the Southern African context. Translated into English, the term means a person who is born with both male and female 'parts'.
LESBIAN	A term used to refer to a woman, trans person or non-binary person who tends to have a romantic and/or sexual orientation towards women or non-binary femmes.
LGBTQIA+	An acronym standing for lesbian, gay, bisexual, transgender, queer, intersex and asexual. This is not an exhaustive list, as denoted by the inclusion of the plus symbol, which nods to the varying sexual orientations and gender identities that exist around the world.
LOBOLA	Also known as *lobolo,* lobola is a customary practice of marriage whereby the bridegroom's family and kin transfer certain goods to the bride's family in order to validate a customary marriage. Historically this was in the form of cattle, but today monetary payment is preferred, depending on the bride's family.
MSM	An acronym standing for men who have sex with men. MSM may or may not identify as gay, queer or bisexual.
NECKLACING	A practice of extrajudicial torture and execution whereby a burning rubber tyre is forced around a person's neck. Under apartheid, necklacing was sometimes used within the Black community to punish those who were perceived to have collaborated with the apartheid government.
NON-BINARY	An umbrella term for people whose gender identity does not sit comfortably with 'man' or 'woman' (also often referred to as genderqueer). Non-binary identities are varied and can include people who identify with some aspects of binary identities, while others reject them entirely.
OUTED	When an LGBTQIA+ person's sexual orientation or gender identity is disclosed without their consent.
PANSEXUAL	A term that refers to a person whose romantic and/or sexual attraction towards others is not limited by sex or gender.
PASSBOOK (DOMPAS)/ REFERENCE BOOK	An identification book or document that every person of colour or anyone who was not classified as white had to carry under the pass laws of apartheid. The book was made up of two parts. One part had a laminated identity card that featured the name of the bearer, their ethnic affiliation, the date the card was issued, the signature of an official, and a black and white portrait photograph. The other part included five sections which listed information on permissions to enter urban areas, record of required medical

examinations, names and addresses of employers, work status and receipts for tax payments. Colloquially, among the Black South African population, these passes were often referred to derogatorily as the dompas, an Afrikaans term literally meaning 'dumb'/'stupid pass'.

PATRIARCHY

A social hierarchy that privileges and prioritises men over women and other gender identities.

PENCIL TEST

A racist, dehumanising test that was devised to assist authorities in racial classification under apartheid. When officials were unsure if a person should be classified as white or of colour, a pencil would be pushed into their hair. If the pencil fell out, signalling that their hair was straight rather than curly, kinky or coily, the person 'passed' and was 'classified' as white.

PEOPLE/PERSON OF COLOUR (POC)

A term used to denote someone who is not considered white. The term is used to emphasise the common experiences of systemic racism amongst people of colour.

PINKWASHING

A term with multiple meanings, but that commonly refers to the appropriation of the LGBTQIA+ movement in order to promote some corporate or political agenda. The term is used to describe the practices of entities who market themselves as 'gay-friendly' to gain favour with progressives, while simultaneously masking aspects of their practices that are violent and undemocratic.

PRONOUNS

Words we use to refer to people's gender in conversation – for example, 'he' or 'she', or gender-neutral pronouns such as 'they'.

QTIPOC

An acronym standing for queer, trans and intersex people of colour.

QUEER

An umbrella term used by those who reject heteronormativity. Although some people view the word as a slur, it was reclaimed by the queer community, who have embraced it as an empowering and subversive identity.

SAFE SPACE

An environment that enables all persons, including sexual and gender minorities, to be free to express themselves without fear of discrimination or violation of their rights and dignity. Individual actions and reactions are key in upholding or violating a safe space.

SANGOMA

A traditional African healer who specialises in treating people's spiritual and physical diseases by looking into their past and future and connecting them with the ancestors. Healers believe that they are called by their ancestors to take on this important and respected position in society.

SEX

Sex is distinct from gender. Sex is assigned to a person at birth on the basis of biological sex characteristics (genitalia) and reproductive functions.

TRANSGENDER	An umbrella term used to describe people whose gender is not the same as, or does not sit comfortably with, the sex they were assigned at birth. Some transgender people are binary-identified and others are not.
TRANSITION	The steps a trans person may take to live in the gender with which they identify. Each person's transition involves different processes. For some this involves medical intervention or gender-affirming healthcare such as hormone therapy and surgeries (medical transition), but not all trans people want or are able to have this. Transitioning might also involve things such as telling friends and family, dressing differently, changing one's pronouns (social transition) and changing official documents (legal transition).
TRANSMISOGYNOIR	A term that characterises the marginalisation of Black trans women and trans-feminine people and captures the intersection of transphobia, racism and misogyny. It is used to denote the fact that Black trans women experience a different, racialised form of misogyny that is compounded with transphobia.
TRANSMISOGYNY	A term capturing the interlocking discrimination of transphobia and misogyny. Transmisogyny includes negative attitudes, hate and discrimination toward transgender individuals who fall on the feminine side of the gender spectrum, particularly trans women and transfeminine people.
TRANSPHOBIA	The fear or dislike of someone based on the fact that they are transgender, including the denial/refusal to accept their gender identity.
WHITE SUPREMACY	A racist ideology in which people defined and perceived as white are central to, superior to and should dominate people of other races, and the practices based on this ideology.
WSW	An acronym standing for women who have sex with women. WSW may or may not identify as lesbian, queer or bisexual.
ZULU	A Bantu ethnic group and language of Southern Africa situated within the Nguni people. They are a branch of the southern Bantu and have close ethnic, linguistic and cultural ties with the Swazi and Xhosa. The Zulu are South Africa's largest ethnic group, with an estimated population of 10 million, residing mainly in the province of KwaZulu-Natal.

The Queer Spectacular:
Zanele Muholi and Visual Redress

Candice Jansen

Zanele Muholi photographs a Black history for the present. Queer life appears as personifications of a necessity to be seen and an urgency to be known by a different gaze. The Black LGBTQIA+ history that Muholi records, one portrait at a time, is not a fictional past. Their portraits become monuments. Their figures may pose as history, but Muholi's portraiture rather presents a record of existence that insists: 'we exist in the visual archive [in order] to teach people about our history, to re-think what history is all about, to reclaim it for ourselves'.[1] Muholi and their people are of a cusp generation, old enough to have had an apartheid childhood and to remember what apartheid felt like. Yet, the feeling of apartheid, not as memory but as vision, still frames how South Africans see Black queer bodies as threatening, un-sacred, and tragic – never as national history. Muholi's portraits speak to shed light on 'this silencing of our histories and contributions'.[2] Their visual archive is a place 'where we bring forth our own narratives'[3] that 'lives on beyond us'[4] and beyond Muholi themself, who, after their first exhibition, *Visual Sexuality* (2004) at the Johannesburg Art Gallery, stepped into a historical void of queer practice in African photography.

Muholi's queer practice undercuts hetero-colonial-apartheid genealogies of time. Alana Kumbier calls this time of the archive 'normative time, characterised by linear progression, firm past/present distinctions, and generational logics of inheritance'.[5] By photographing from and within lived experiences of Black LGBTQIA+ community, Muholi presents queer stories as political visions that subvert oppressive visual norms, and transfigures them into new visual principles. Muholi queers these notions of time to shape how histories and futures can be seen in the present. Their collective intervention, between photographer and photographed, arrives at a queer visual place that Kumbier calls 'a different modality for living historically, or putting the past into meaningful and transformational relation with the present'.[6]

Visual history may preoccupy Muholi as a photographer and as an activist, but their practice is future-looking, photographing in what Tina Campt calls a 'grammar of black feminist futurity'.[7] Campt understands this as a 'grammar of possibility that moves beyond a simple definition of the future tense as *what will be* in the future'.[8] This grammar 'moves beyond the future perfect tense of *that which will have happened* prior to a reference point in the future. It strives for the tense of possibility that grammarians refer to as the future real conditional or *that which will have **had to** happen*.'[9] The tense of Muholi's portraiture becomes, as Campt would call it, 'a performance of a future that hasn't yet happened but must',[10] empowering imagination 'beyond current fact'.[11] Muholi's activist queer practice visualises from the limits of history and confronts us with how far we still need to travel in our images to reimagine South African identities. They un-fix Black queer representations from the bondage of the present and project prefigured self-images that appear to be 'living the future *now*'.[12]

This queering of time, as Muholi describes, means to 'contrast'. The drama of their portraiture unsettles and blackens visions which stir 'that confusion, that mix, that fix', which they claim 'is based on confusion, on confusing'.[13] Contrast, Muholi explains, 'is when two opposing forces clash. Contrast is about *difference*.'[14] Contrast is a queer gesture through which Muholi reinvents the difference of race, gender and sexuality and the difference of time, space and embodiment to redress a visual difference once denied by apartheid. Their visual intention grew from the struggle for the visibility of Black LGBTQIA+ lives, made invisible with stigma, violence and the classificatory nature of South African institutions. By living their future now, and refusing the current precarity of Black queer experience, Muholi's portraiture inhabits what Campt claims as 'a future against all odds'.[15]

Contrasting is not a quiet practice. It is a spectacular one that returns us to a formative distinction in South African cultural studies made by Njabulo Ndebele in his anthology, *The Rediscovery of the Ordinary* (1991). The title essay was presented as a keynote address at the conference on New Writing in Africa: Continuity and Change held at the Commonwealth Institute, London, in 1984. It was a time for South Africans to think beyond apartheid; a time that called for different ways of reading Black writing beyond what Ndebele calls 'the spectacle'. Apartheid had confined the aesthetics of Black experience in literature into the categorical, in which the Black body is represented in either pain or protest and thus overdetermined by politics or the demonstration of a collective experience. Ndebele does not conceive of 'the spectacle' as a singular mode of representation. He presents a genealogy of 'the spectacle' in varied terms of social absurdity, dramatisation and struggle, which share visual ground. The spectacle, he writes, represents 'the complete exteriority of everything: the dramatic contrasts ... the lack of specificity of place and character so that we have spectacular ritual ... turned into symbol'.[16]

Ndebele believed that 'the ordinary' was a practice bound up in an attention to detail or intricacy that was concerned with 'intimate knowledge, observation, analytical thought [and] the sobering power of contemplation, of close analysis, and the mature acceptance of failure, weakness and limitations'.[17] It posed a necessary challenge to 'the spectacle'. Muholi presents us with how far we have come since Ndebele's distinction, blurring binaries that may no longer serve South African emancipation. They demonstrate that visibility need not be incompatible with interiority. Their backgrounds may lack specificity, but Muholi's characterisation does not. Their photography is ritual that queers visibility by surfacing gender and sexual identities in exteriorising ways. The exterior can become the interior made visible. Seeing should be meaning in their visual activism that makes their figures shine with spectacular imagination. If 'the spectacle' implies an objectifying gaze, Muholi in contrast evokes 'the spectacular' as reinvention; as a means with which to dull the monotony and the violence of the everyday. Muholi's portraits do not present a spectacle of queer Black life. They represent a spectacular recuperation of its visibility that does not diagnose Black queer vulnerability, but rather surfaces vulnerability in the flesh. They give it a look. They wear it as armour, disguise and purpose.

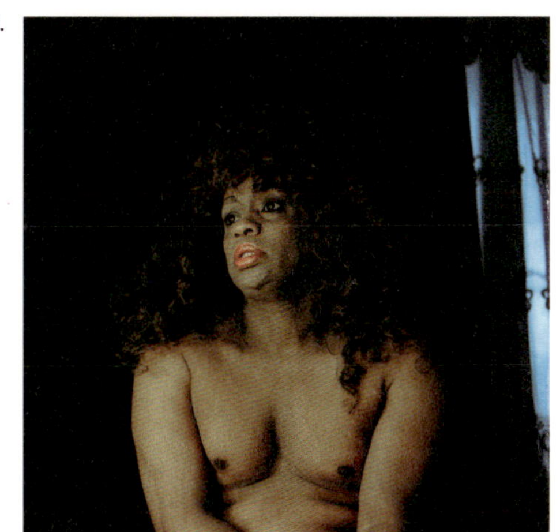

I.

Notice the amber light above which 'La Rochelle II' (2007) is seen. Their triumph is laid bare and lit from below. The burnt shadows between skin folds look touched by the hand, not the camera. La Rochelle II is cast in a soft yet heroic light that warms the almost blackened room. A patterned lace curtain is draped as if hung in a house or a bedroom. Their ordinariness takes on the spectacular warmth of a blue night in which a red lip of colour looks as if to speak. They sit on their perch, ready for flight or for repose. La Rochelle II appears both as naked reality and optical projection of their mind, and Muholi's vision. Their exposure is a vulnerable spectacle. Domestic nostalgia is placed visibly behind them. Their back is to the veil. They face what is to come with a gaze fixed outside of the frame, offering a means to be seen. Muholi may have photographed them, but they exposed themselves to the light.

I. Zanele Muholi, La Rochelle II, 2007

Only Half the
Picture

2003–2006

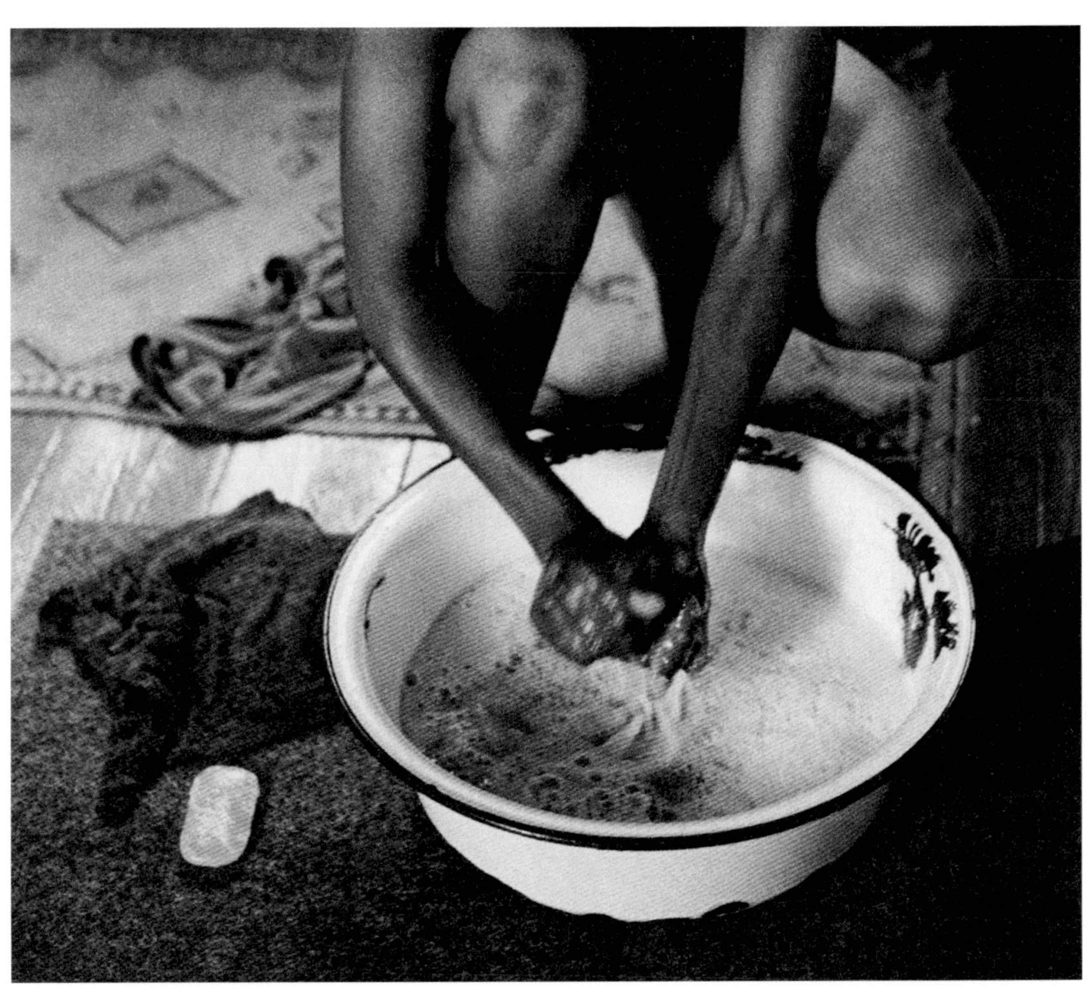

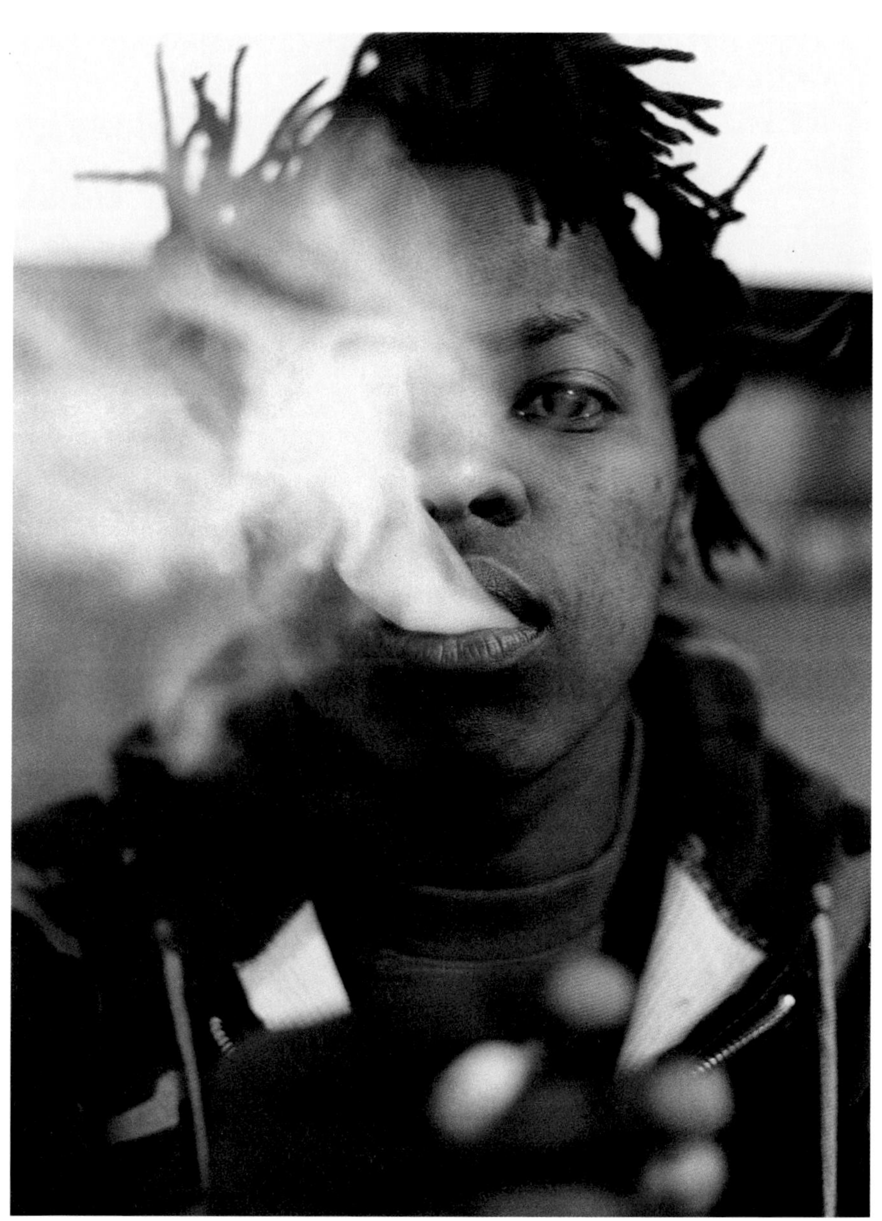

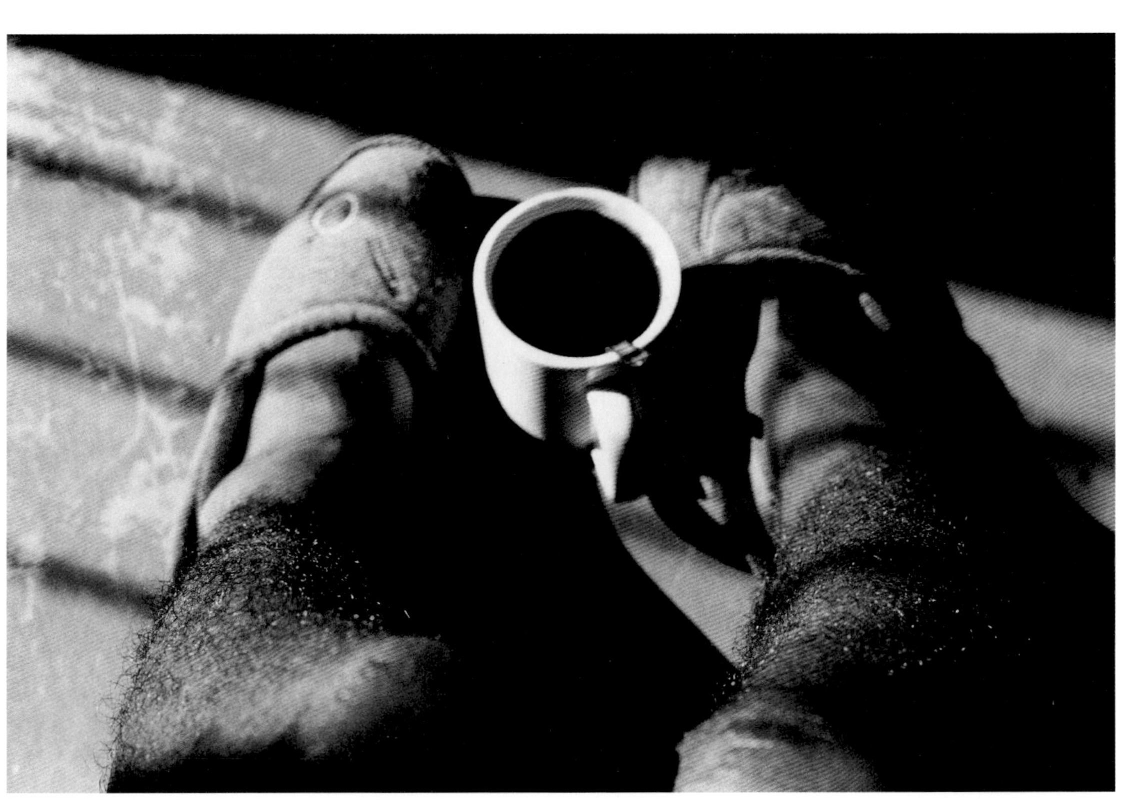

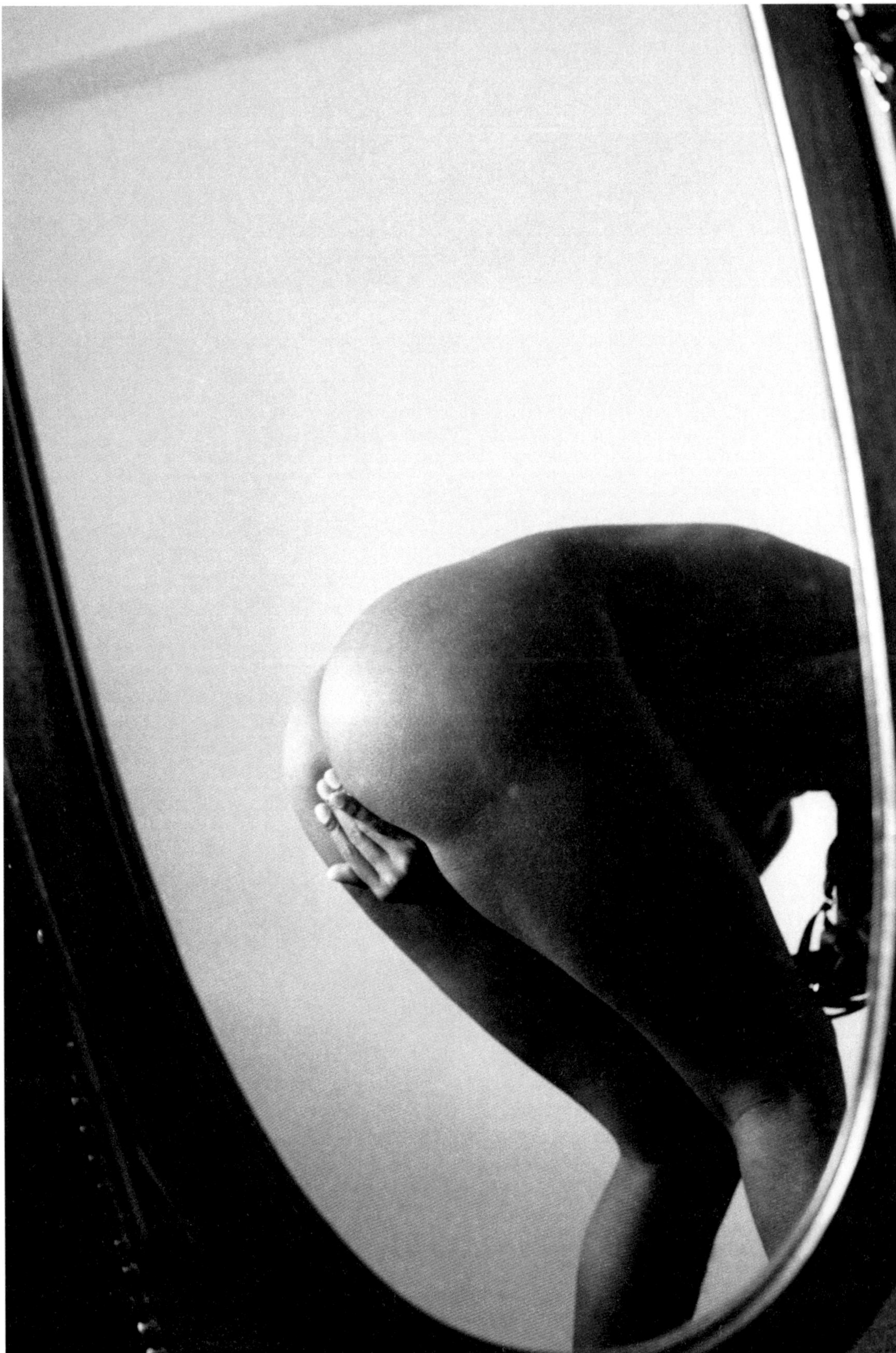

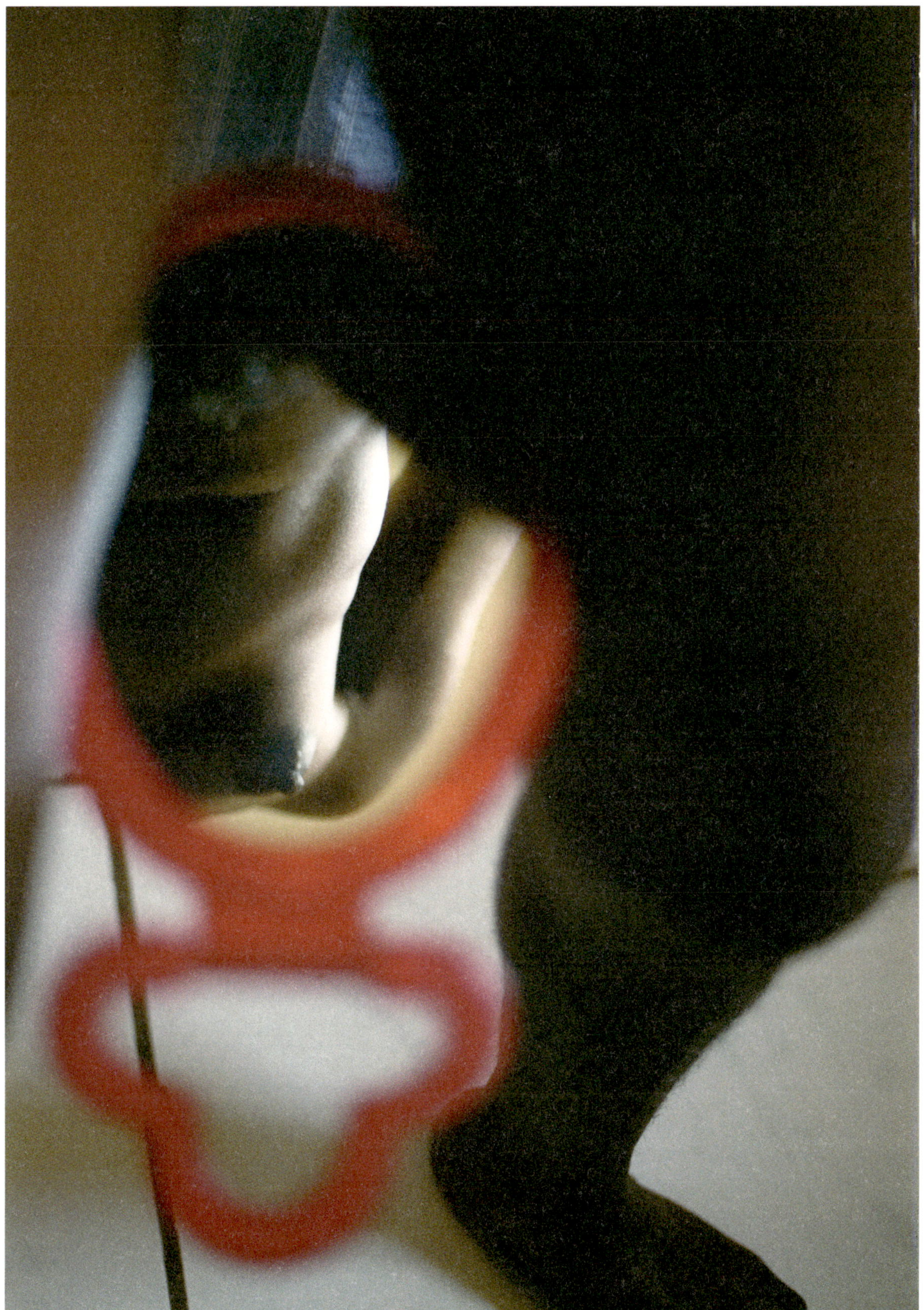

O.B. 2290/12/2004
Cas: 753/12/2004
ATT: Rape + Assault G.B.H.
Tel: (011) 936-1199.
D/Inspector Qilingana.
SUID-AFRIKAANSE POLISIEDIENS
C.S.C
1 6 DEC 2004.
C.S.C
MEADOWLANDS: SOWETO
SOUTH AFRICAN POLICE SERVICE
Roem

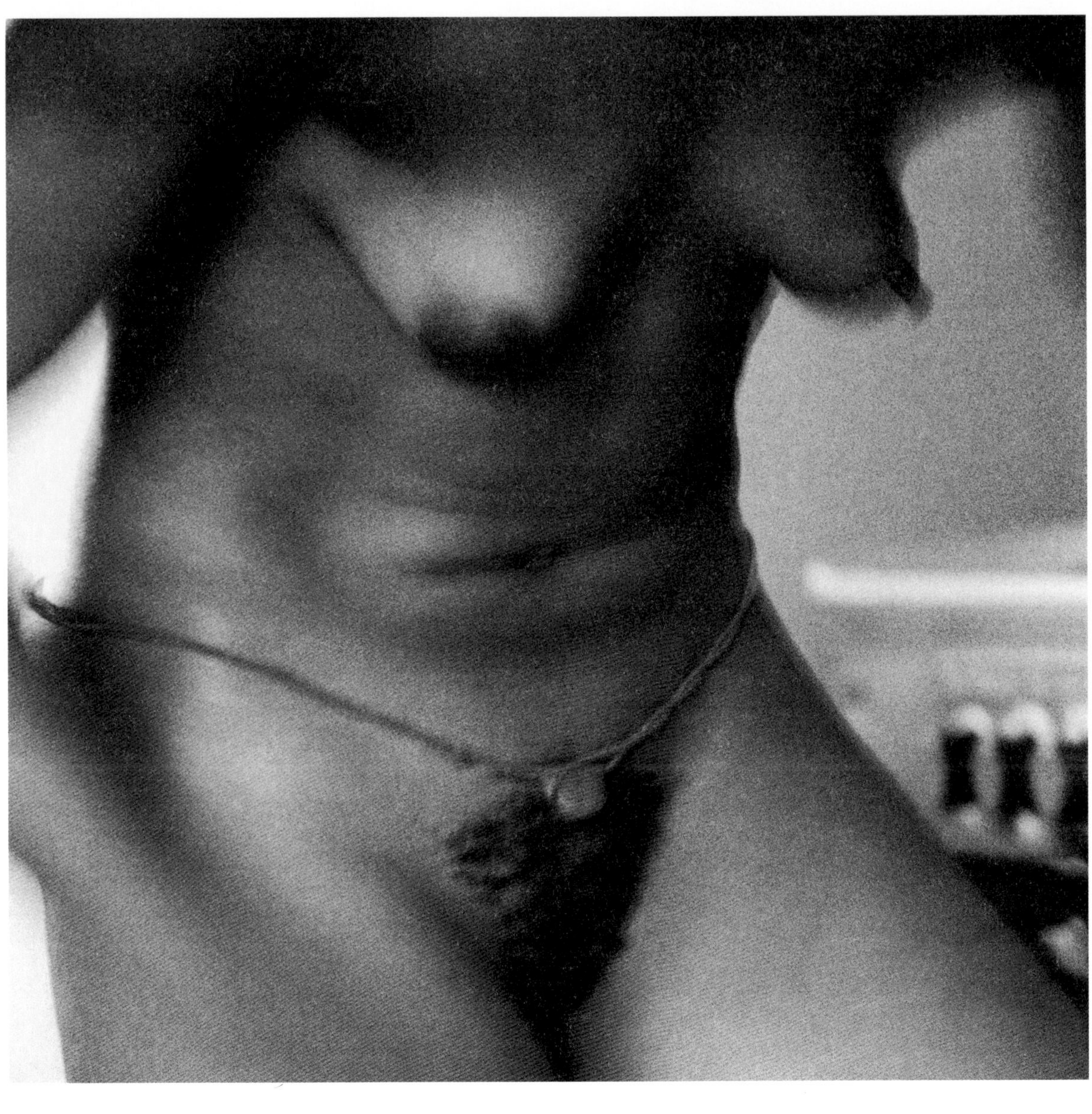

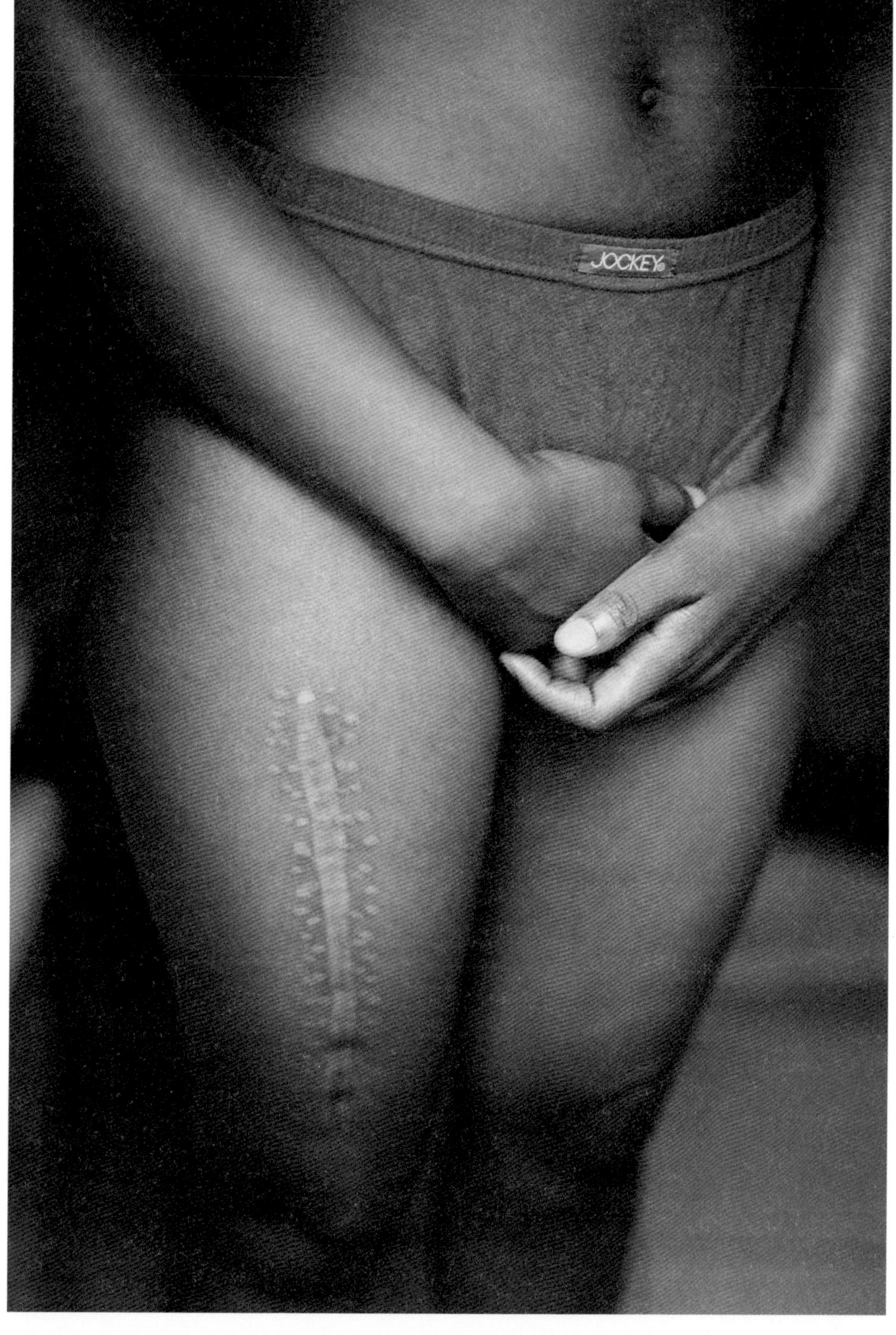

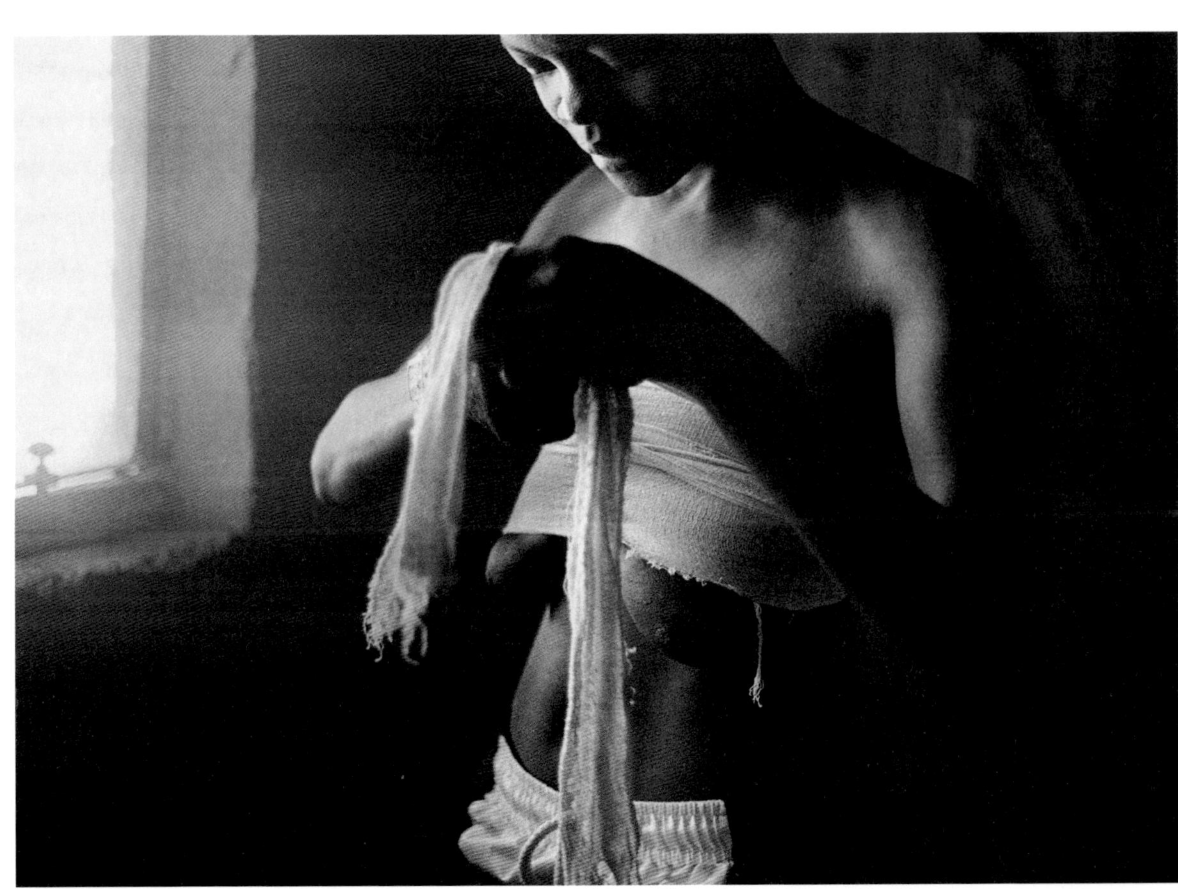

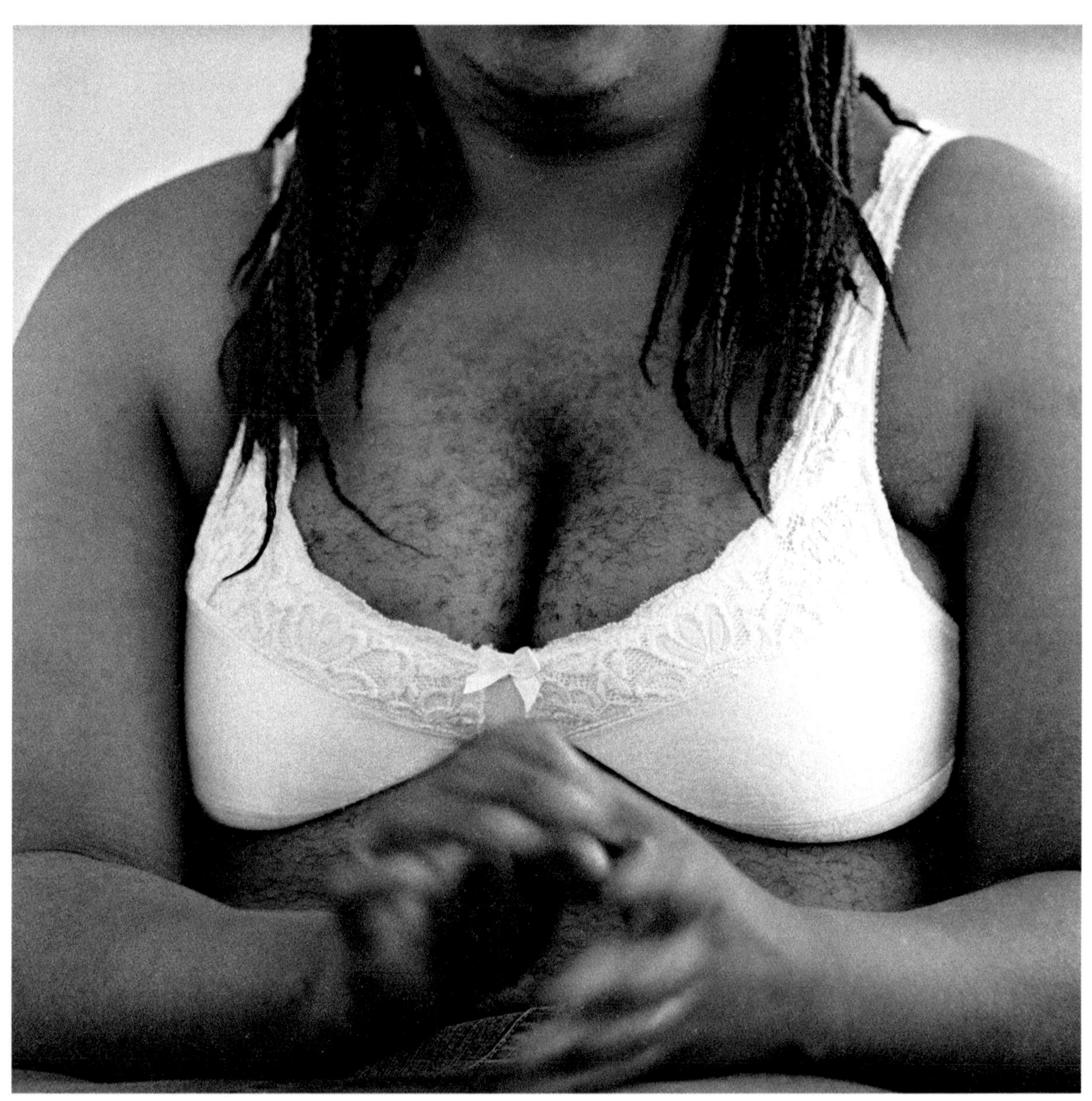

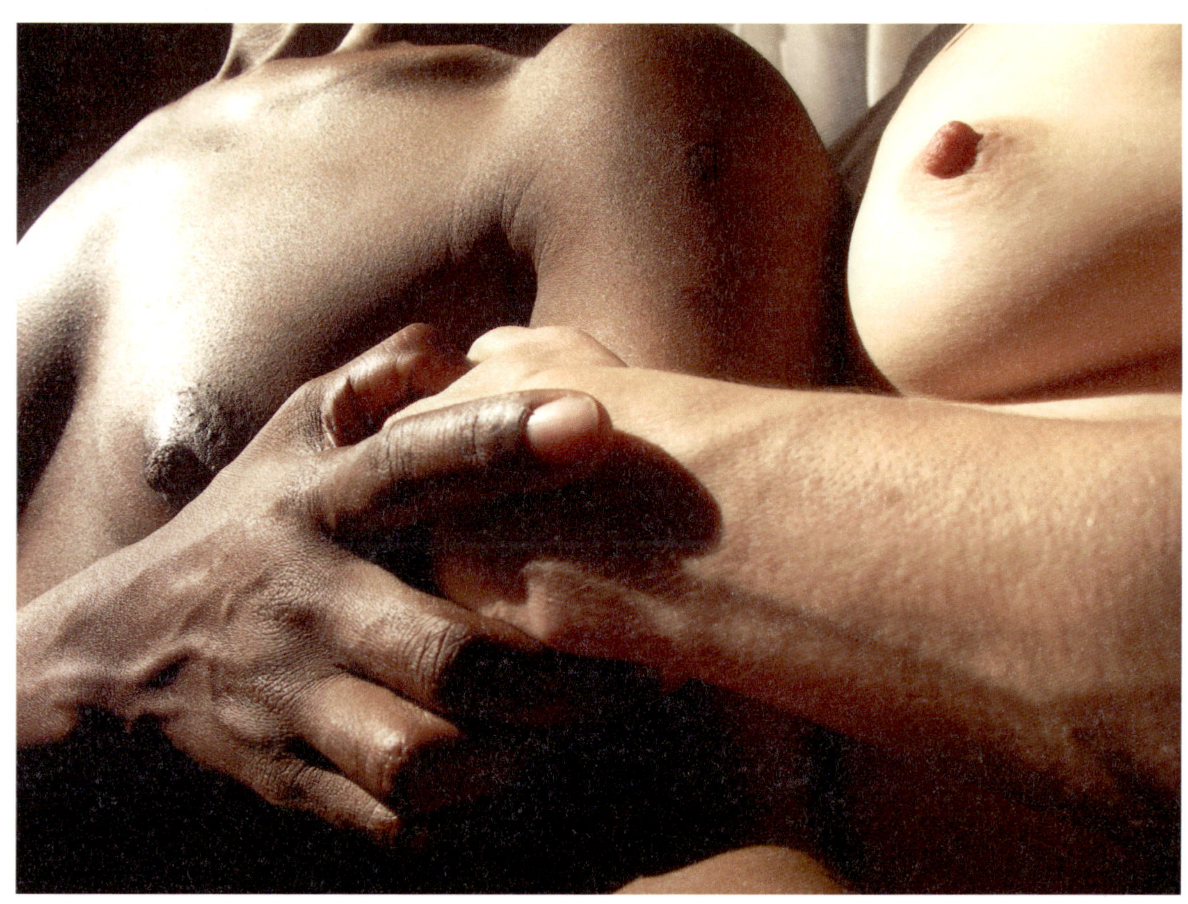

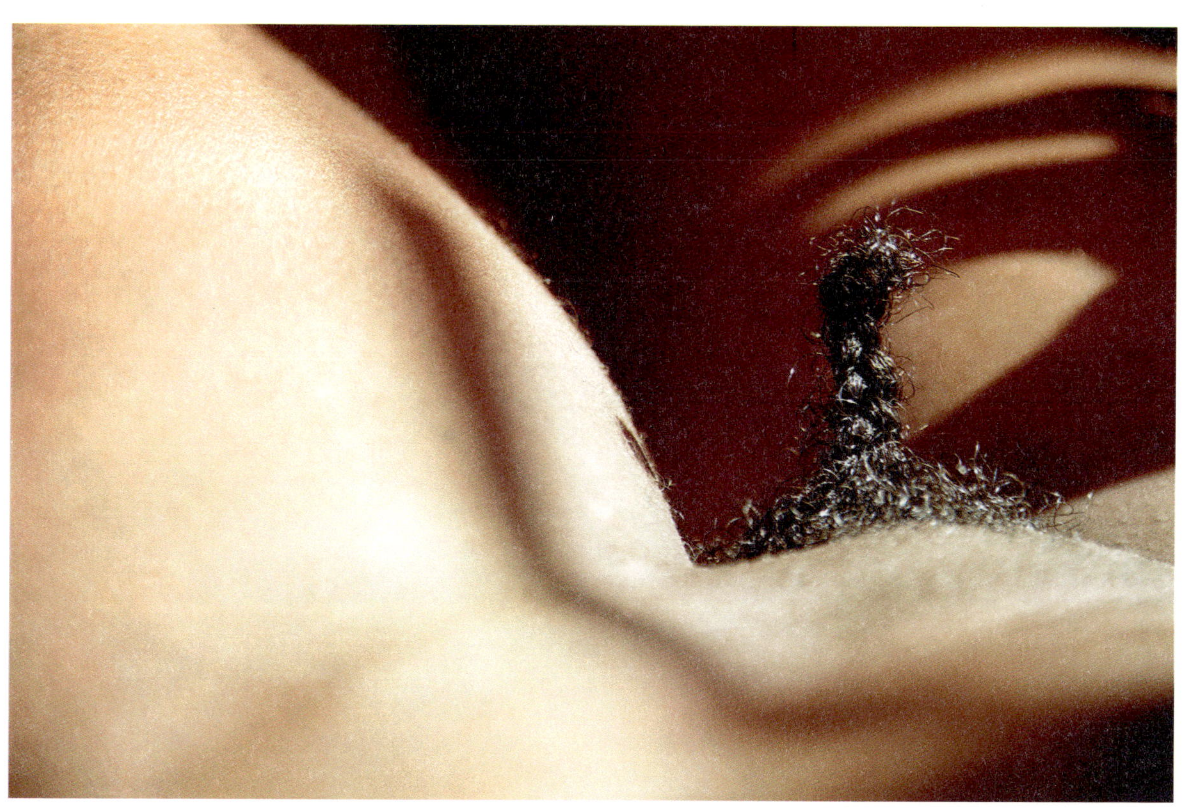

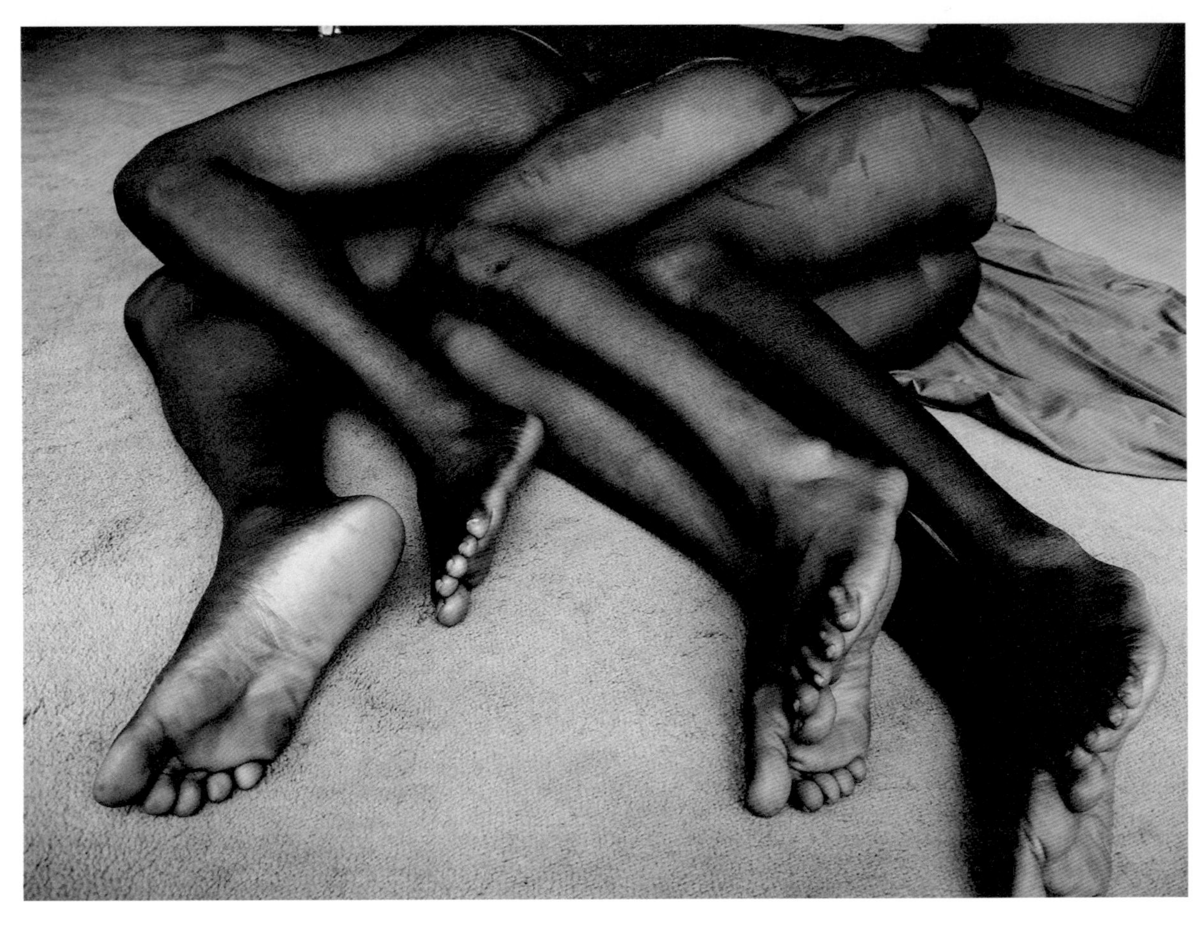

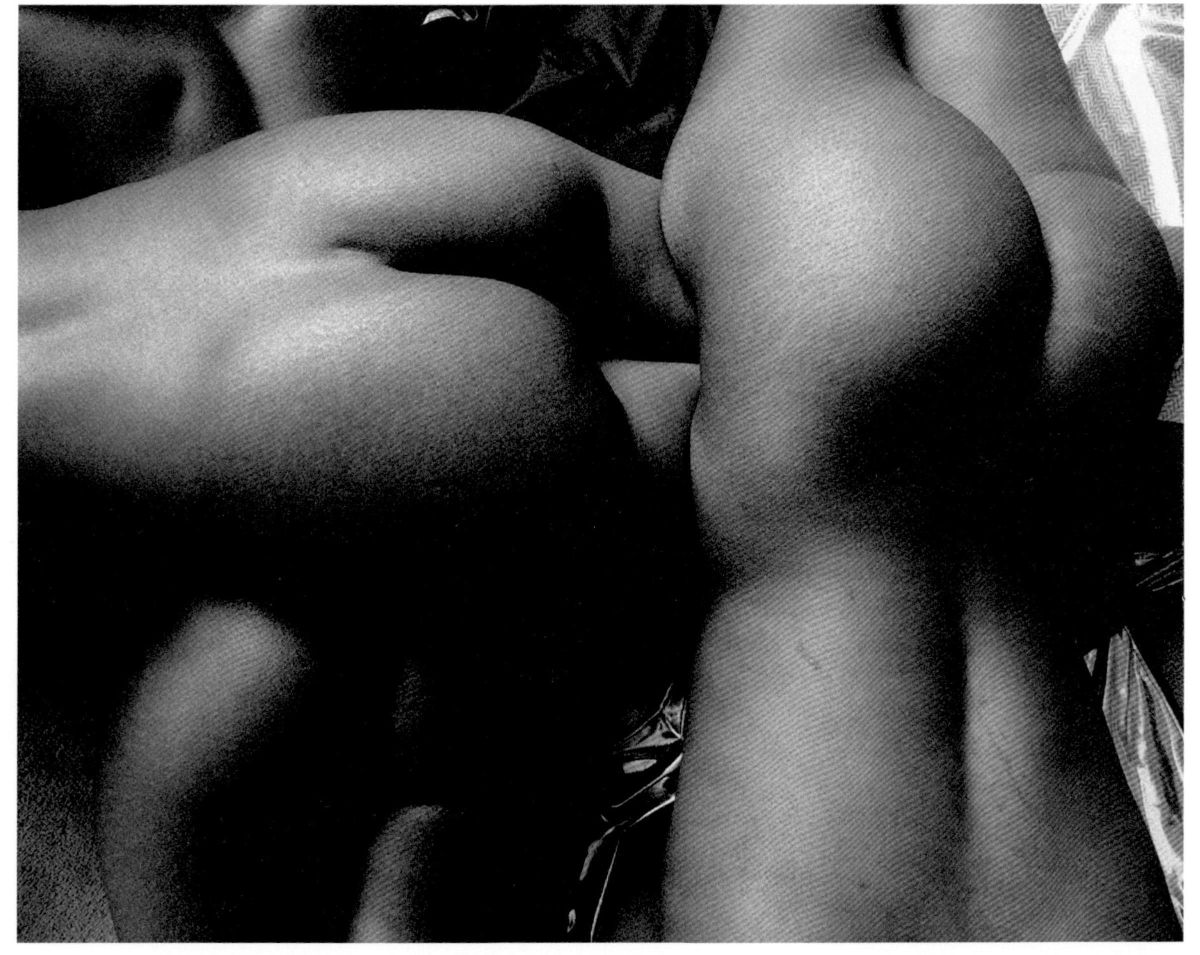

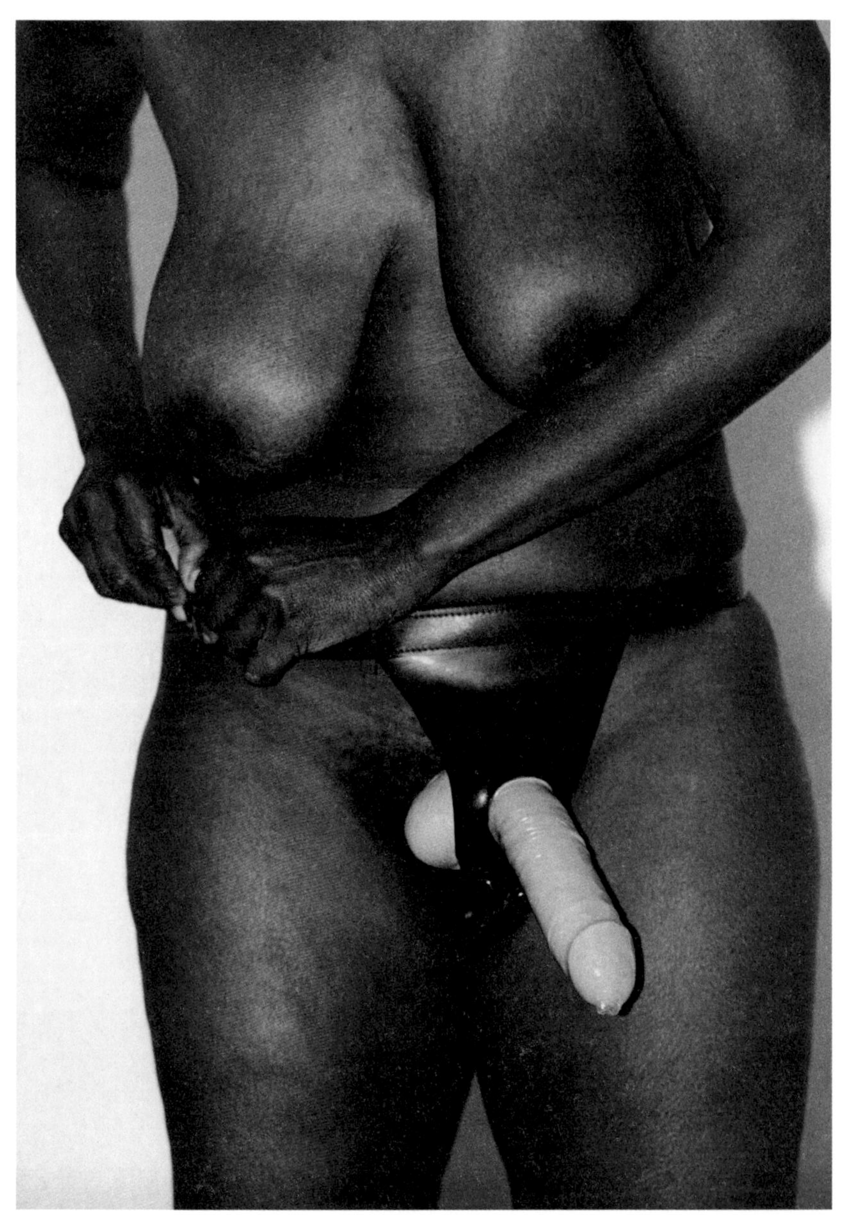

Community and Collectivity

Pamella Dlungwana

Uphathe umphako –
ukhumbul' ekhaya

Community and
Collectivity

Pamella Dlungwana

Uphathe umphako –
ukhumbul' ekhaya

ngizon' bona   *i'll see you / farewell*

Horror Café is packed, the eye lands on female bodies dressed head to toe in white, and a mixture of celebration and sadness permeates the air. I know the space to be a reggae hangout, specifically on Thursdays when Bongo Muffin's Apple Seed takes the decks and spins some seriously homophobic anthems as women gyrate and men hop about, lost to the music and the promise of the evening's close.

Tonight the club is hosting a farewell and fundraiser for Zanele Muholi, who is packing their bags for Toronto, Canada. The night has been arranged as a surprise for the activist by friends and colleagues proud to see them off to a strange land. It speaks to the spirit of the night, with everyone present wishing to contribute what little they can to ensure that, when they arrive in Toronto, Muholi need not ask any stranger for help, nor travel, as it were, like *uqhuma etsheni.*[1] Tonight is about celebrating one of our own and extending a desire that when they land they feel as warm away as they have in our collective bosom. Everyone present wants to give Muholi a little something for *umphako* – that lunchbox one fills for long journeys. *Uphathe umphako – ukhumbul' ekhaya.*[2]

This shy Black queer community is unafraid to buff the club in dance, as there are no jeering crowds or passive-aggressive bar huggers with questions of, 'So, who's the man and who's the woman?' As the speakers thump Brenda Fassie and Lebo Mathosa beats, and the air thickens with perfume and sweat, women hold each other closer, kisses are planted on full lips, and love disputes are initiated or resolved. Muholi becomes an accordion from the many hugs they give and receive – this one from POWA (People Opposing Women Abuse), that one from FEW (Forum for the Empowerment of Women), this other one from *Behind the Mask* magazine, those cute girls from the poetry circle and, oh, shame that little curfew breaker is shaking at the thought of being found out. Everyone wants to say their goodbyes, and none of them knows that this is but a dry run of the many farewells one will have to bid Muholi as they launch themself and the spirit of this community to a snooze-button-weary international audience.

•

BRABANT ROAD, WOODSTOCK, CAPE TOWN, SEPTEMBER 2008

don't illustrate

Mine is a humble apartment, and Muholi and Olivia have littered the floor with images, loose pages from poetry books, and spaghetti cables from laptops and chargers. This intimate workshop is focused on one photographer and two poets, all looking through each other's works, finding kin and building a legible document.

My house has become a lab and we vie from tea cup to screen, image and text, to produce 'What Do You See When You Look At Us?' This is the radicle of what is to become Muholi's practice as an artist and activist. Olivia and I become the beta of many writers Muholi chooses to work with in animating the message in their work and expanding the spotlight their success will shine on them.

'I'm not asking you to illustrate. It's important we all find some connection in each other's work, or this doesn't work.' The tea party will grow to include writers like Napo Masheane, Lebo Mashifane, Milisuthando Bongela, Andiswa Dlamini, Cheryl Clarke and Hlonipha Mokoena.

•

QUEENS – PARKTOWN, JOHANNESBURG, OCTOBER 2009

angisebenzi namavila   *i don't work with lazy people*

It could pass for an internet café, there are laptops and cameras, projects in various stages of post-production, and people clicking away hardly looking up but for an adapter for this or a hard drive with that. I count six people in one room, another three or four in the lounge, and the hinges on the front door are hoarse from the many ins and outs.

It's almost 8am and Muholi's house has been abuzz with activity from I can't tell when. A group of young photographers is headed out for a visit with a family in mourning, another lot has a workshop with a girls' school group, and yet another is packing for the Eastern Cape. The remaining lot are editing material for Inkanyiso, a BlogSpot created by Muholi as a forum for queer and visual (activist) media. They continue to train and co-facilitate photography workshops for young women in the townships.

This is Muholi's new family. Young queer individuals who have come with the desire to learn photography, flex their writing skills and document the activities of their community. There is no place for holiday makers here: everyone needs to have a clear idea of the contribution they want to make and what lessons they want in exchange. Everyone is a student and a teacher. Muholi is currently abroad, but the people I find at the house are as busy unsupervised as they would be with an overseer with a whip and the blazing sun as assistant.

It is this group of active self-motivated young adults who will inspire Muholi to establish a scholarship for young photographers at the Market Photo Workshop. Unbeknownst to them, their actions plant the seed which today has benefitted many aspirant queer photographers. So far Muholi has paid full fees for more than fifty students to study at Market Photo Workshop.

•

GREATMORE STUDIOS, CAPE TOWN, JULY 2012

it's serious, mzala, asidlali   *it's serious, my friend, we're not playing around*

We are snowed under with applications for Muholi and Lindeka Qampi's Photo XP Workshop. It has been years in, and they have spent what time they have between exhibitions, residencies and shoots hosting workshops for young girls across the country and have decided that, as they prepare for another exhibition in the city, they will host one at this residency space.

A full week-long programme, it attracts youngsters and practising artists from all over the city. Greatmore, a decidedly masculine space from the mere composition of those artists in residence at the time, is quietly challenged by the presence of young lesbians from the townships of Gugulethu, Langa, Nyanga, Athlone and Salt River.

Muholi and Qampi are a formidable duo, who amuse and instruct with an ease and familiarity that is encouraging to participants unfamiliar with the equipment they have been given. Muholi's motto is 'give cameras, not candies' – outside educational sessions they lend equipment freely. The workshop closes with an exhibition, and the facilitators make sure that as much effort is placed in the preparations for this event as would be for any other exhibition. The response to the call for applications, it turns out, was a trial run for the event itself, as Greatmore buckles at the reception the exhibition enjoys.

•

NEW YORK, USA, SEPTEMBER 2016

sisonke vele   *we're in this together*

We are all together in one city, and it's crazy. The Inkanyiso crew are in Chelsea, and we arrange to meet. I recognise them by the many bags they have on them, three to a person, with a camera bag and hand-held recorder for each one. Terra and Lerato are tired: they have been on the road for they can't remember how long. I have seen them in different cities under different circumstances, and fatigue is always camouflaged with smiles, healthy humour, and an ever-present curiosity about where they are and with whom they share that space. I last saw Terra in Paris in 2014, editing a film they had done in Cape Town, and Lerato was responsible for a Muholi solo exhibition in the same city a few years later. This particular trip has seen them in multiple cities throughout the US, and they have one more stop before they head home.

Together with Muholi, they have plans for more workshops, exhibitions and expansion when they land back home. Again, I find myself in a room with too many laptops, cables and hard drives. Muholi is pacing as they explain why they choose to work so closely with these two.

'They know what they want, who they are, and they demand a lot out of themselves. I need to look up and see people who are hustling for themselves, and these two are business people; they have their own things waiting for them when they get home. *Sisonke la, asilali, siyaspana.*[3] Period.'

I cannot count the number of Muholi exhibitions Lerato has helped curate. The pair are currently on the road in South Africa documenting testimonies from *Faces and Phases* participants for a documentary they are co-producing.

•

KZNSA, BULWER ROAD, KWAZULU-NATAL, 2019

ikhono lethu   *this is our talent*

I can only see the shadow for the substance in this case, but I enjoy the work and Muholi's movements via Instagram and the many WhatsApp videos and messages Muholi sends at ungodly hours.

They have been travelling back and forth to our mothercity, Durban, for a year whilst organising another major exhibition in Cape Town. For *ikhono lethu*, an exhibition hosted by the KZNSA, they have opted to work with local artists, commissioning interpretations of *Somnyama Ngonyama* versus only exhibiting their own work and enjoying a traditional homecoming exhibition.

In this act Muholi has passed on the mic, sharing focus on their work and newly minted celebrity with artists largely unseen outside of Durban and mostly unheard of in contemporary South African art circles. This is the DNA of Muholi as an individual operating within a larger whole. As the number of seeds in their palm grows, so too do they share the bounty with those around them. Our local currency once had a half cent, and in the last decade and a half I've enjoyed watching Muholi perform the alchemic feat of splitting a cent so that all could eat, grow and become.

Being

2006–ongoing

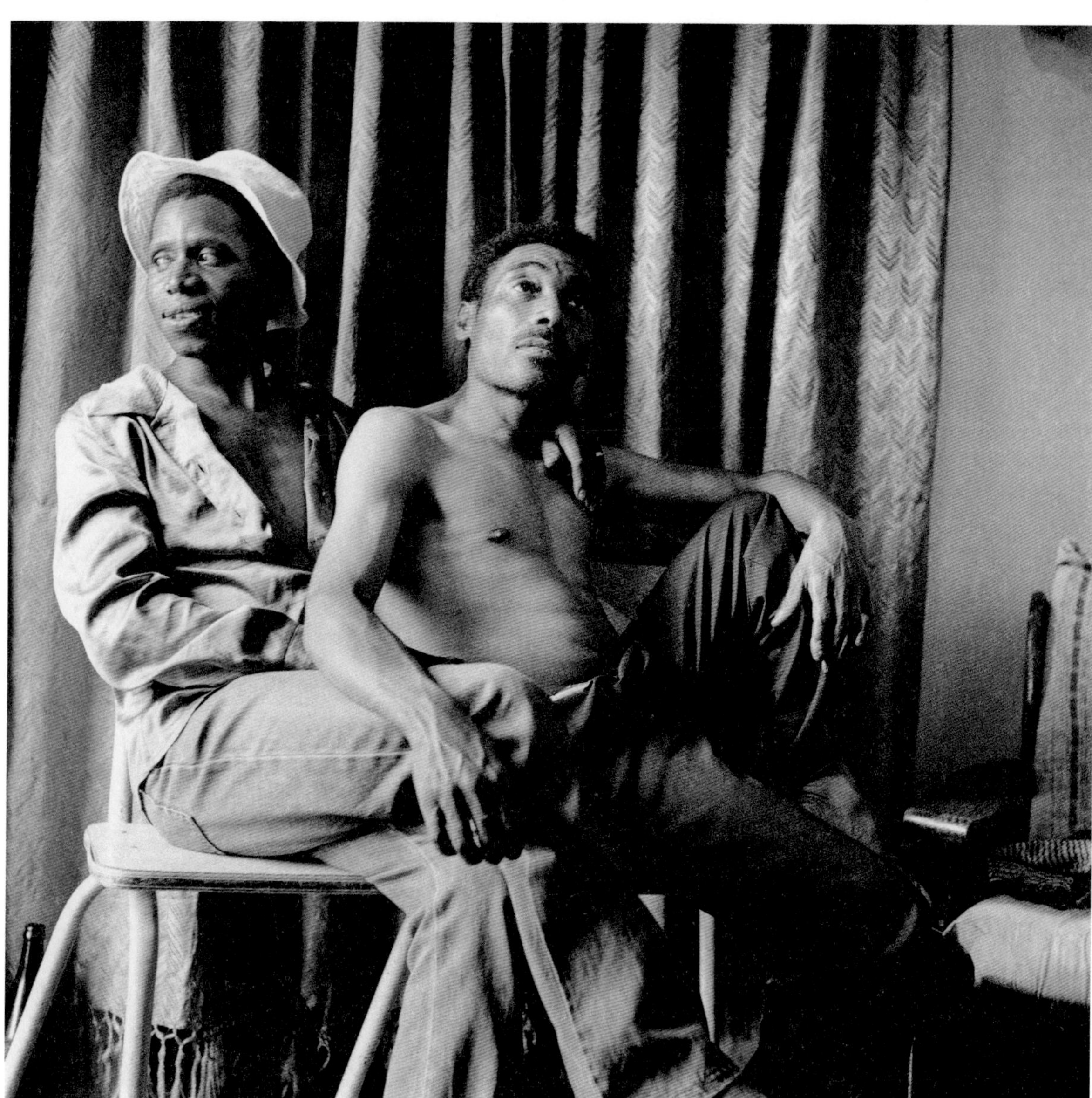

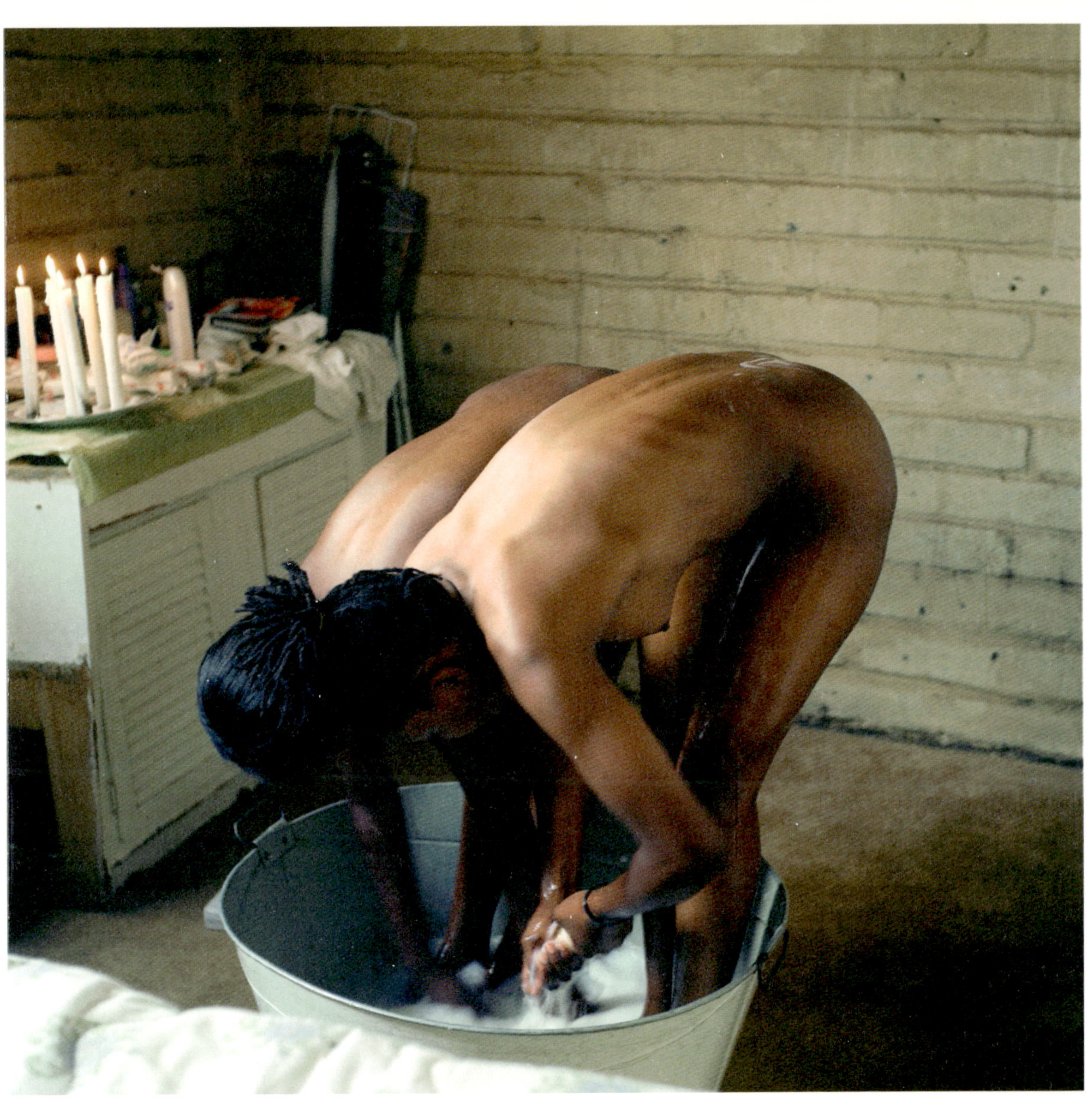

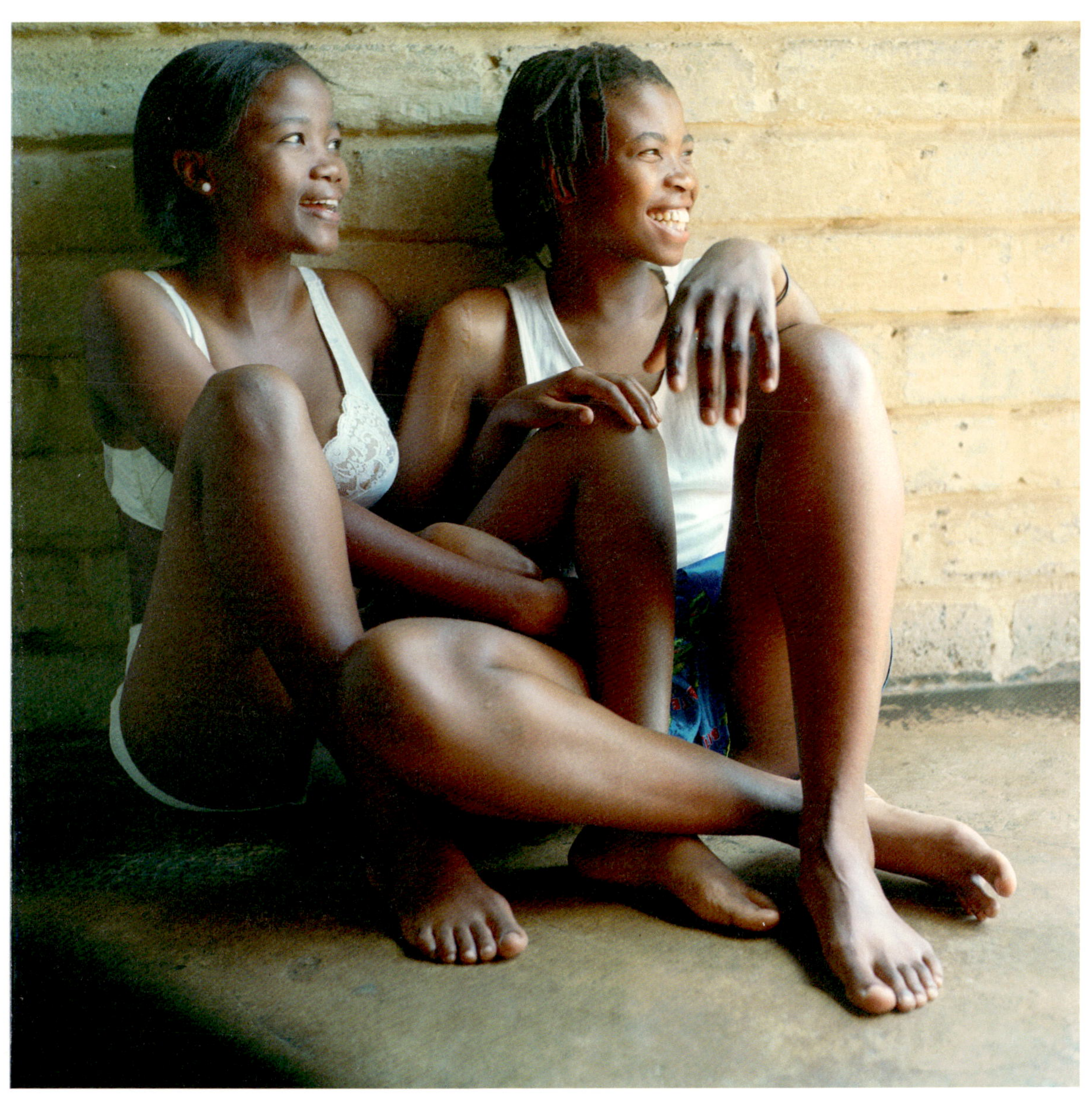

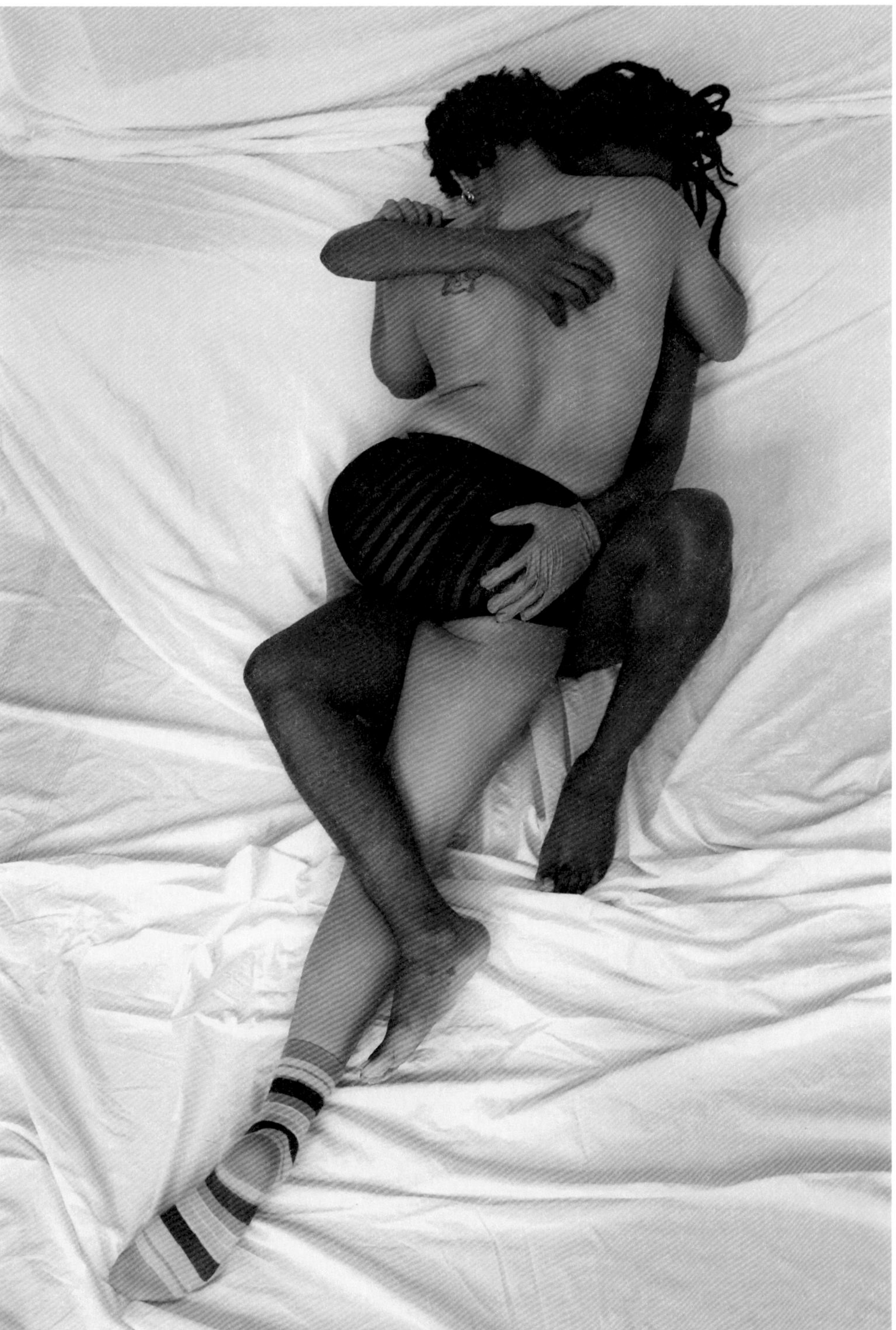

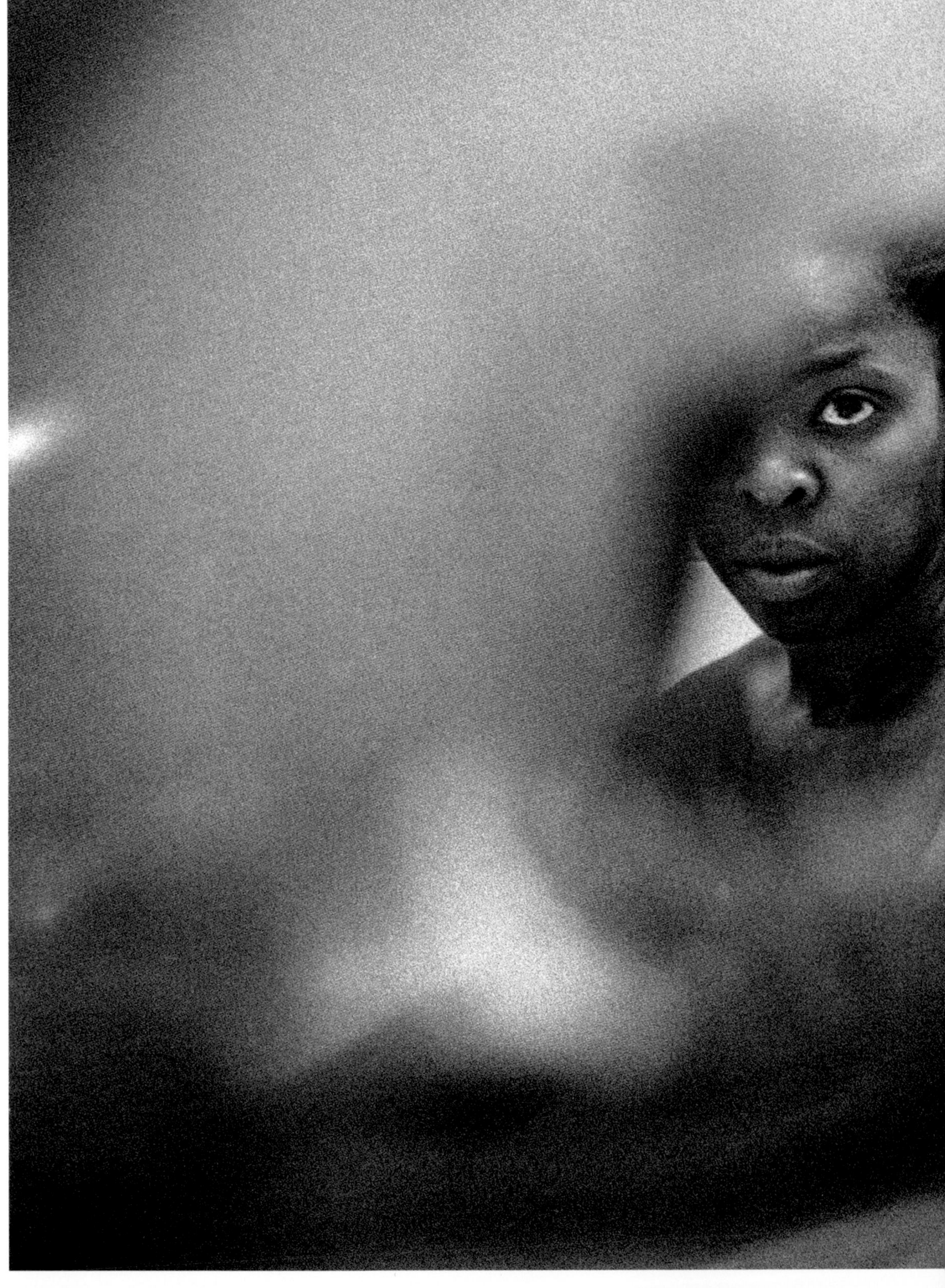

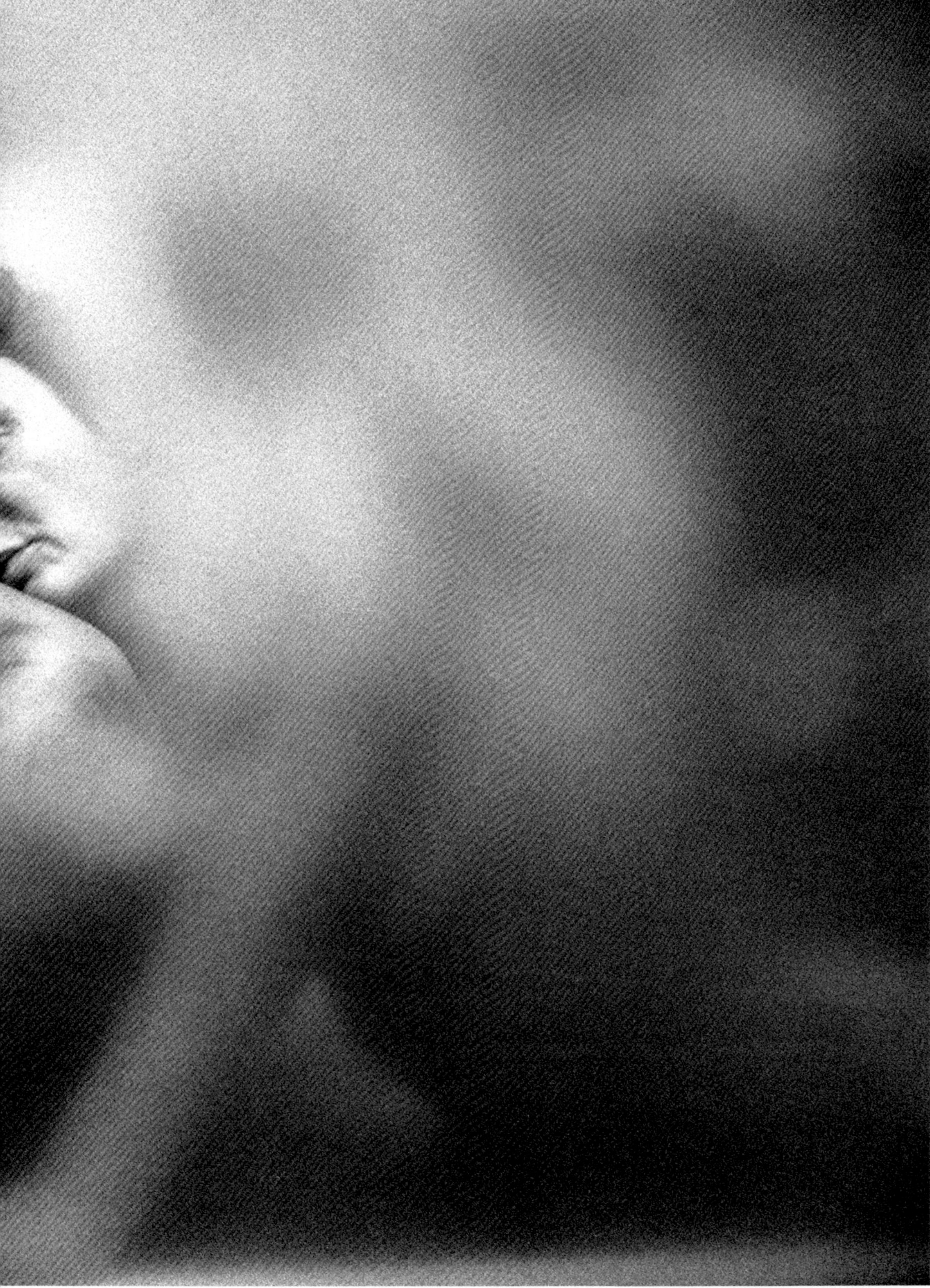

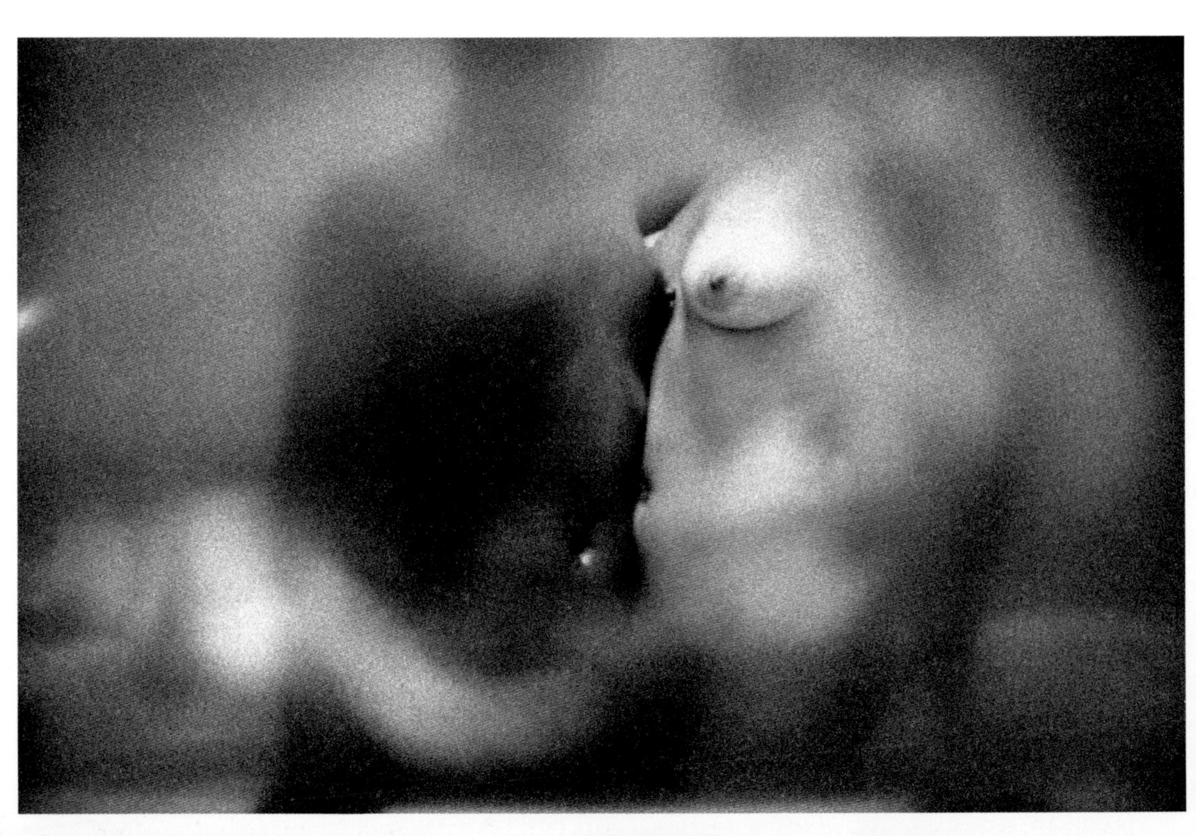

47 Hompi and Charles Januarie, KwaThema, Springs • 2007

48,49 Katlego Mashiloane and Nosipho Lavuta, Ext. 2, Lakeside, Johannesburg • 2007

51 LiZa I • 2009

54 ZaVa II, Paris • 2013

Letter III:
The Archive Other/wise

Renée Mussai

Dear Muholi,

Lately, I have been infatuated – obsessed – with a word: 'otherwise'. With all that it holds and all that it implies: open-ended and accommodating, it seems infinitely generous; obliging, almost. Discerning. Relational: alluding to circumstances *different from those present*. It suggests change. And fecundity. It can be a promise or a threat. An opening. Rebellious. Conditional. What might the notion of *otherwise* connote in relation to your practice, I wonder – your living, growing archive of potent visual activism?

THE ARCHIVE OTHER/WISE. I've been reading – and rereading – a lot these past few months. 'Without positive obsession,' Octavia E. Butler writes in the opening lines of *Parable of the Sower*, 'there is nothing at all.'[1] It is as though the word is pursuing – accompanying – me in my promiscuous literary wanderings, continuously reminding me to *think, feel, see differently*; to embrace and 'shape change', like the protagonist(s) in Butler's seminal speculative fiction. Or else ...

In her profoundly brilliant meditation *In the Wake: On Blackness and Being*, Christina Sharpe urges us to 'call on our capacities to read, think, and imagine *otherwise*'.[2] Saidiya Hartman's sublime *Wayward Lives, Beautiful Experiments: Intimate Histories of Social Upheaval* conjures an archive of young Black women eluding photographic capture: 'radical thinkers who tirelessly imagined other ways to live and never failed to consider how the world might be *otherwise*'.[3] And in *On Decoloniality*, Catherine Walsh and Walter Mignolo collaboratively present only one viable option for our collective future: a movement towards 'the *otherwise* that is the decolonial *for*'.[4]

Still mourning her recent passing, I revisited Toni Morrison's remarkable collection of essays, *Playing in the Dark: Whiteness and the Literary Imagination*.[5] Here, Morrison writes about the racial *other* as a 'dark and abiding' presence against which 'privileging and privileged differences' are measured. 'How could it be *otherwise*?' she asks.

Other/wise... Both a proposition and a promise: imbued with fertile, alternate potentialities and indigenous knowledges. To me, your visual activism and photography – your archive – is birthed from the intimate communal private/public spheres that prioritise the 'otherwise' as an imaginative, generative site of defiance; queerness not only exists within it but fuels and powers, *defends, proclaims, and propagates* it.[6]

THE ARCHIVE AS REVOLT / ASPIRATION. I keep thinking how *Somnyama Ngonyama* and *Faces and Phases* share the same counter-archival impulse: surging through your growing archive of the self, and your living archive of Black lesbian and bisexual women, trans men and gender-non-conforming individuals; how both series insist on 'keeping and putting breath back in the Black body in hostile weather' (Christina Sharpe), despite 'climates of virulent anti-blackness everywhere'. *We revolt simply because ... we can no longer breathe*.[7] How does one survive – breathe – in 'atmospheric conditions' saturated with the toxic haze of homo/trans/queer/xenophobia and the undying threats of epistemological, linguistic, ontological-existential, physical and gendered violences? [...]

And yet you keep creating space for collective being, and collective breathing. You tell the story from 'inside the circle' (Saidiya Hartman).[8] You imagine and reimagine. You visualise, and visualise again. You dare. It takes so much courage ... to be, to breathe, to survive.

THE ARCHIVE AS INSURGENCE. As I reflect, I think of your archive as a transvisual 'campaign of inscription'[9] – a provocation and a liberation, a queering pictorial revolt against the dehumanisation that black, brown or queer humans experience simply because of the colour of their skin, because of whom they love, because of who they – you, we – are.

Do you remember when you first saw the hundreds of photographs of anonymous African Americans collected by W.E.B. Du Bois exhibited at Autograph?[10] An ancestral photographic lineage pre-dating *Faces and Phases* by more than one hundred years... Thinking back, I am reminded of how you answer Du Bois's (counter)archival promise – his nineteenth-century *otherwise*, if you will – by delinking it from the confines of patriarchal heteronormativity, by offering a revolutionary collection of photographic portraits in which alternate kindreds and dissident sexualities manifest as generative [queer] sites of power, of named presences and self-determinations that not only trouble normalcy in all its modes – including homonormativity – but categorically refuse its centrality and/or its relevance.

THE ARCHIVE AS ELIXIR. And it made me think of the many different ways you make visible, citable and legible their radical presences, and commemorate – celebrate – their beautiful and precarious lives in *Somnyama Ngonyama* and *Faces and Phases* (in *Brave Beauties*, too). And the way you do so again and again in your 'photo follow-ups' – like a physician, bound by a pact of long-term/lifelong care – and the solicitude implicit in these continuous acts of 'queer returns', to borrow the title of Rinaldo Walcott's insightful collection of essays.[11]

Combating erasure with remedial visuality, your camera both does and undoes: it sutures the continual injuries inflicted on those of us who are female, queer, trans, dark(er)-skinned, poor or differently abled, and insists on the potency of individual agency and collective autobiography to create a recuperative archive for the future – a site of being, belonging and becoming, an urgent and necessary antidote.

I worry about you, often, about the effects on the mind and body from endless suturing, archiving and documenting – all this holding of space – and also, perhaps especially, the hyper-imaging of yourself in *Somnyama*. How do you hold on to yourself, amidst all of this? 'The worst injury', Claudia Rankine writes in *Citizen*, 'is feeling you don't belong so much / to you'.[12] Remember that you must *support the substance* while you *sell the shadow*, to borrow Sojourner Truth's potent words,[13] and breathe, breathe, please, as you continue to perform the difficult and taxing creative labour of visualising the world anew, and *otherwise*.

THE ARCHIVE AS INSISTENCE. You, and each of your participants and collaborators, refuse to be silenced, refuse to be unseen. Sharply in focus, they look at you, at your camera's lens, and only then into the eyes of the viewer... They appeal to our capacity to affect and to be affected: to transform how we look, how we see, how we *watch*. 'One needs to stop looking at the photograph', Ariella Azoulay posits in *The Civil Contract of Photography*, 'and instead start watching it.'[14]

To watch their faces, to engage their eyes, is to look into yours: for it is you that they look out to – assertive, self-possessed, defiant – with 'unintimidated, unblinking, and unflappable resilience'.[15] Their gazes, no longer 'oppositional' – not a combative *against* but a generative *for* – calling on us to 'recognise and restore their citizenship through our viewing'.[16] This pact of recognition between you and them signals a process in which the 'I' (eye) and 'they' (as pronoun, as non-binary, as community) are intimately entwined: in which a mutual validation of existence – a momentary embrace of Gayatri Spivak's strategic essentialism – occurs, and in which Sylvia Wynter's *genres of being human* are made legible through modes of multiplicity and agential referent-we's – in which, as Wynter writes, 'everything is praxis'.[17]

[THE ARCHIVE AS] RESISTANCE. A recent occurrence... Because of geo-political / socio-cultural ideologies, a planned feature celebrating your work must be 'discreet': no queer (LGBTQIA+) politics, please; 'performative' self-portraits only. 'Would that be okay?' they ask. 'How do I respond to this?' you say, exhausted already from the intolerable weight imposed by this (non)invitation: a (non)invitation that ends with four bracketed words, afterthoughts masquerading as helpful tips in parentheses: 'just drop the lesbian'.

How, indeed, does one respond to an invitation to perform an act of [queer] disavowal? Regardless of how well-intentioned the proposal was, how legitimate their motivations and how understandable the desire for discretion – in a place where Sharia law is strictly enforced, where cross-dressing is illegal, and where, in the twenty-first century, consensual homosexuality is punishable by public flogging, jail or death – did they not realise the casual epistemic violence implicit in this request? The carelessness – the linguistic brutality – inherent in the words chosen? The symbolic murder? The ontological negation, the subjugation?

Here, photography becomes a 'silence that silences'[18] – were it not for a (non)'performative' self-portrait, inadvertently, therapeutically, born from the wound caused by each such moment, each threat of erasure and revocation of rights: triggering the transformation of oppressive forces into creative (s)urges, insult into compliment.

THE ARCHIVE AS COMMEMORATION. While I understand that 'a kind of wilful critical blindness'[19] may prove lifesaving at times, there are so many silences yet to be broken, as Audre Lorde reminds us in 'The Transformation of Silence into Language and Action', still relevant as ever.[20] And what is photography if not a language? A language that speaks with many voices and in multiple frequencies: some images scream, while others whisper; some utter bold commands and others register quietly, preserving their ability *to rupture silences* for moments of emergency.[21]

I think of the radical intimacy of your archive and the many silences it refuses, re-re-membering dispossessed figures whose voices were disavowed, whose bodies were violated. I think here, for instance, of the late activist Fezekile Ntsukela Kuzwayo, and your visualising – inhabiting – her on the day she died, ten years after she accused former South African president Jacob Zuma of rape.

And I think of you at Constitution Hill, enveloped in a grey prison blanket in *Bayephi* (2017) - staging a visual protest to honour the women who marched on Pretoria in 1956, not only against apartheid but for freedom and equality. Sixty years later the same striped blanket frames – births – you in *Zamile* (2016), conjuring the memory of the late Noxolo Nogwaza, Eudy Simelane and Girly Nkosi of KwaThema[22] and all those lost to – as well as those surviving and defying – gender-based violence, hate crimes and oppression in South Africa, and beyond.

Commemorative, corrective and curative, your revolutionary visual archive – from *Faces and Phases* to *Somnyama Ngonyama*, from *Brave Beauties* to *Being* – provides a requisite blanket in times of precarity.

Speaking of commemoration: this month marks the 30th anniversary of Rotimi Fani-Kayode's passing. His practice – like yours, a photographic communion between art and advocacy – was infused with beautiful rituals of cultural and sexual

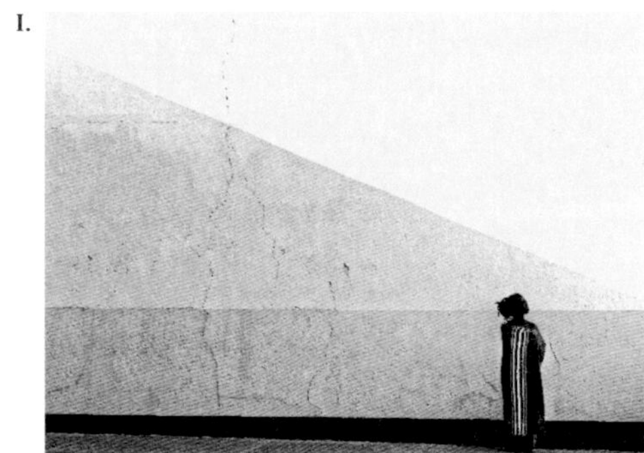

I.

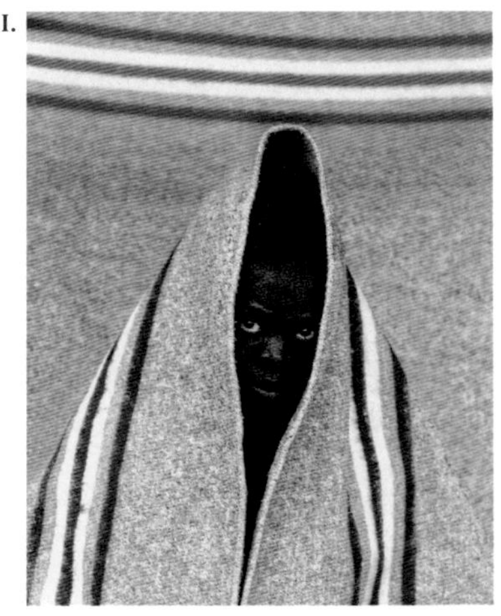

II.

difference, altering the field of contemporary [queer] visual culture irrevocably. And if anyone has continued and amplified his legacy, it is you.

As I write this letter, I am oscillating between the wild and serene sonic spheres of Julius Eastman and Miles Davis... With the tunes of *Gay Guerrilla* and *All Blues* drawing to a close, allow me to thank you: because you, my dear friend, have generously, courageously, gifted us an intimate visual atlas that not only maps different architectures of being, but also forges an opening, a 'dream book for existing otherwise'.[23] And for that, we are forever in your debt.

See you in 2020, perhaps in our library-cum-lounge-cum-studio, inhabiting my pleated garments once more to create new insurgent (self)imaging worlds amid endless books ... in beautiful pursuit of the promise inherently present in the notion of *otherwise.*

Until then, please be well. And don't forget to rest, and breathe...

Love, always.
Renée

LONDON, DECEMBER 2019

III.

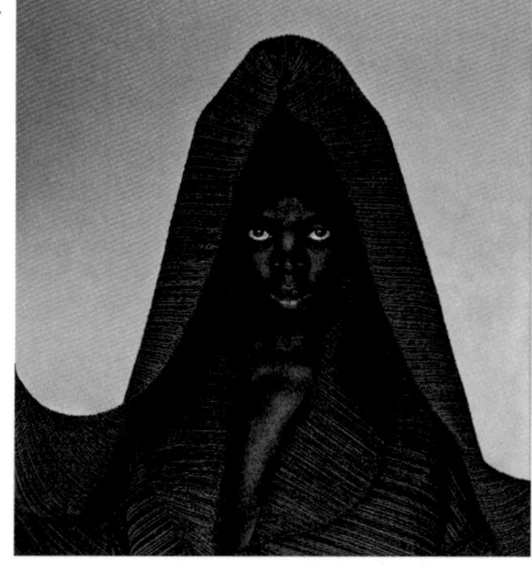

I.   Zanele Muholi, Bayephi III, Johannesburg, 2017

II.   Zanele Muholi, Zamile, KwaThema, 2016

III.   Zanele Muholi, Thembeka II, Newington Green, London, 2014

Faces and
Phases

2006–ongoing

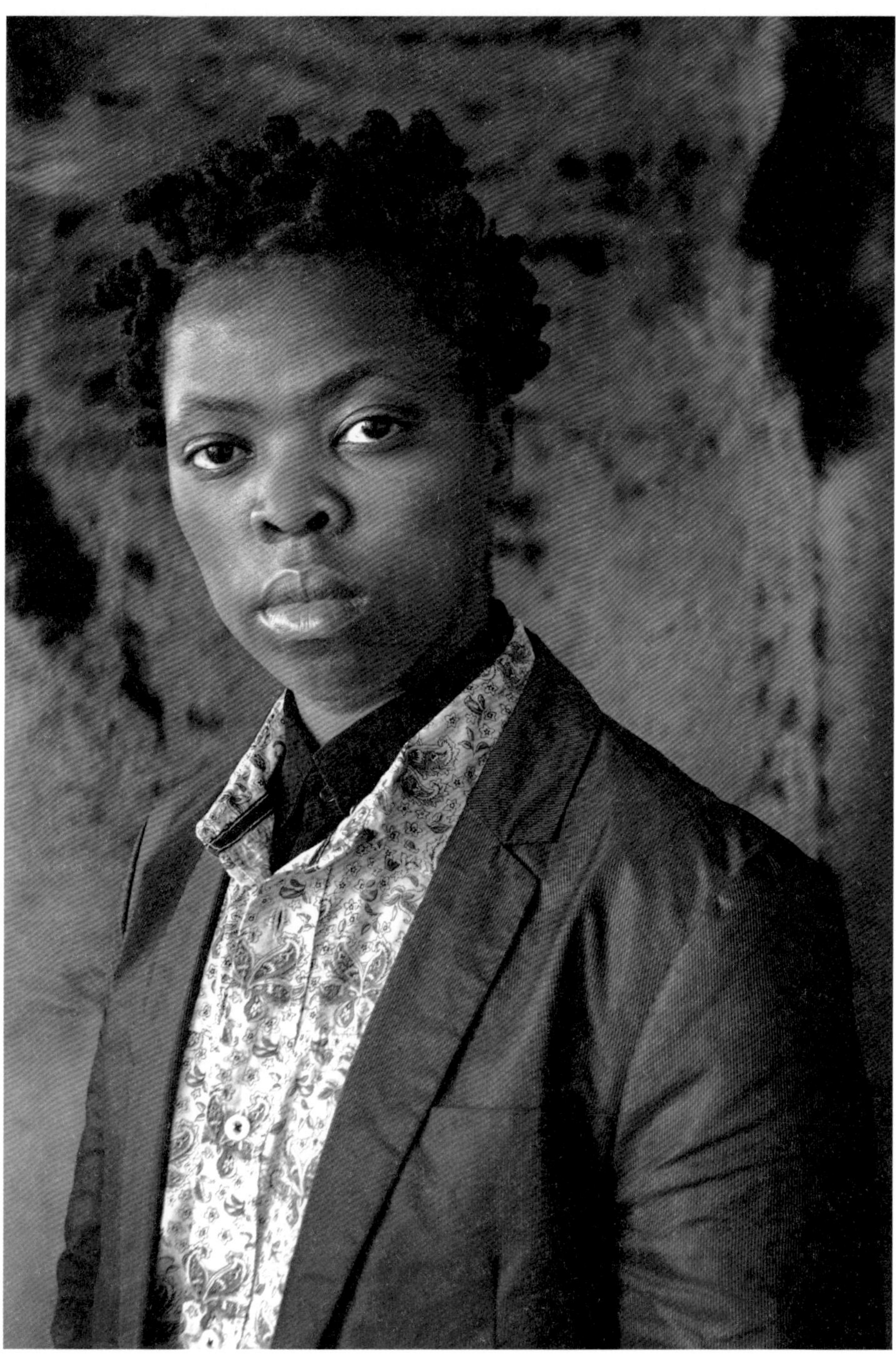

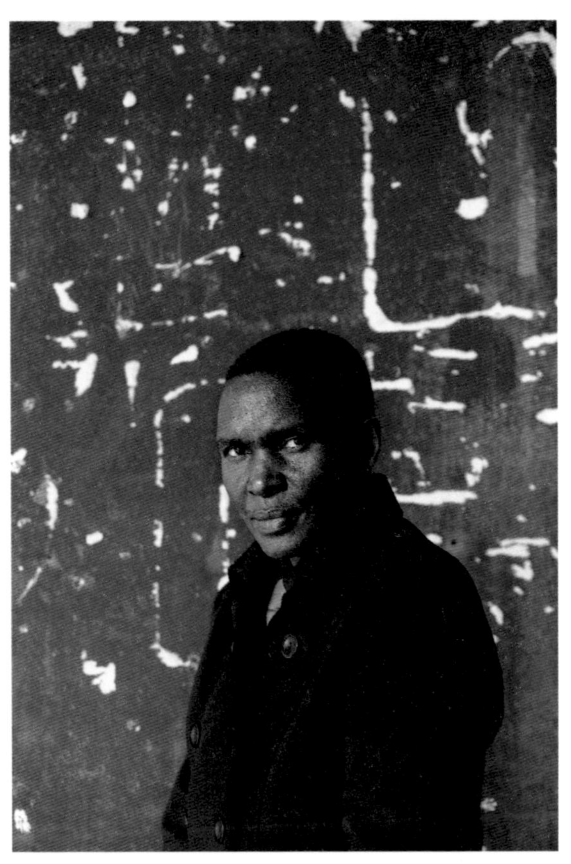
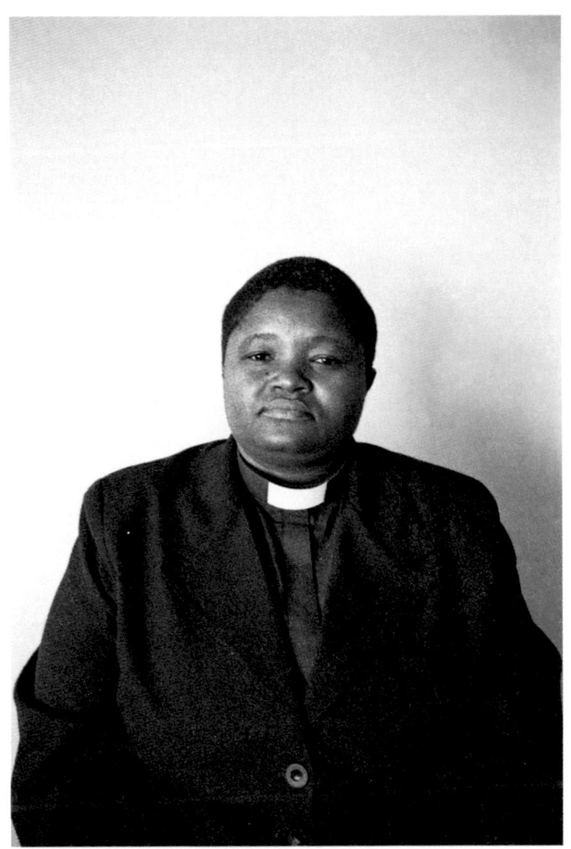
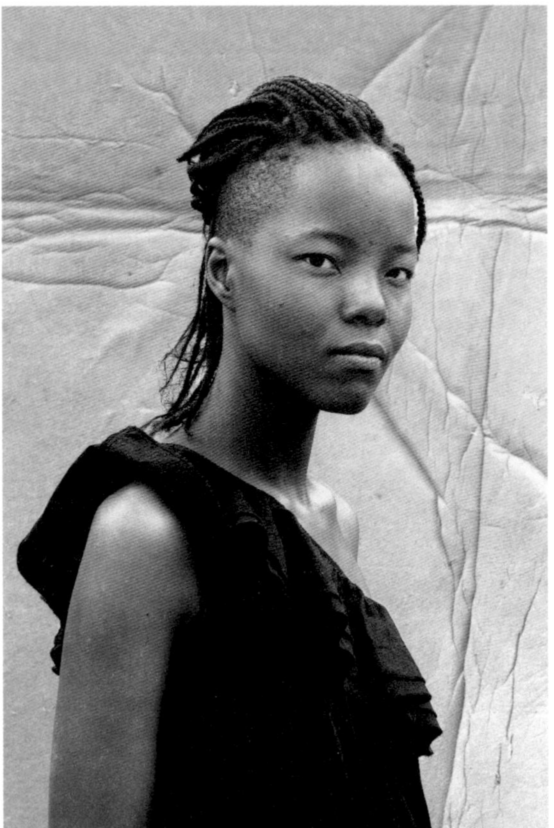
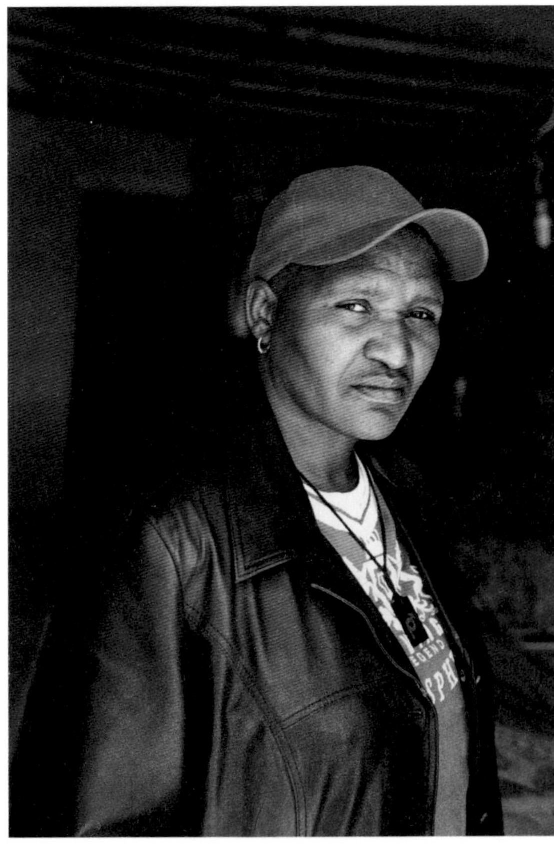

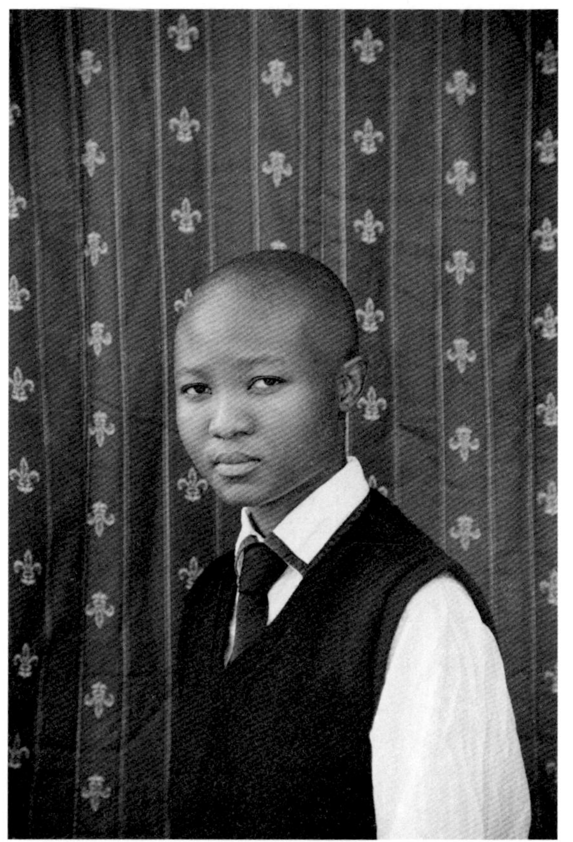
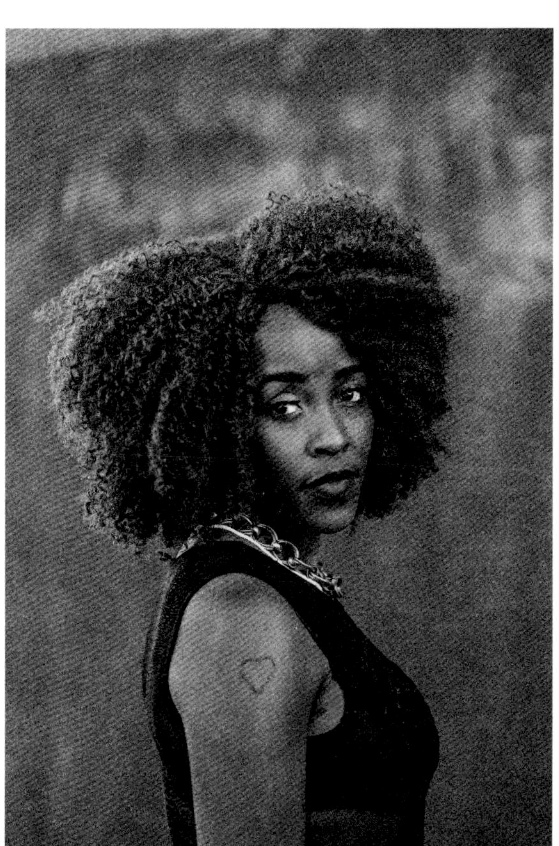
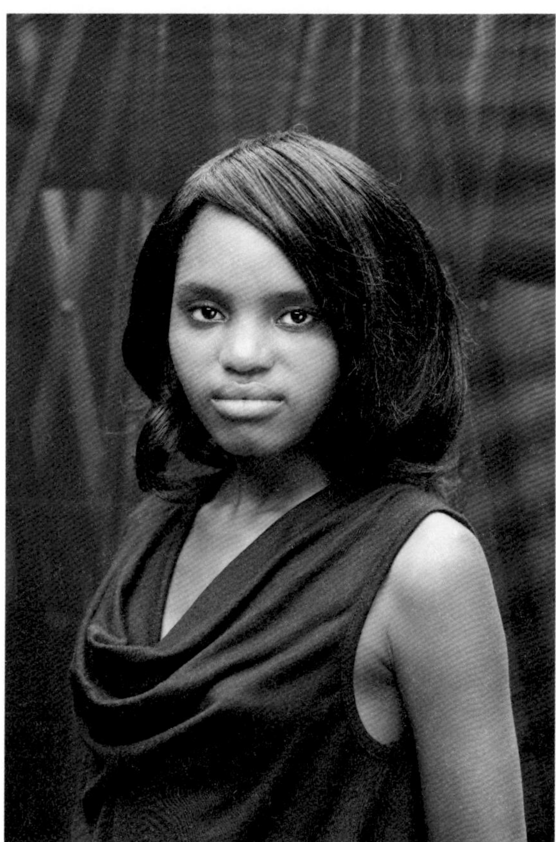
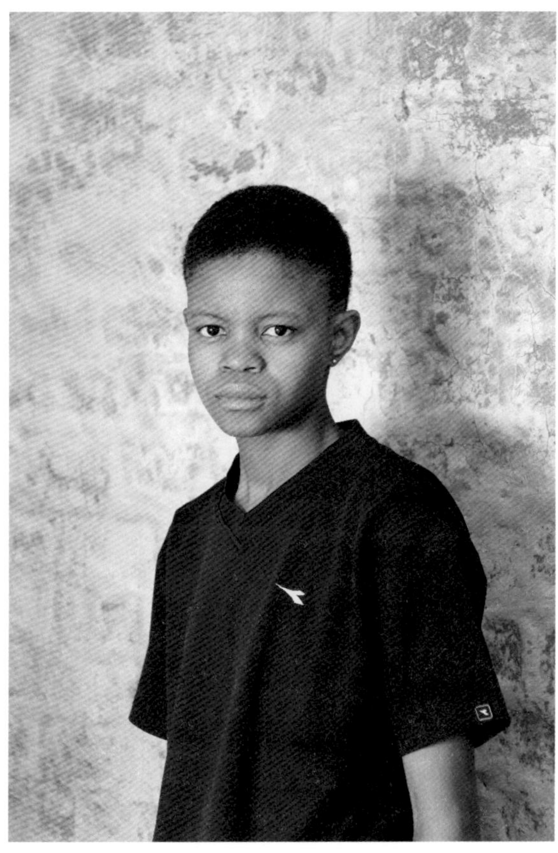

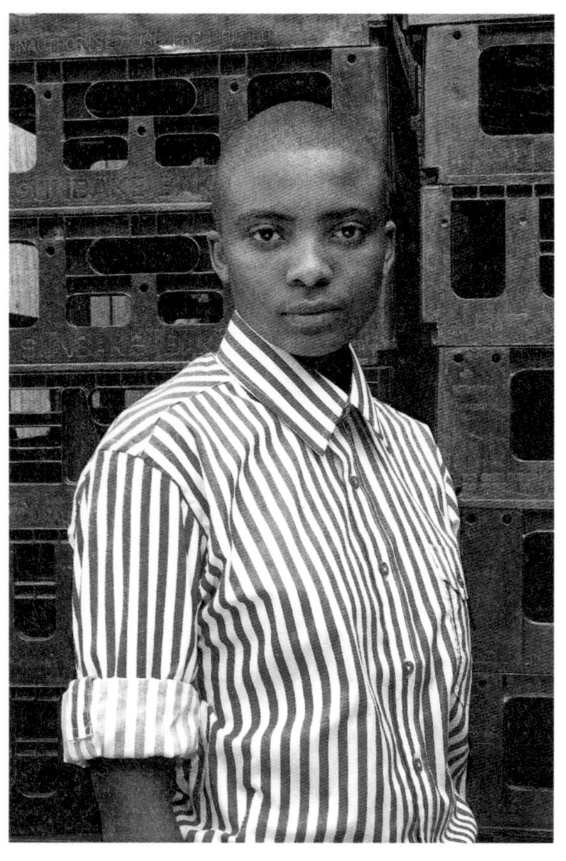

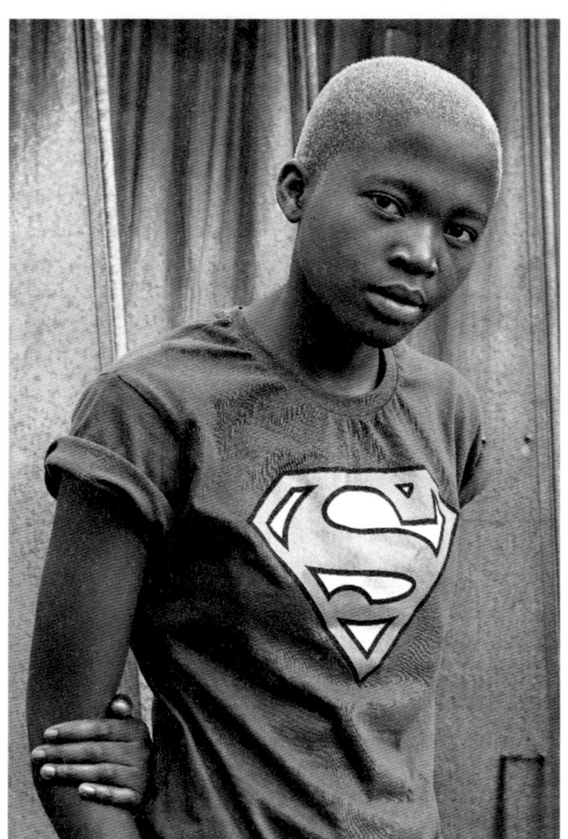

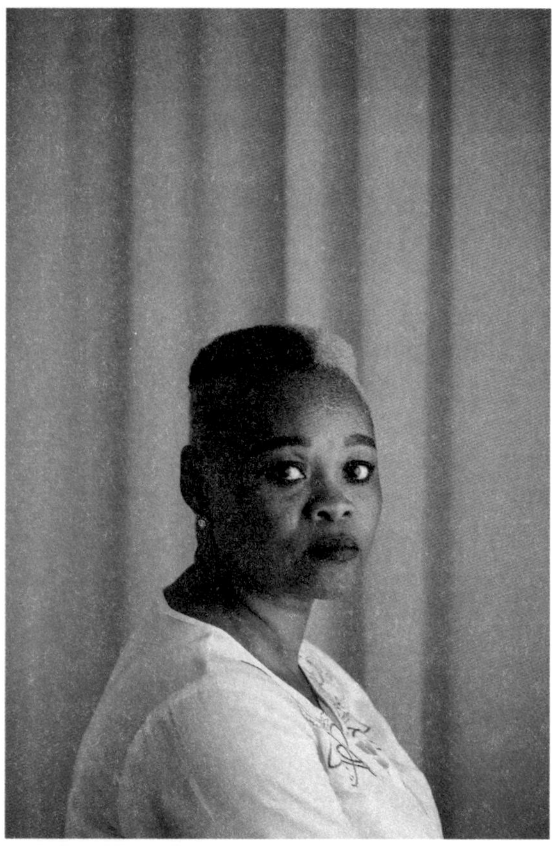

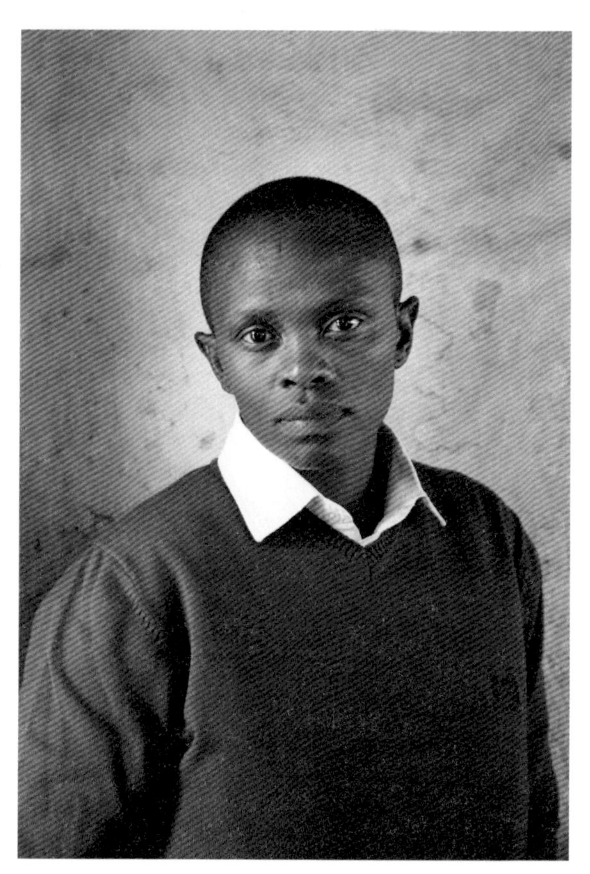
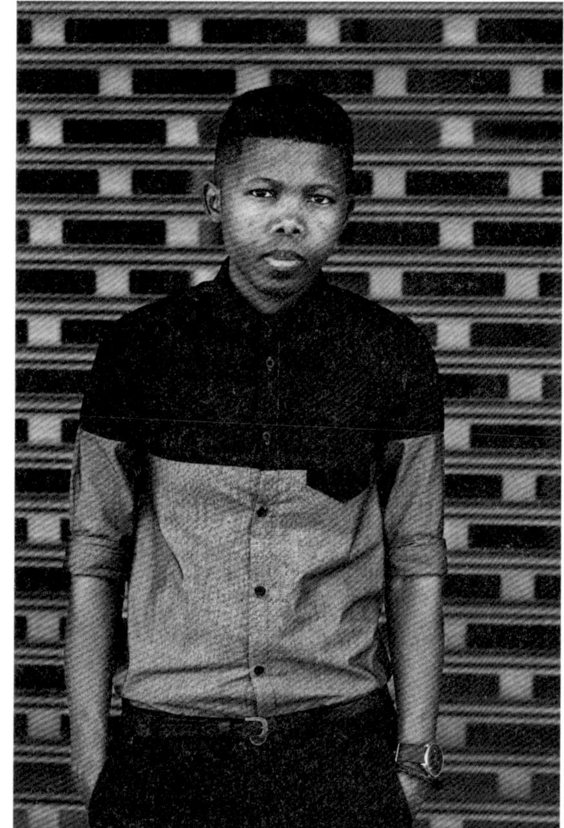
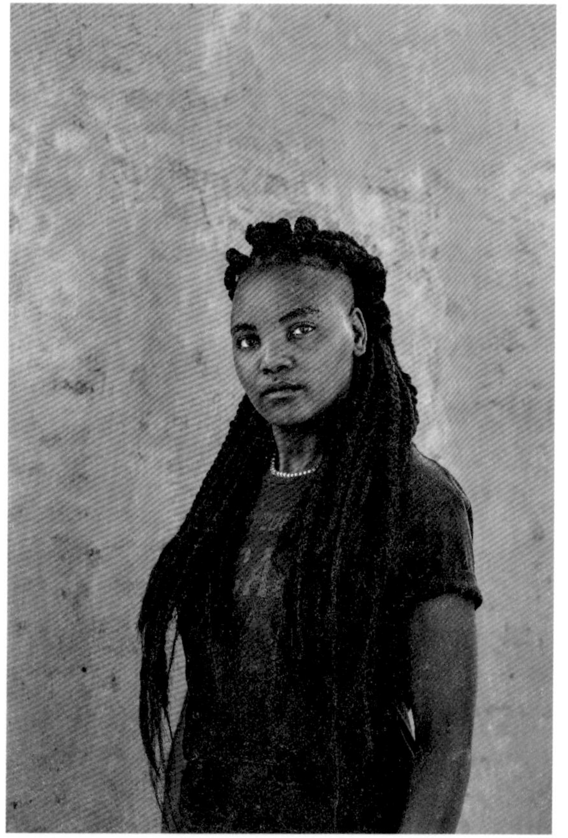

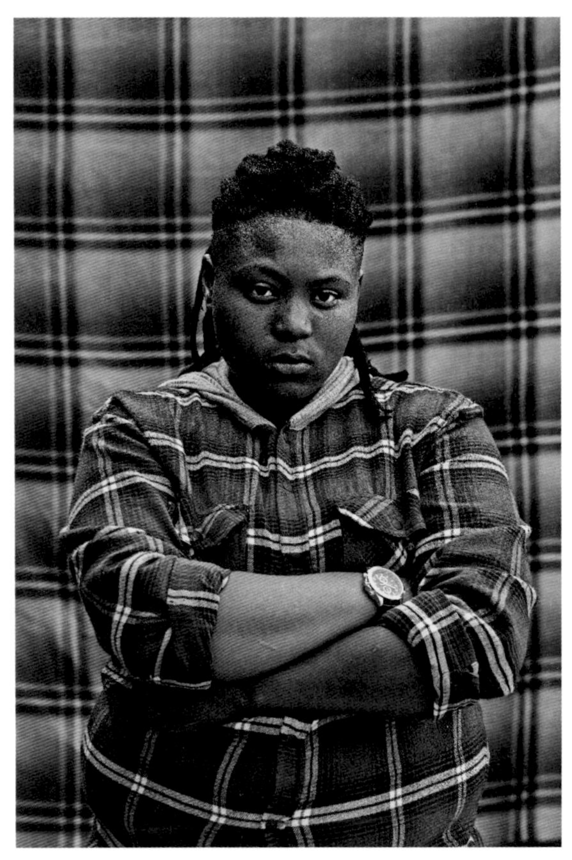

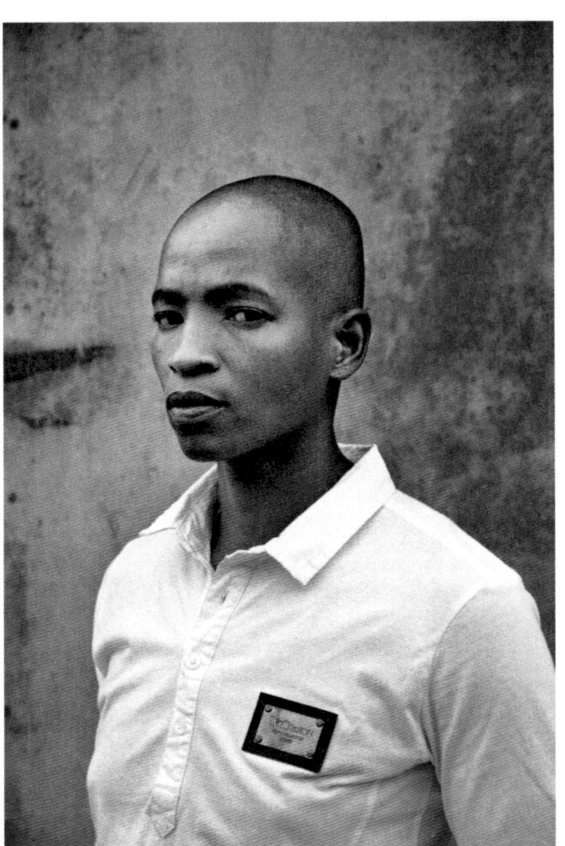

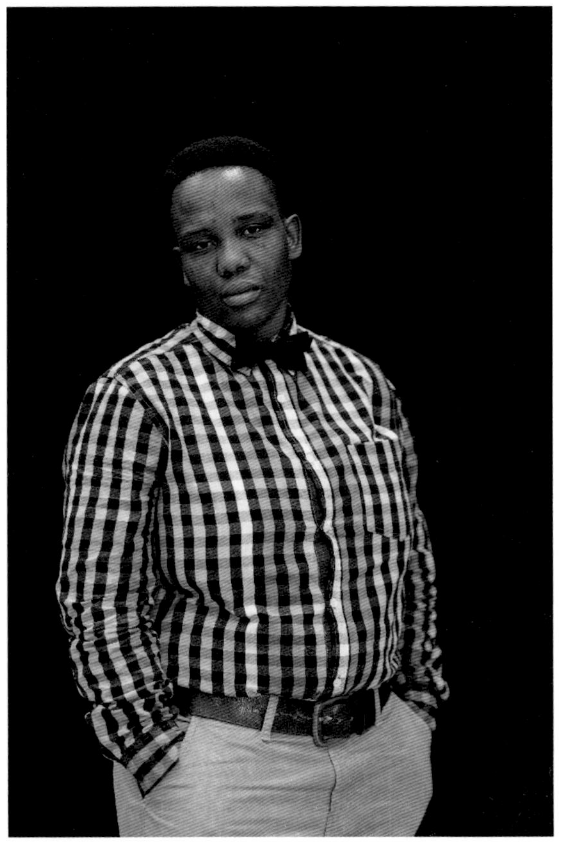

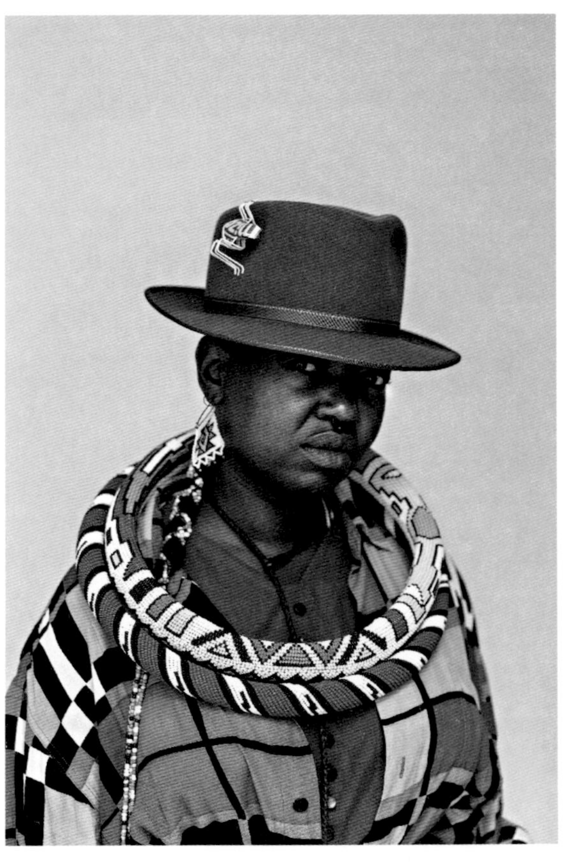

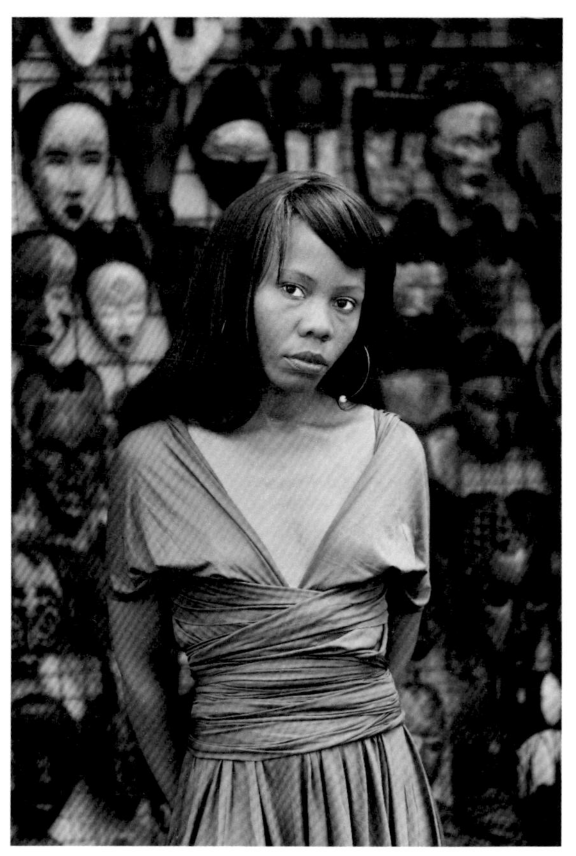

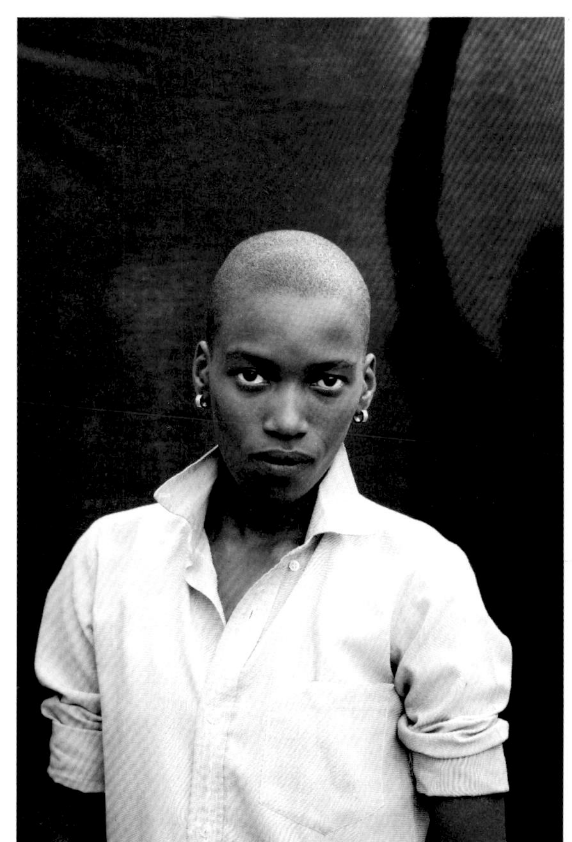

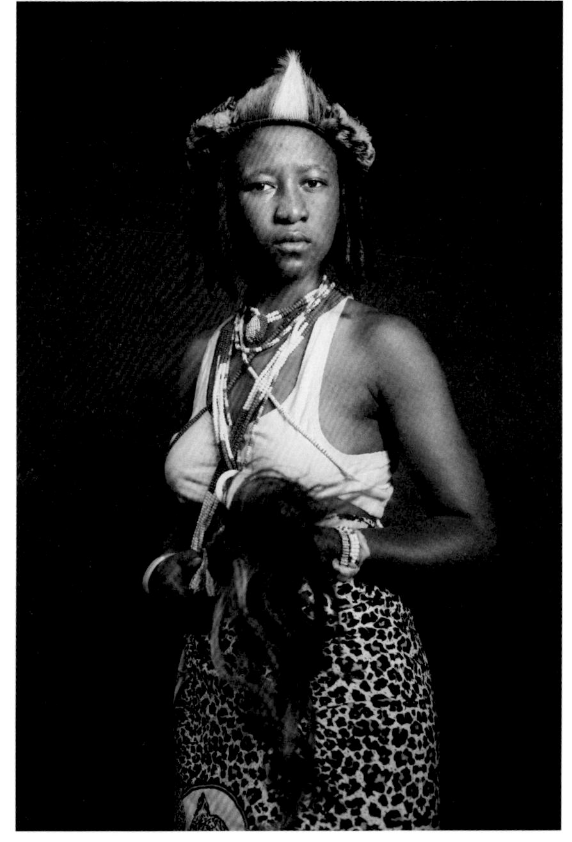

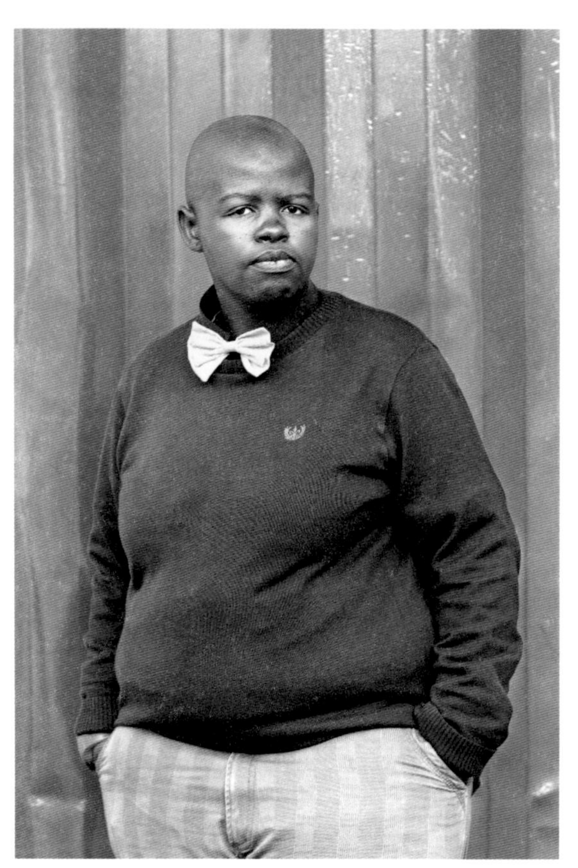

I AM NOT A VICTIM BUT A VICTOR
Lungile Dladla

They call February the month of love, I call it the month of change…

In February 2010, I was walking with Mathapelo ('one who prays') along Swazi street. It was around 7pm, a few hours after my aunt's funeral. My friend was accompanying me to my house and the street was not busy that day. A guy came walking in the opposite direction; we paid no attention to him because we did not think of anything bad. In a blink of an eye he was right behind us with a gun; he said '*Futsek nina siya le manje*' (voetsek, we going that direction now). Shaking and scared, we listened to him.

He led us to a field. The strange thing about him was that he knew the place so well that he told us exactly where to walk because that place has dangerous holes we could fall in. When we got to his place of horror he instructed us to lie on the ground face down and hands behind our backs.

We did as told because we feared for our lives as he had a gun in his hand and threatened to use it if we did not do as he said. He undressed us and said, 'Today *ngizoni khipha ubutabane.*' ('Today I will rid you of this gayness'). I said a little prayer because I knew what was coming. He then tied both our hands and feet. My friend kept on negotiating with him not to rape us and I was absentminded the whole time. It felt like my body was there but my mind was so far away. I just remember my friend saying, 'Please if you rape us use a condom.'

He asked why was I wearing guys' clothes; my tongue was tied, I couldn't say anything, so I kept quiet. He covered our faces with our clothes then he started raping my friend; when he was done he then untied my feet, spread my legs apart and forcefully penetrated me, I was crying and praying. When he was done he got dressed and said, 'I'm going now, I will tell you when you should go.' Then he started walking, I could hear his movements as he was moving through the grass. From a distance he told us to get dressed and go. We tried to untie each other's hands then dressed; in the dark we managed to get out of those fields.

Then I told my friend that I'm going straight to the police station. It was around 11pm. She said it was too risky but I told her that I did not care. We got to the police station; the police officers took us to some room. We told them what happened and as we were talking they stopped and asked me, '*Nawe*, you were raped? How? That is impossible, you're a guy!' What they said hurt me even more. I then asked them how I could be male *namabele* (with breasts)! If it was not for the girl I used to go to school with, those stupid people would have not taken my statement.

They told us they did not have a crime kit yet but the police station is next to the clinic. As they were taking our statements one of the officers said that it's not the first time they heard of a rape case in that area. In my mind I thought, 'why then didn't you go patrol the veld?' We left the police station around 12–1am. I could not sleep that night as I could smell that guy on my body. In the morning we went back to the police for the tests, they took them, gave us some pills then told us to go, they will call us.

Time went and they never called until Kaya FM covered my story and demanded to know what happened. They told them that the case was closed because the suspect is unknown. A year later, the case was reopened; they found the guy and arrested him. In court it was revealed that he had been charged with 17 cases of rape. He was sentenced to life for all his crimes. I cannot say I was happy with that but it was better than nothing.

When I thought that the worst has past, hell broke loose as my life turned upside down. I was not treated well at home and I got very sick in December 2011 due to stress.

In January 2012 I was admitted to hospital; I was very sick and I thought I was dying. The doctors did a string of tests to figure out what was wrong with me. The tests came back and I was diagnosed HIV positive. On top of that I had lung infection and PCP (Pneumocystis pneumonia). At that point I could not breathe or walk, I thought it was the end of me. I stayed in hospital for two months, and when I was discharged my CD4 count was a single digit – everyone thought I was not going to make it.

However, I started taking ARVs and I must say I am healthier than ever before. My CD4 count is over 300 and my viral load is low. One thing I still need to overcome is the fact that whenever I take my medication, I am reminded of what the bastard did to me! However, my inner self is strong, I am going to beat this. HIV is not my life, I'm not going to let it get to me. I am not a Victim but a Victor.

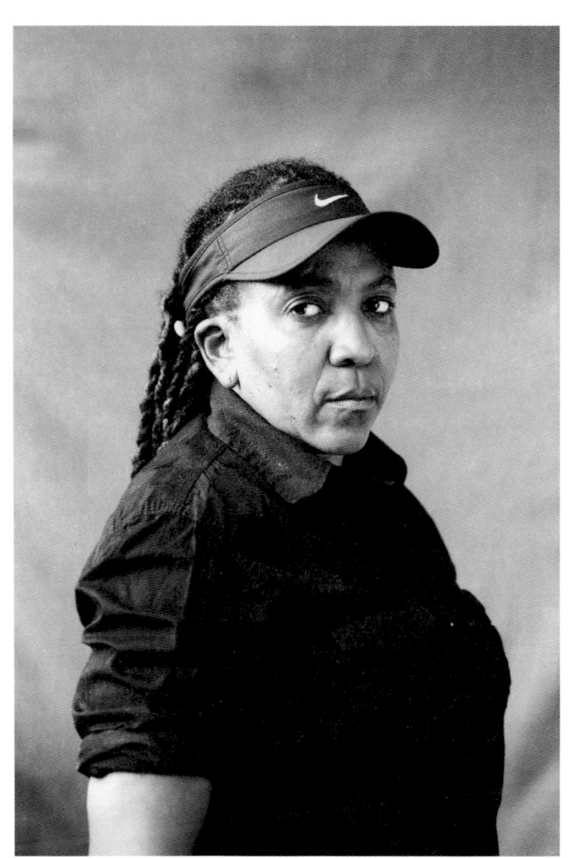
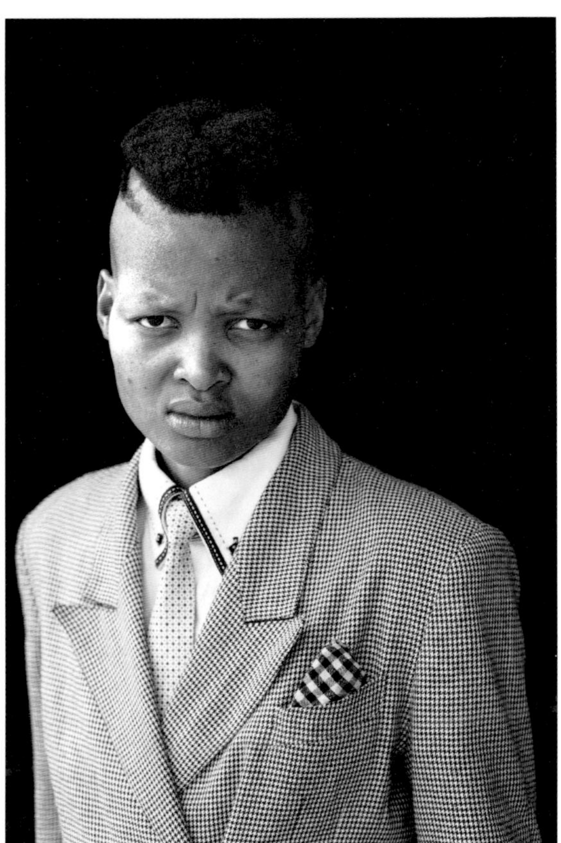
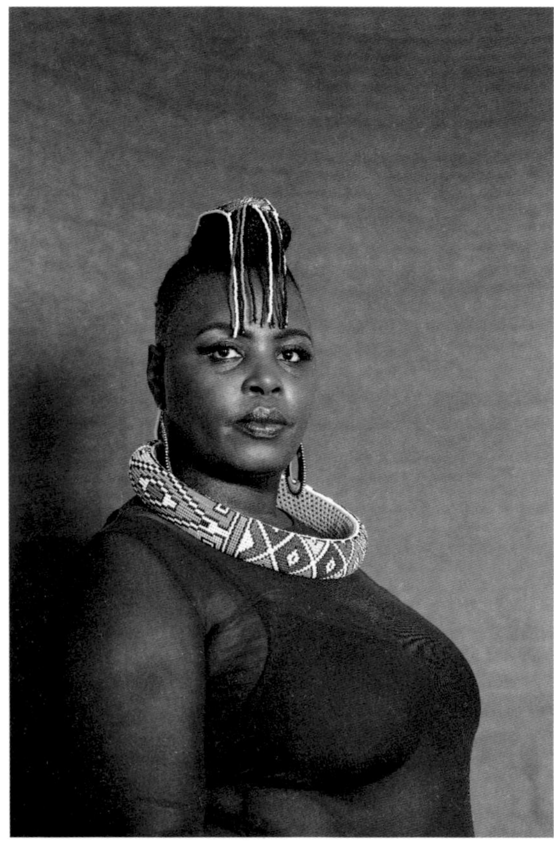

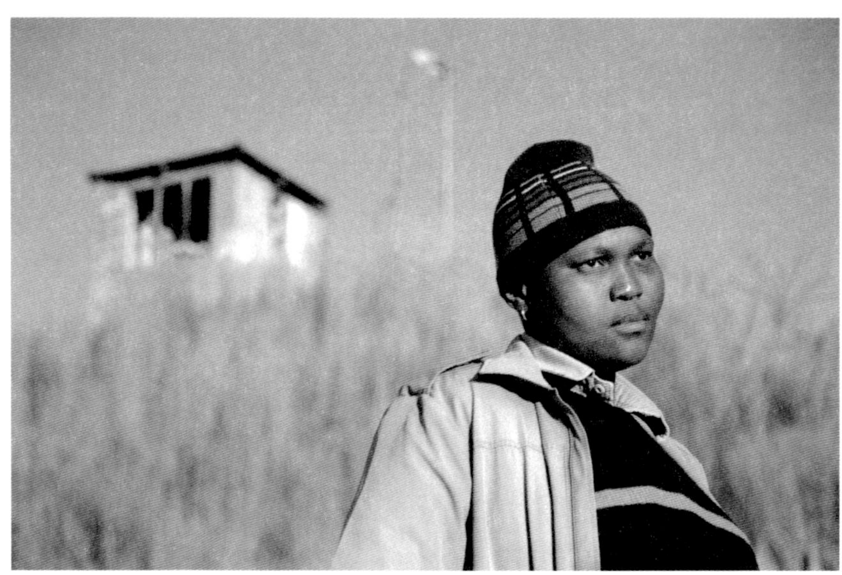

Busi Sigasa 1982–2007

REMEMBER ME WHEN I'M GONE
Busi Sigasa

For I ...
Wrote stories for the nations to read
Stood without fear and told my story
I smiled and greeted without judging
I influenced positive living to the sick
I planted seeds of hope to the hopeless
I groomed and grew
the younger ones whose parents died
I created artistic designs with my hands
I crafted and drew beautiful pictures
I installed education
l reasoned to some
I represented the minority to the majority
I made nations aware
I wronged some and made some happy
I survived against odds
I swallowed my medication even as hard as it was
sometimes
I did so to remain strong and true
I lived my life regardless of my status
I fought for women to be taken into serious
consideration by our government
I wrote and said 'my' spoken word
I fought and showed many that there's nothing
wrong with being diabetic, epileptic and HIV
I represented many of the HIV infected lesbian sisters
I told the truth never mind the judgements
I lived and I'm still living
I loved and prayed to my GOD
I prayed without hesitation, for
I believe/d
I was a big sister to my younger sisters
I listened to my mother's teachings
I became friends with father
I'D DIE FOR MY FAMILY,
I LOVED THEM SO!

I captured moments with my camera
I brought forth what was unseen to the nations
through the power of image, pen and paper
I struggled to make it life
I was taken for a ride by some whom
I thought were friends
I showed my rapist how strong I was
Regardless that he poisoned my blood with his HIV
I believed and prayed
I stood low and respected all regardless of their age,
colour and size
I say along with others
I had a unique voice
I had a message to deliver and a vision to see
I tried,
I fell and I never succeeded sometimes
I was patient while to some
I was strange
I was loved by some and was hated by some,
STILL I did my thing
I loved and appreciated beautiful women
I loved them more than life itself
Some would say ...
I am full shit!
but spiritually I was full
I was fed with GOD's glory that's why I praised HIM
I praised HIM more than I praised friends
I am my mother's daughter
I made history and marked historical books of this
world
SO ... REMEMBER ME WHEN I'M GONE!
FOR ... without no doubt
I am in peace with my maker and creator.

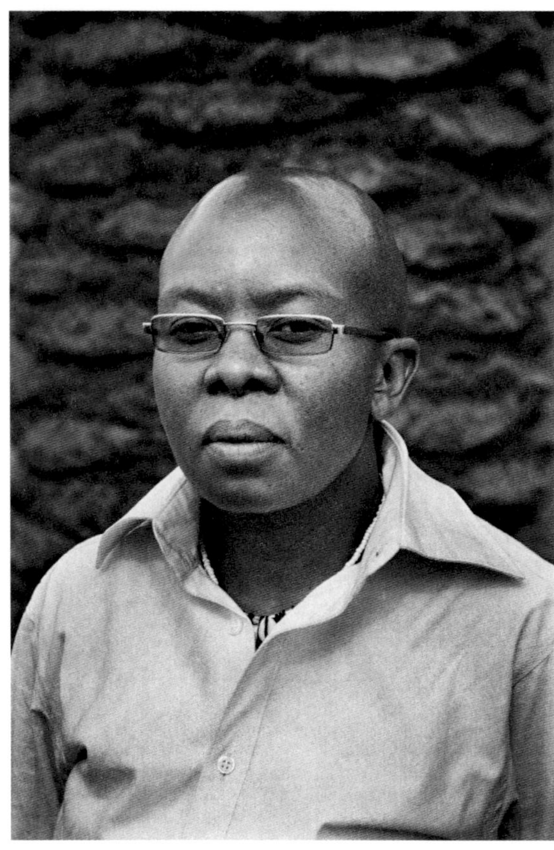

Nkunzi Nkabinde   1975–2018

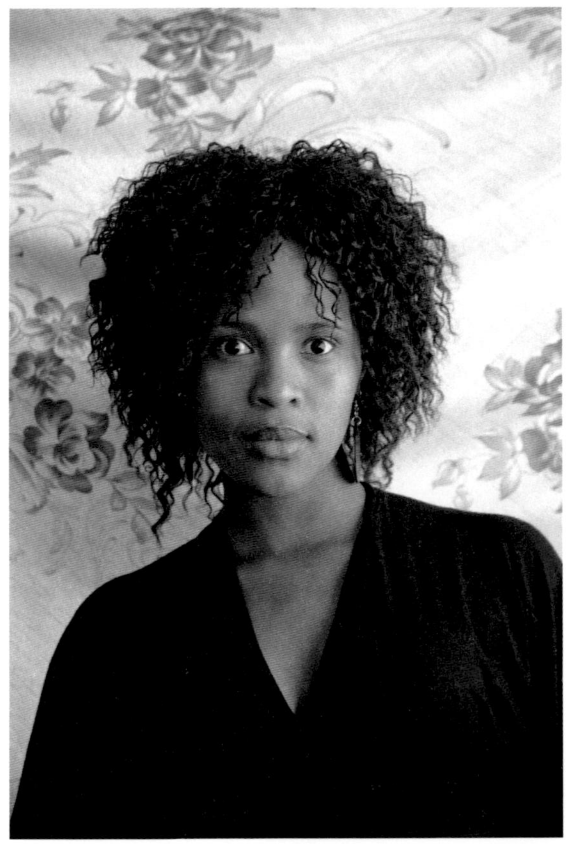

Sosi Molotsane   1987–2018

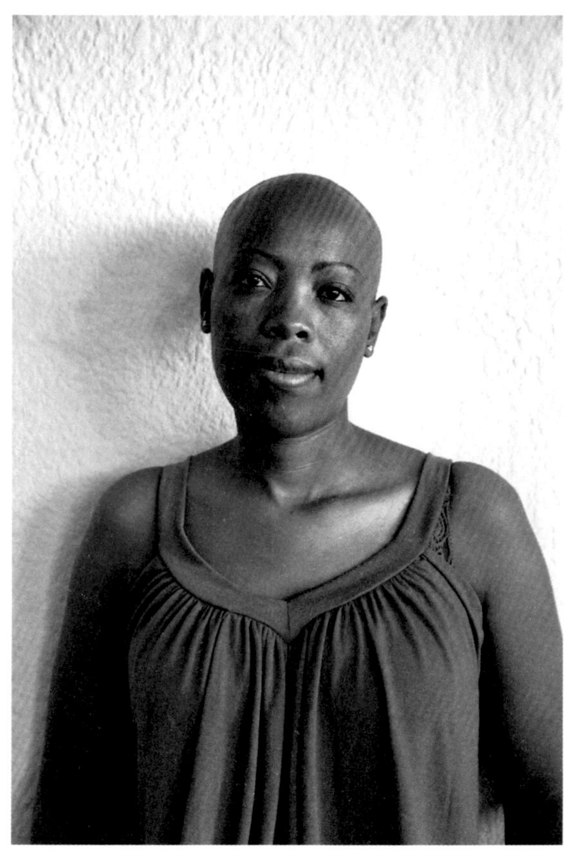

Penny Fish   1973–2009

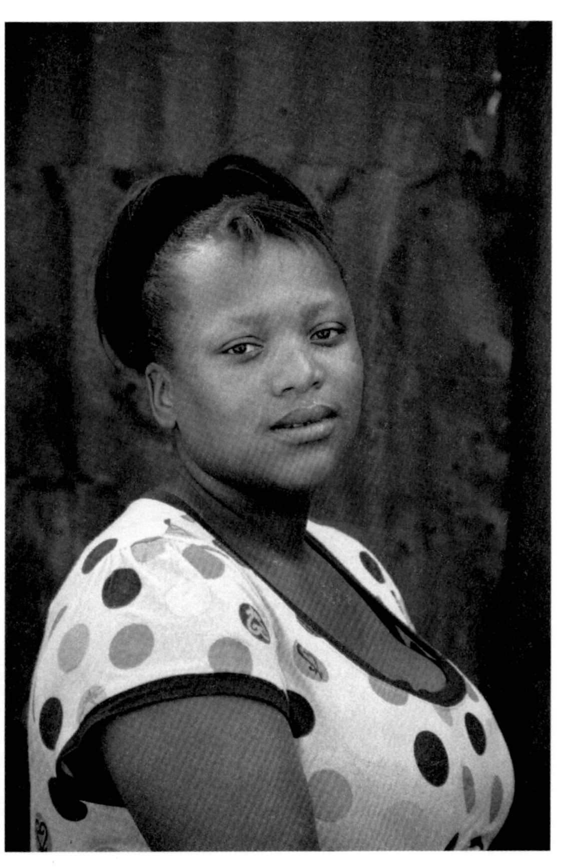

Nosizwe Cekiso   1986–2009

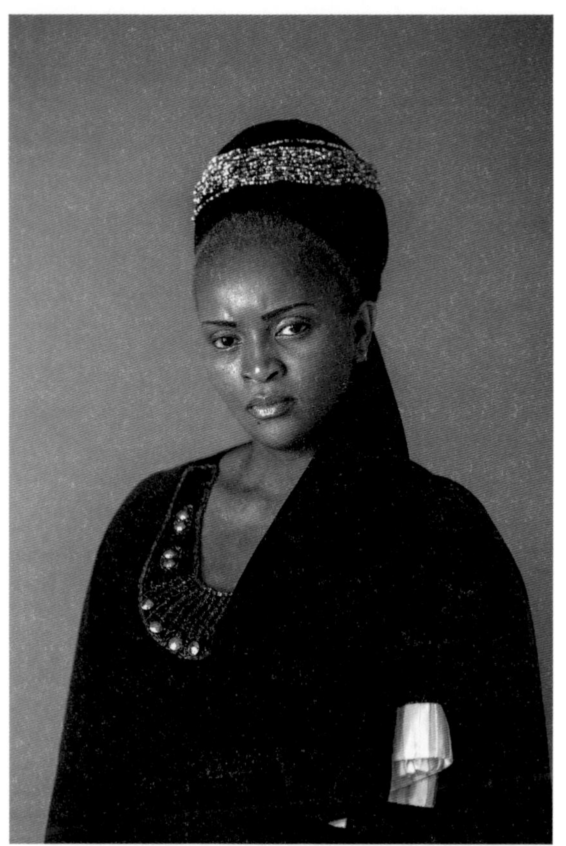

MaGesh Zungu 1977–2017

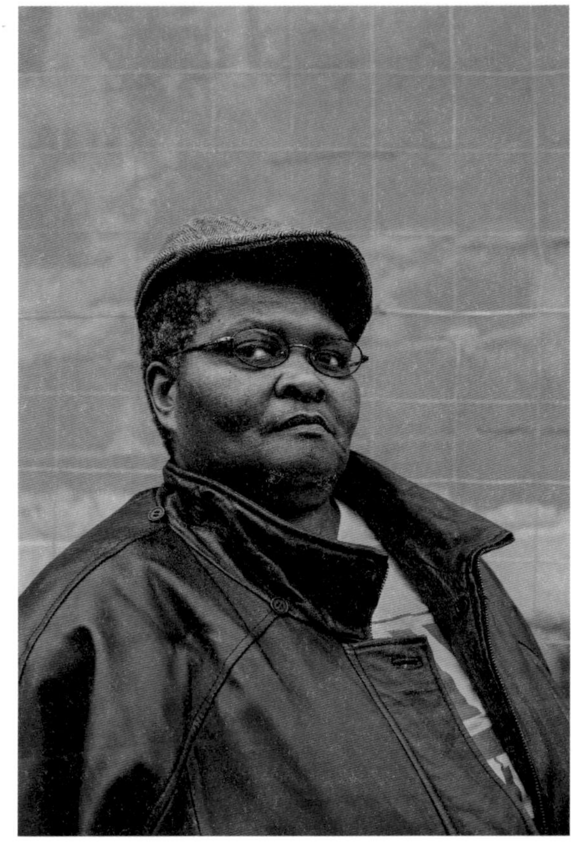

Menziwa Biyela 1949–2019

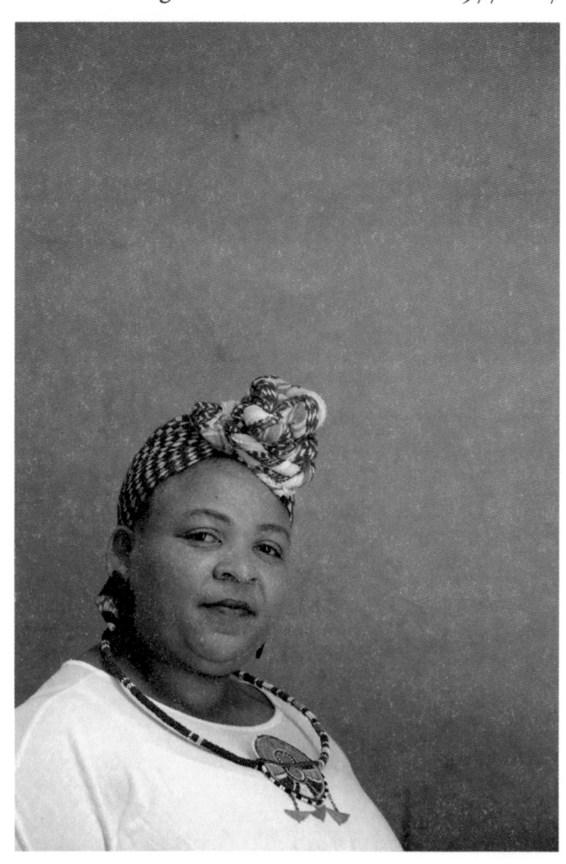

Phindile Madlala 1972–2019

63   Zanele Muholi, Vredehoek, Cape Town • 2011

64,65   Pastor Fezeka Royo I, City Hall, Johannesburg • 2017   Nokuthula Dhladhla, Berea, Johannesburg • 2007   Refilwe Mahlaba, Thokoza, Johannesburg • 2010   Zandile Malinga, Daveyton, Gauteng • 2017

Tumi Nkopane, KwaThema, Springs, Johannesburg • 2010   Funeka Soldaat, Makhaza, Khayelitsha, Cape Town • 2010   Phila Mbanjwa, Pietermaritzburg, KwaZulu-Natal • 2012   Thandi Mancane Selepe, Braamfontein, Johannesburg • 2010

66,67   Lerato Dumse, KwaThema, Springs, Johannesburg • 2010   Mbali Pearl Zulu, KwaThema, Springs, Johannesburg • 2010   Sindi Shabalala, Parktown, Johannesburg • 2007   Smangele Mzizi, Constitution Hill, Johannesburg • 2016

Nonhle Kunene, Durban • 2018   Nomthandazo Mohotlhoane I, KwaThema, Springs, Johannesburg • 2017

68,69   Monde Pharlane, Daveyton, Gauteng • 2017   Gazi T Zuma, Umlazi, Durban • 2010   Kekeletso Khena, Green Market Square, Cape Town • 2012   Nhlanhla Mofokeng, Katlehong, Johannesburg • 2012

Futhi Mkhize, Durban • 2015   Skye Chirape, Amsterdam • 2016   Sharon 'Shaz' Mthunzi, Daveyton, Johannesburg • 2014

70   Lungile Dladla, KwaThema Community Hall, Springs, Johannesburg • 2006

72   Sthesh Gonya, Parktown, Johannesburg • 2013   Vuyelwa 'Vuvu' Makubetse, Daveyton, Johannesburg • 2013

Indlovukazi Mapule, Durban • 2018

74   Busi Sigasa, Braamfontein, Johannesburg • 2006

76,77   Nkunzi Nkabinde, Braamfontein, Johannesburg • 2008   Penny Fish, Vredehoek, Cape Town • 2008

Sosi Molotsane, Yeoville, Johannesburg • 2007   Nosizwe Cekiso, Gugulethu, Cape Town • 2008

78   MaGesh Zungu, Brooklyn, New York • 2015   Menziwa Biyela, Verulam, Durban, KwaZulu-Natal • 2015

Phindile Madlala, Durban, KwaZulu-Natal • 2016

Thinking Activism:
Zanele Muholi and Queer Photography Histories

Sarah Allen

Zanele Muholi was drawn to photography through activism, galvanised by the twin desire to see themself reflected in a new era of democracy in South Africa and to raise awareness of how that same democracy was still failing them. An activist sensibility defines their practice. Placing Muholi within a nexus of specific work made by queer photographers not only allows us to locate Muholi within broader transnational lineages but also allows us to appreciate their particular contribution crafted by re-enforcing or re-centering activism.[1]

COLLABORATE, DOCUMENT, ARCHIVE

'I am re-writing a black queer and trans visual history of South Africa for the world to know of our existence, resistance and persistence'[2] — ZANELE MUHOLI

One of the earliest queer photographic contexts that Muholi was influenced by is found within lesbian feminism which developed primarily in North America and Western Europe in the 1970s in response to second-wave feminism and gay liberation. Joan E. Biren, one of the photographers associated with this movement, was of particular influence. Muholi has stated: 'Her work related to what I wanted to achieve, and it still means so much to me in ways that you won't believe'.[3]

The post-Stonewall years in which Biren's work can be situated saw increased possibility for publicly imaging the social, community and family aspects of queer life. In Biren's two self-published books, *Eye to Eye: Portraits of Lesbians* (1979) and *Making a Way: Lesbians Out Front* (1987), lesbians were depicted with families, at work, at play, at rest (see right). The focus was resolutely on social life rather than the sexual – a means through which Biren intervened in the narrow lesbian stereotypes available to her: 'the image of lesbian as vampire and the faux lesbian – images shot by photographers such as David Hamilton of women who were not necessarily lesbians but who were engaged in intimate lesbian scenes'.[4]

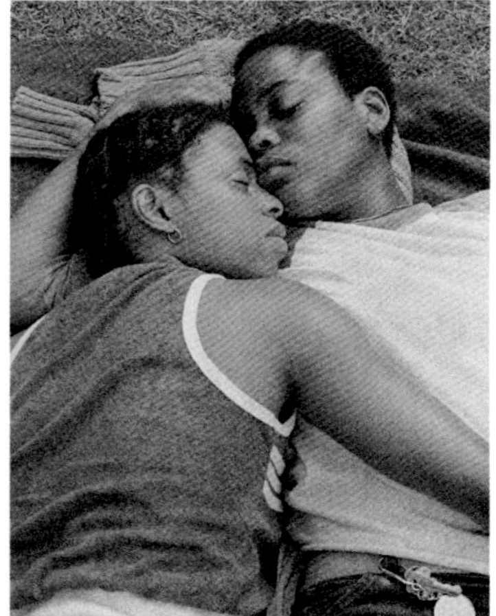

I.

For Biren, the approach to photographing individuals was rooted in 'collaboration, not domination'.[5] Consent and collaboration also define Muholi's photographic approach, symbolised in their insistence on the term 'participant' as opposed to 'subject'. A critical element of this collaboration, and one which takes a cue from Biren, is the importance of giving voice to participants. Nowhere is this more apparent than in *Faces and Phases* (2006–ongoing), Muholi's series now numbering several hundred portraits of lesbians, gender-non-conforming individuals and trans men – a family album writ large, and a homage to both the individual and the collective. Participants appear alongside testimonies. 'I am a young black lesbian woman and pride myself in knowing who I love and who I want to share my life, soul and body with,' writes Phila Mbanjwa in the *Faces and Phases* publication (see p.65, bottom left). Lungile Dladla, a survivor of 'corrective rape' who contracted HIV from the attack, affirms, 'I am not a Victim but a Victor' (see pp.70–1).

81

At the heart of Muholi's practice are questions of visibility. A key expression is the insistence on naming of participants – a choice which has profound implications, as it can act as a second 'coming out' for those pictured.[6] Biren was equally committed to naming participants, drawing inspiration from Audre Lorde's sentiment: 'that visibility which makes us most vulnerable is that which also is the source of our greatest strength'.[7] When Muholi came to write their thesis for their MFA in Documentary Media in 2009, it was Biren's quote on visibility which opened the paper: 'Without a visual identity we have no community, no support network, no movement. Making ourselves visible is a political act. Making ourselves visible is a continual process.'[8] Muholi has taken Biren's concept of 'continual process' to its ultimate expression in adopting *Faces and Phases* as a lifelong project, a living archive. This drive to archive extends to documentation of many facets of Black queer life, such as pride, protest, weddings and funerals.

An important way in which Muholi's work marks a departure from Biren is in its inclusion of images of private intimacy between same-sex couples – enforcing its normality and redressing its suppression within racist, heteronormative and patriarchal image regimes. Secondly, Biren and many of her contemporaries, such as Tee Corinne and Cathy Cade, were white photographers and documented white individuals in the majority. This is markedly different from Muholi, who is telling a specifically Black queer history from within. Given this, Muholi's work could also be positioned in relation to a trajectory of queer African American photographers: for example, Lenn Keller, who documented Black queer lives in the San Francisco Bay Area from the 1980s, and Lola Flash, who for decades has made work addressing Black queer experience and was a photographer for ACT UP (AIDS Coalition to Unleash Power).

For Muholi, creating this Black South African queer archive is a deeply political act. They note: 'absence, for me, is an active process of silencing, one that condones and facilitates the ongoing violence against women's bodies in general and the bodies of Black queer (wo)men in particular'.[9] Muholi's archive thus seeks to evidence lives and histories which testify to inequality and injustice felt by individuals who cannot access the rights enshrined in South Africa's progressive constitution. Moreover, by representing Black queer lives absent from the visual landscape in a new era of democracy, Muholi ultimately reveals a more democratic view of post-apartheid South Africa. Ushering this archive into existence is therefore the means through which Muholi has spoken of claiming their full citizenship, insisting that the so-called Rainbow Nation deliver on its promise of inclusion.[10]

SELF-PROJECTIONS: TOWARDS AN ACTIVIST SELF-PORTRAIT

'When I position myself in my own frame, I do so on my own terms attempting to articulate my own way of seeing and wanting to be seen'[11] — ZANELE MUHOLI

Self-portraiture has proven to be a uniquely suited genre for queer photographers to stage scenes in order to explore hybrid identities and multiple subjectivities.

In their approach to self-portraiture, which sees them project myriad characters, archetypes and personas, Muholi joins an arc alongside the work of artists such as Maud Sulter. Sulter's series *Zabat* (1989) recast Black women, including herself, writer Alice Walker and artist Lubaina Himid, as the nine muses of antiquity, characters consistently depicted as white throughout history.[12] If some of Muholi's work may appear to engage in similar re-enactments – *Babhekile II, Oslo, 2015* riffing on Vermeer's *Girl with a Pearl Earring* or *Thembeka I, New York Upstate, 2015* (p.130), a re-imagining of depictions of the Virgin Mary – this is perhaps not the primary purpose of the image. Muholi's stagings are often much more direct in their specific agenda, the body used as a canvas to project issues onto in the service of 'bringing forth political statements'.[13]

Reading one of Muholi's early performative self-portraits, *Miss Lesbian I, Amsterdam, 2009*, against a work from Lyle Ashton Harris's series *Constructs* (1989) helps illustrate this. In *Constructs #10*, the first in a series of four images, Harris is shown wearing a wig and whiteface (below right). According to the artist, the series is 'a social critique of notions of passing and notions of beauty'.[14] 'Passing' is the ability for a person to be regarded as a member of an identity group other than their own; it can be a form of self-preservation against prejudice, harassment or risk of violence.[15] In *Constructs*, Harris addresses passing as it pertains to race and sexuality, stating, 'clearly I'm not trying to pass'.[16] In *Miss Lesbian I, Amsterdam, 2009* (below left), although Muholi dons a swimsuit, tiara and wig, the presence of body hair and a tattoo places this contestant outside hetero-normative standards of beauty. In addition, the sash proudly proclaims 'Miss Black Lesbian'. Clearly Muholi does not seek to pass either.

A key way in which their approaches diverge is in their positioning to activism. Harris has commented that *Constructs* was not a work of AIDS activism, though it was made at the height of the pandemic in the US.[17] Conversely, Muholi's image speaks to their belief in the importance of queer Black beauty pageants as a space of resistance which redresses the narrative of victimhood that consumes Black queer individuals in South Africa and precludes their claim to beauty.[18] In 1997, Muholi

II.

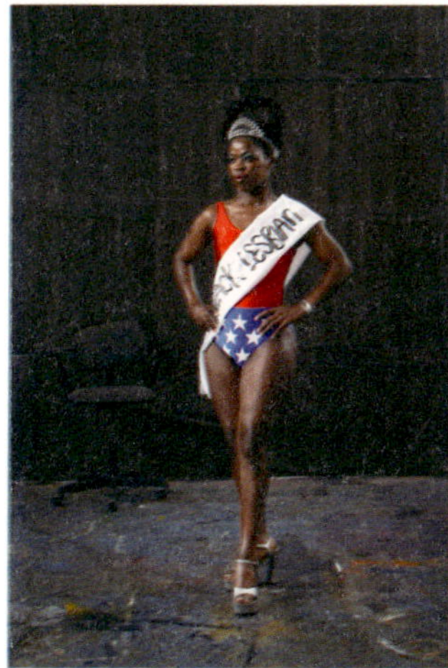

III.

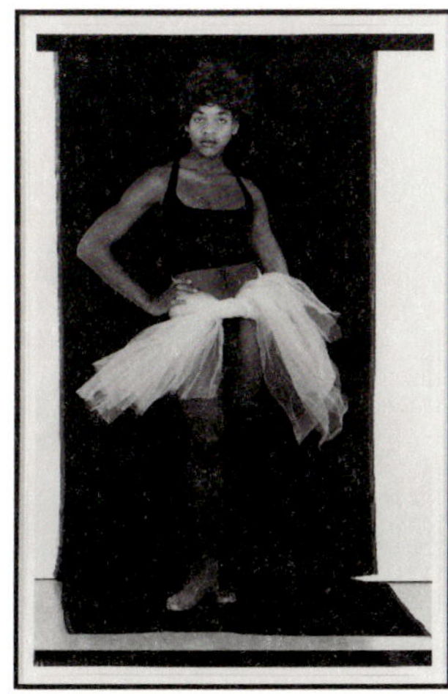

themself won 2nd prize in a beauty pageant hosted by the Black lesbian organisation Nkateko. Later they would stage beauty contests at the Forum for the Empowerment of Women, and their series *Brave Beauties* (2014–ongoing) focuses specifically on beauty pageant contestants.

Muholi's *Miss Lesbian* series seems equally poised to remind us of South Africa's engagement with beauty pageants on the international stage. It was not until 1970 that South Africa allowed Black women to compete in Miss World. However, this

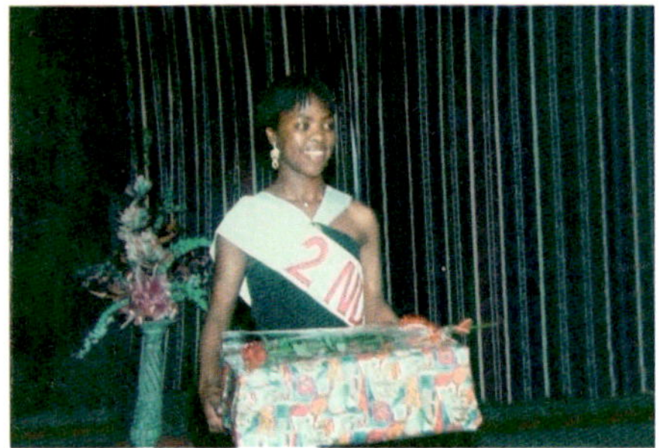

IV.

was only through a dual entry of a white woman to represent Miss South Africa and a Black woman to represent Miss Africa South, a widely criticised approach which determined beauty along racial lines. Whereas Harris choose whiteface to critique canons of beauty, it is interesting to consider how Muholi would later darken their skin through photographic contrast. This approach to darkening skin tone is worthy of far more detailed analysis, yet for this discussion seems important to position in relation to Muholi's experience coming of age during a time when an 'internal war against our own black, African beauty' was being waged – the marketing of skin bleaching creams being just one manifestation: 'many of us conformed and bleached ... even as we resisted and fought against racial hierarchy'.[19]

Somnyama Ngonyama (2012–ongoing) amalgamates many references to such apartheid histories as well as to Muholi's own Zulu heritage, personal experiences and broader histories of Black representation. Rotimi Fani-Kayode's performative portraiture adopted a similar hybrid approach, often fusing an exploration of his sexuality with reference to his Yoruba roots. In his own words, he sought to redress 'the vulgar objectification of Africa which we know at one extreme from the work of Leni Riefenstahl and, at the other, from the "victim" images which appear constantly in the media. It is now time for us to re-appropriate such images and to transform them ritualistically into images of our own creation.'[20] It is a sentiment which speaks to many of Muholi's self-stagings.

In *MaID in Harlem, African Market, 116 St, 2015*, Muholi is shown draped in beads, shells and fly-whisks – a direct comment on anthropological photography which often posed subjects with objects connoting their African 'otherness'.[21] The image critiques a Western fascination with such clichéd objects in a manner not dissimilar to Fani-Kayode's *Dan Mask* 1989, in which the artist is pictured dramatically elevating the mask like a sacred offering.[22]

Yet there are other concerns at play in Muholi's image. Muholi has spoken of how each item might hail from different countries of Africa. They therefore inflect the image with a broader inquiry into questions of global commerce and trade – the

systems and exchanges that saw these products of
African labour arrive in Western metropolitan capitals.
Muholi appears nude, and so a visual equivalence is
made between the consumption of these objects of
African 'otherness' and the same consumption of
the racialised body. Black labour is a subject Muholi
returns to throughout their practice, the title of the
image *MaID* standing for 'my Identity', and the word
'maid' referring to 'the quotidian and demeaning
name given to all subservient black women in South
Africa'.[23]

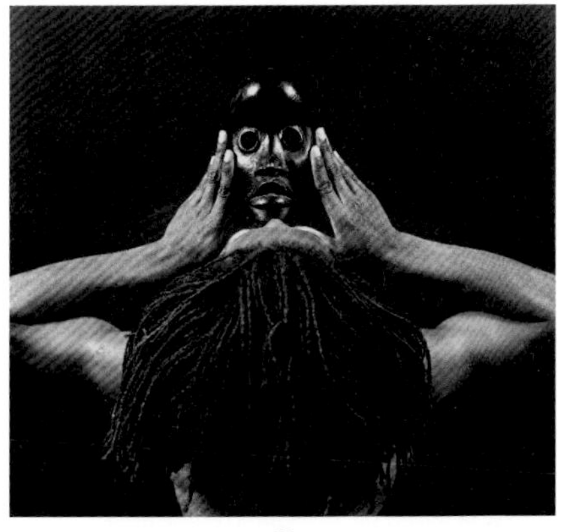

V.

In *MaID in Harlem, African Market, 116 St, 2015*, as with many
images in *Somnyama Ngonyama*, Muholi sourced materials
from the immediate environment they found themself in.
This instant collaboration with place, re-purposing of the
ordinary, working with what is at one's disposal, is activist
in sensibility. In *Vile, Gothenburg, Sweden, 2015*, flour from the
kitchen is used to dull shine on the face. In *Bester I, Mayotte,
2015*, toothpaste is used on the lips (p.126). In *Lena, London,
2018*, an elaborate headdress is fashioned from a hotel
bed runner (p.135). Crucially, and unlike Sulter, Harris or
Fani-Kayode, many of Muholi's transformations are products of an itinerant lifestyle. Each new environment is the
studio, and each image bears the location and date. This is
an act of purposefully inserting and marking the presence
of the Black queer body into places all around the world,
places that may otherwise deny or erase its existence.

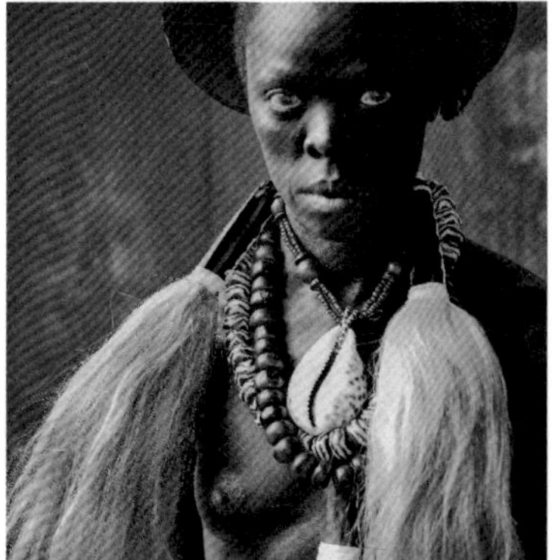

VI.

This brief framing of Muholi's work within broader queer photography histories
reveals the photographer's ability to cross and collapse photographic boundaries –
from traditional portrait photography to expansive documentation of Black queer
life, to images of queer intimacy, to symbolic self-portraiture. While this diversity
alone is enough to differentiate it, the ultimate strength of their contribution lies in
re-enforcing an activist approach throughout the varying types of images created; in
thinking activism at each turn.

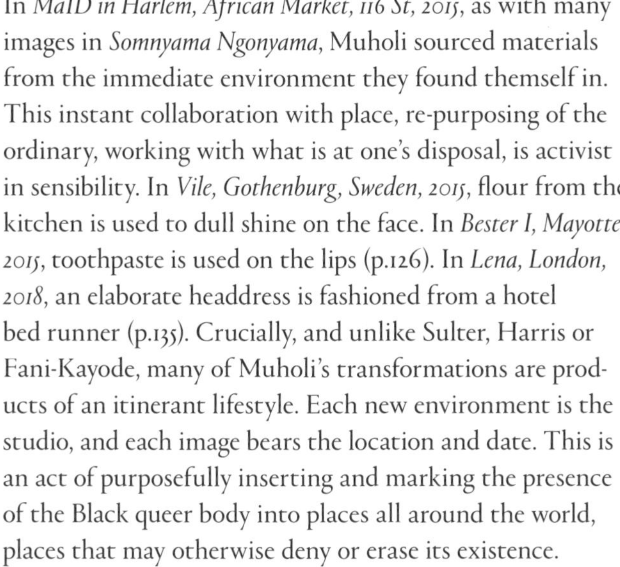

I. Joan E. Biren (JEB), Priscilla and Regina, Brooklyn, New York, 1979

II. Zanele Muholi, Miss Lesbian I, Amsterdam, 2009

III. Lyle Ashton Harris, Constructs #10, from the series Constructs, 1989

IV. Ms Sappho, Club Chameleon, Johannesburg, 1997 (image altered)

V. Rotimi Fani-Kayode, Dan Mask, 1989

VI. Zanele Muholi, MaID in Harlem, African Market, 116 St, 2015

Brave Beauties

2014–ongoing

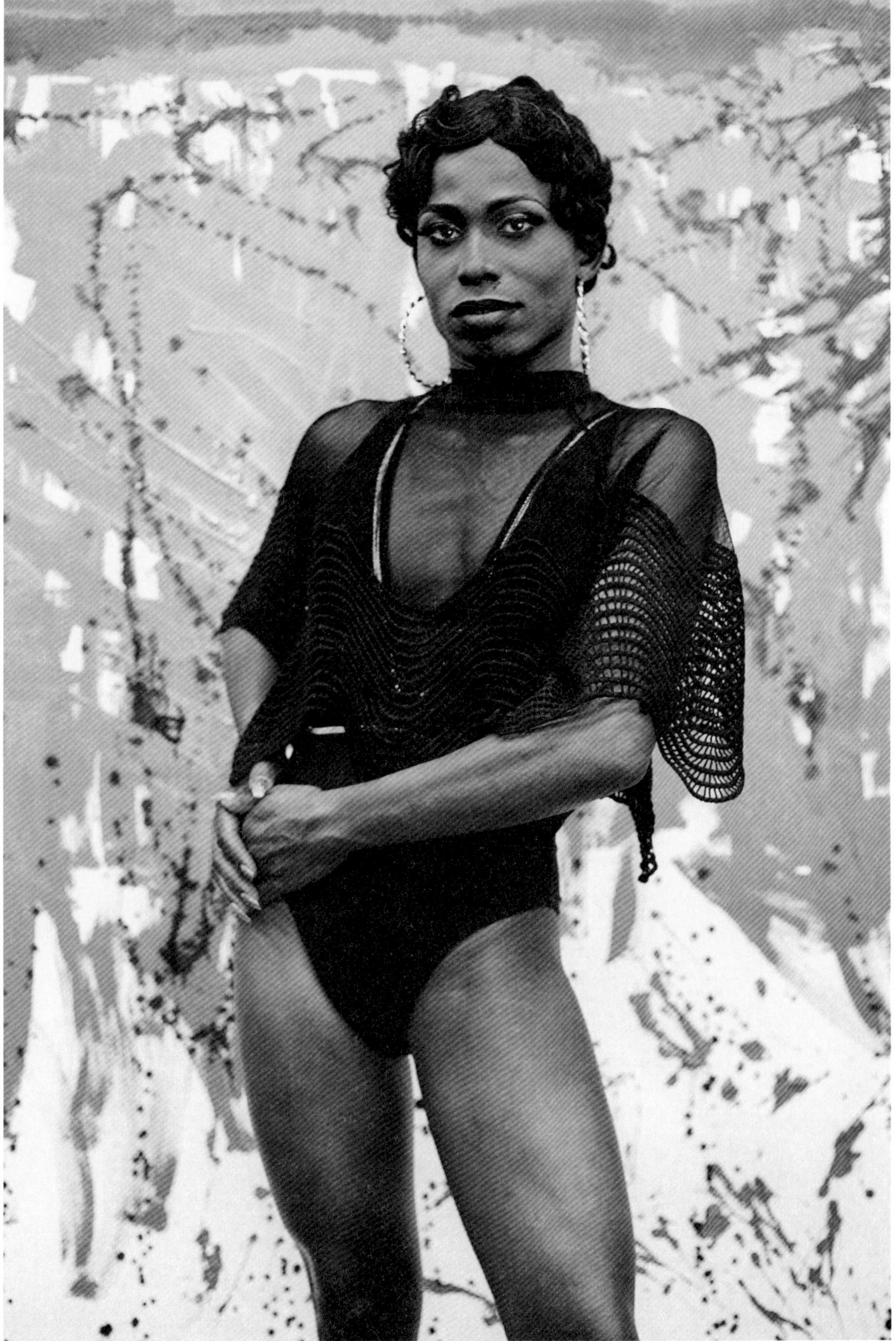

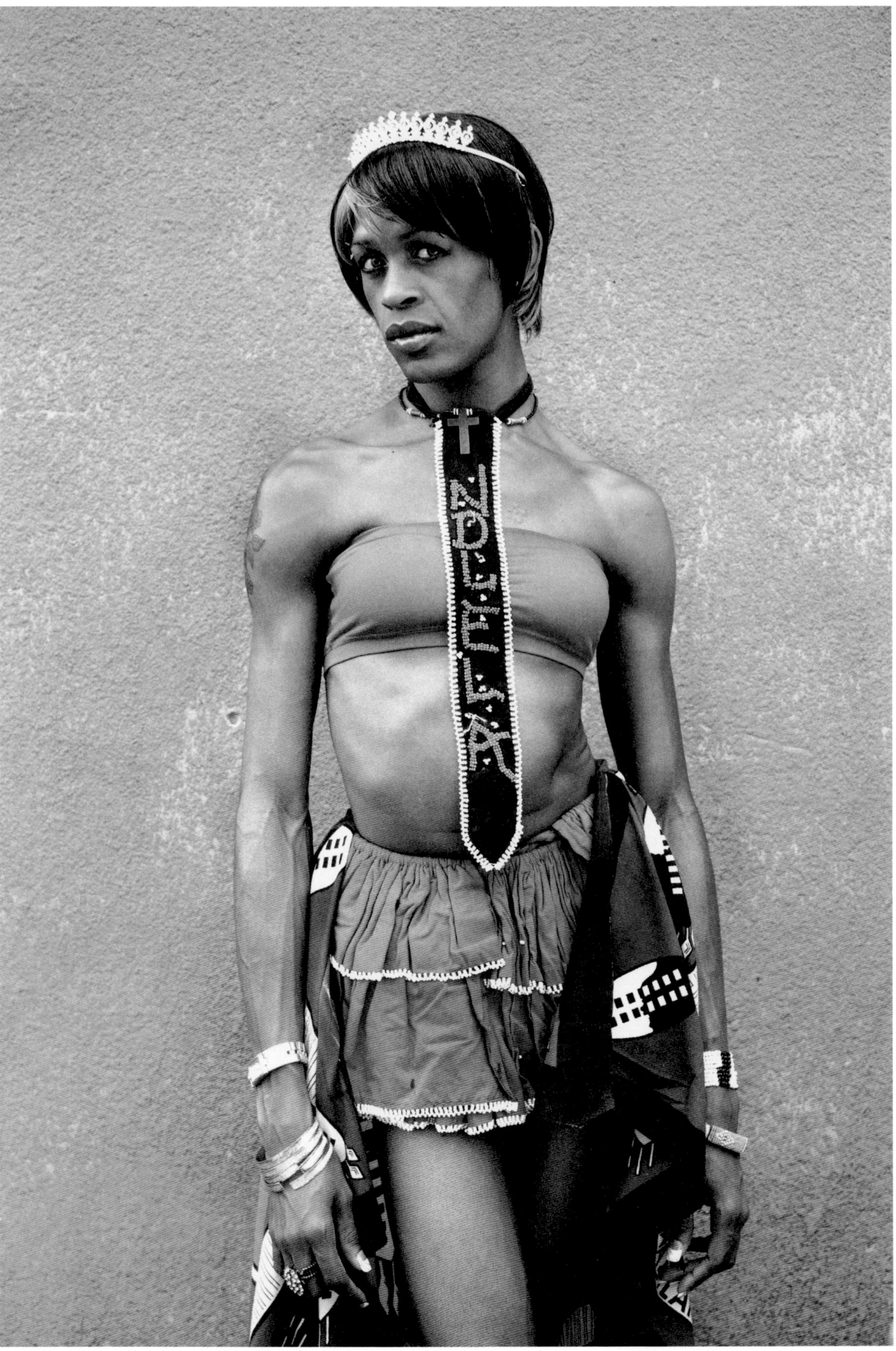

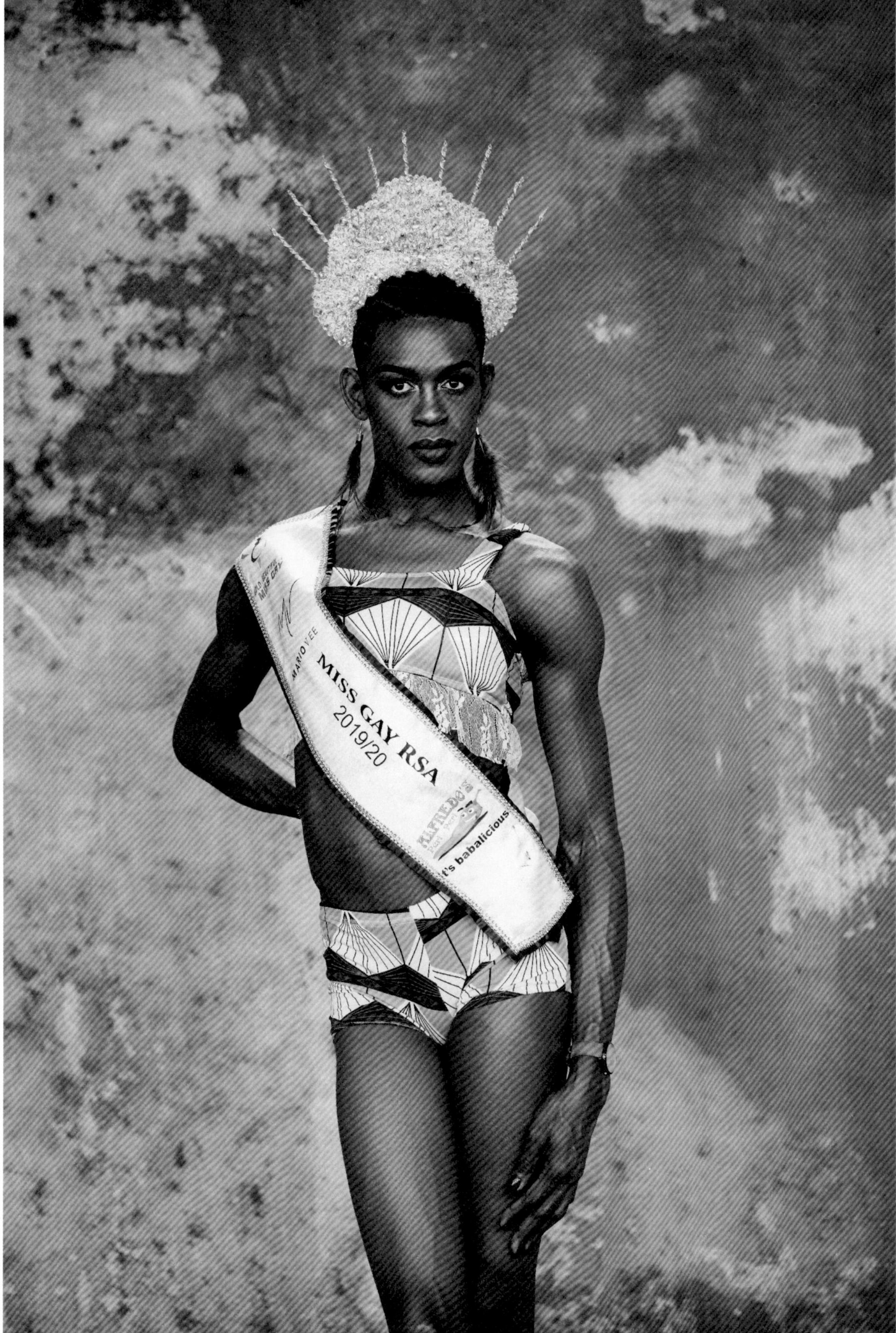
MISS GAY RSA
2019/20
MARIO VEE
It's babalicious

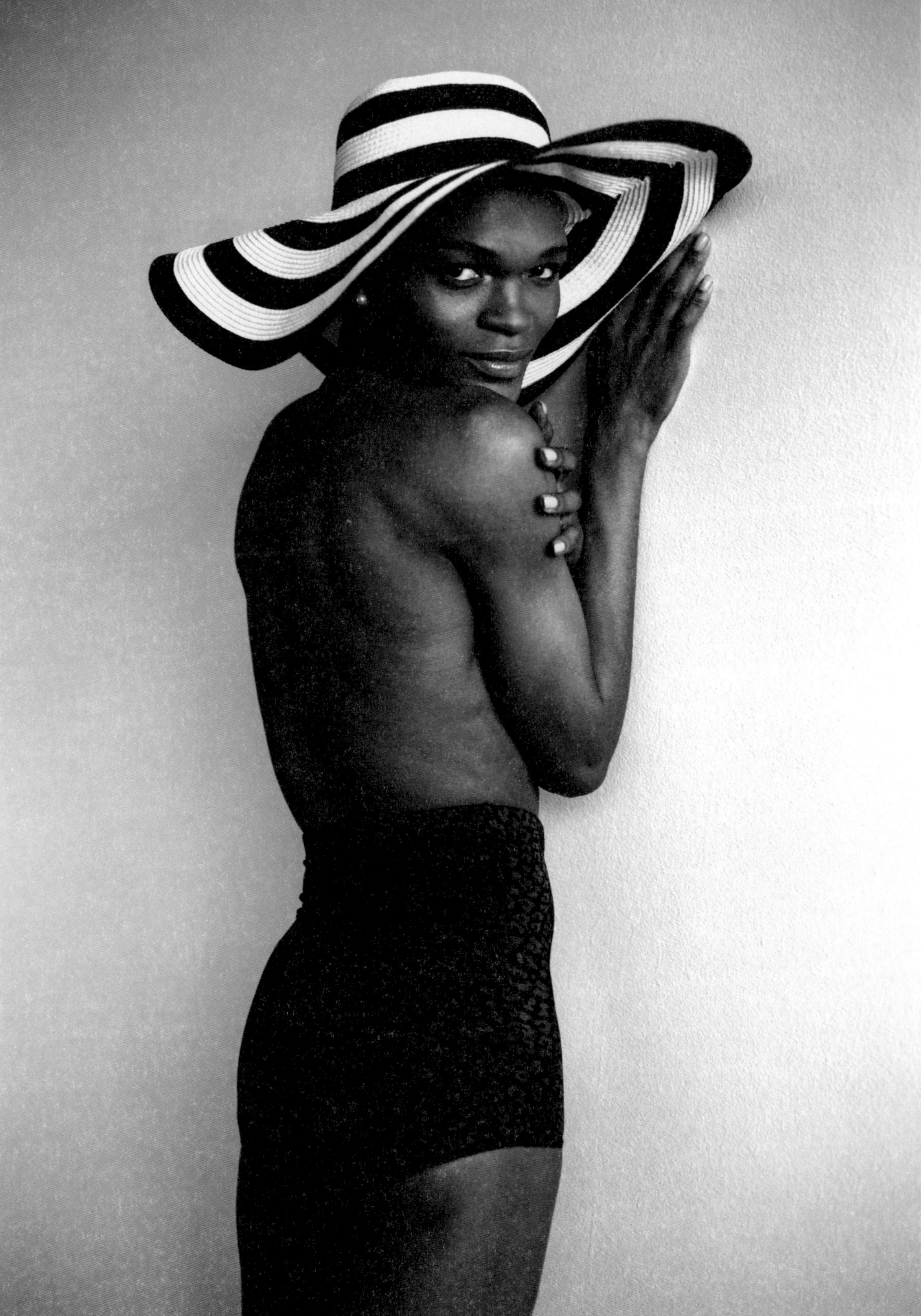

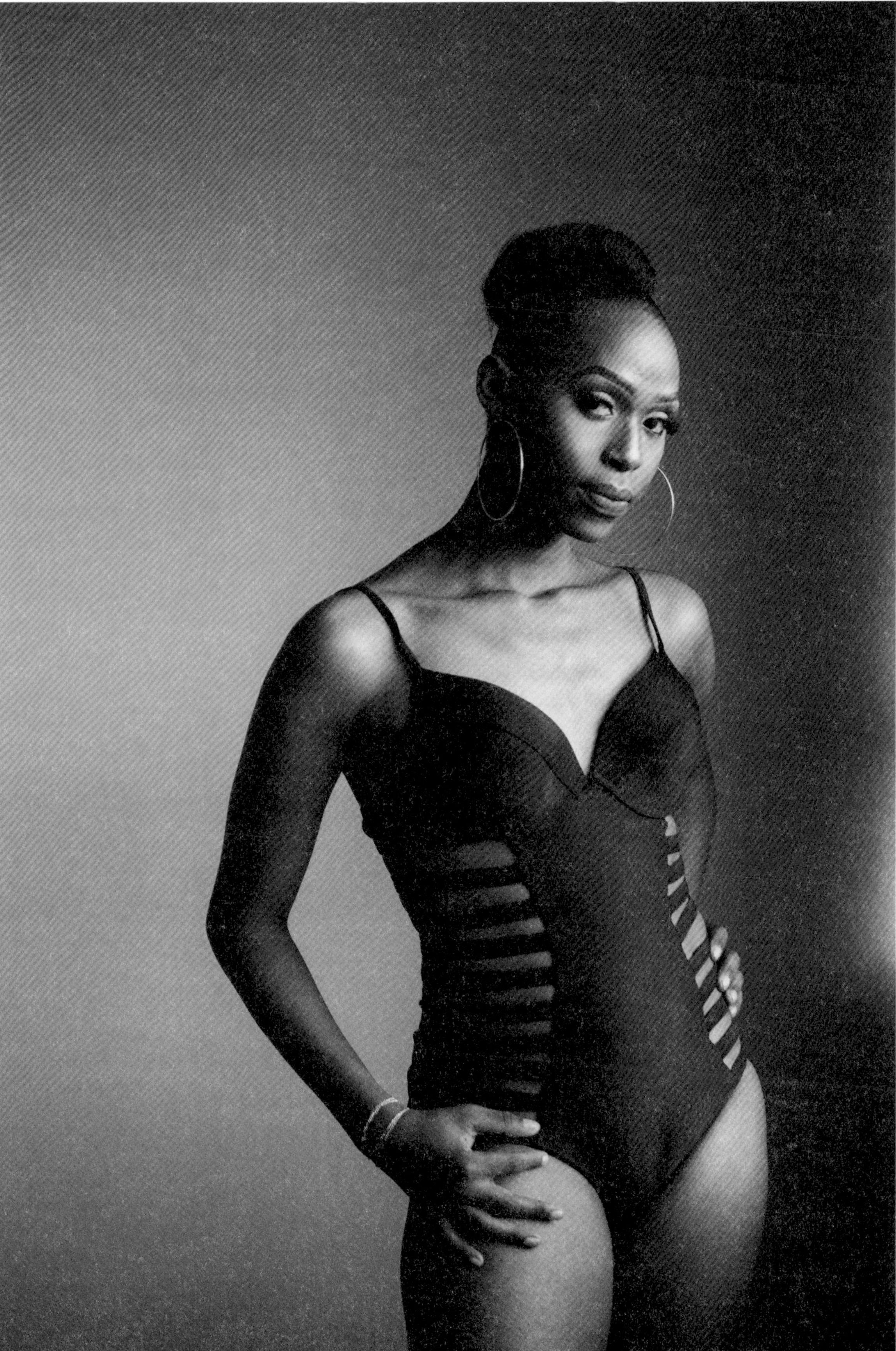

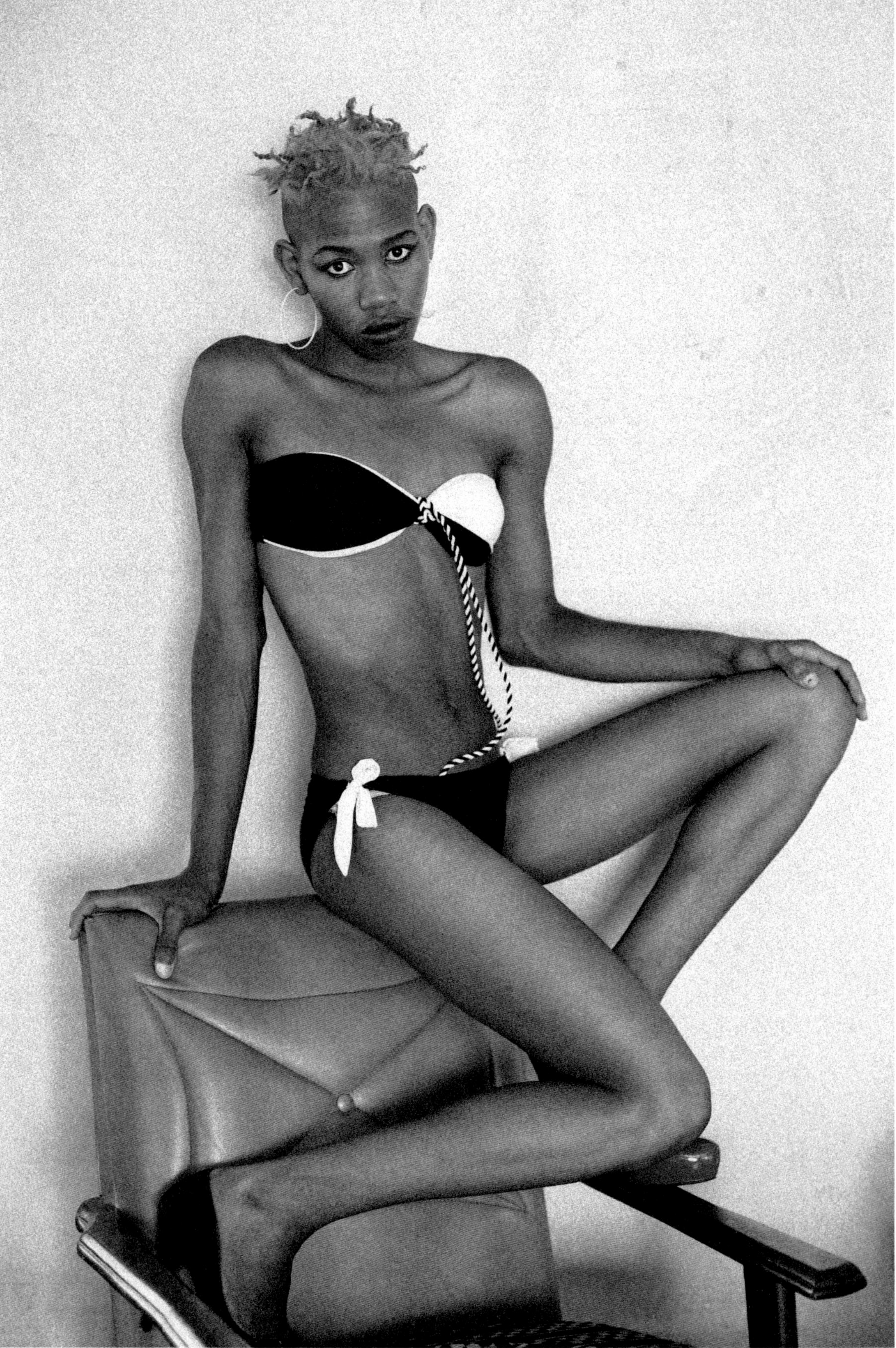

It is very difficult to tell my side of the story.

My pronoun is she or her, but you have those
people who still don't understand me.

Going to school was like an everyday war.

Today I want to break it out, I don't want this
woman in me to die crying.

Don't see my gender, just see me as a person.

Living in a township, people are really not
familiar with the term 'transgender'.

Try and find out more.

Change is good.

Transform.

We are all born from love.

Once they have more knowledge about
transgender people, it's very rare for them
to discriminate that person.

People just need to live, freedom, just live.

Patience shall prevail.

Whatever they were trying to take from me,
they failed.

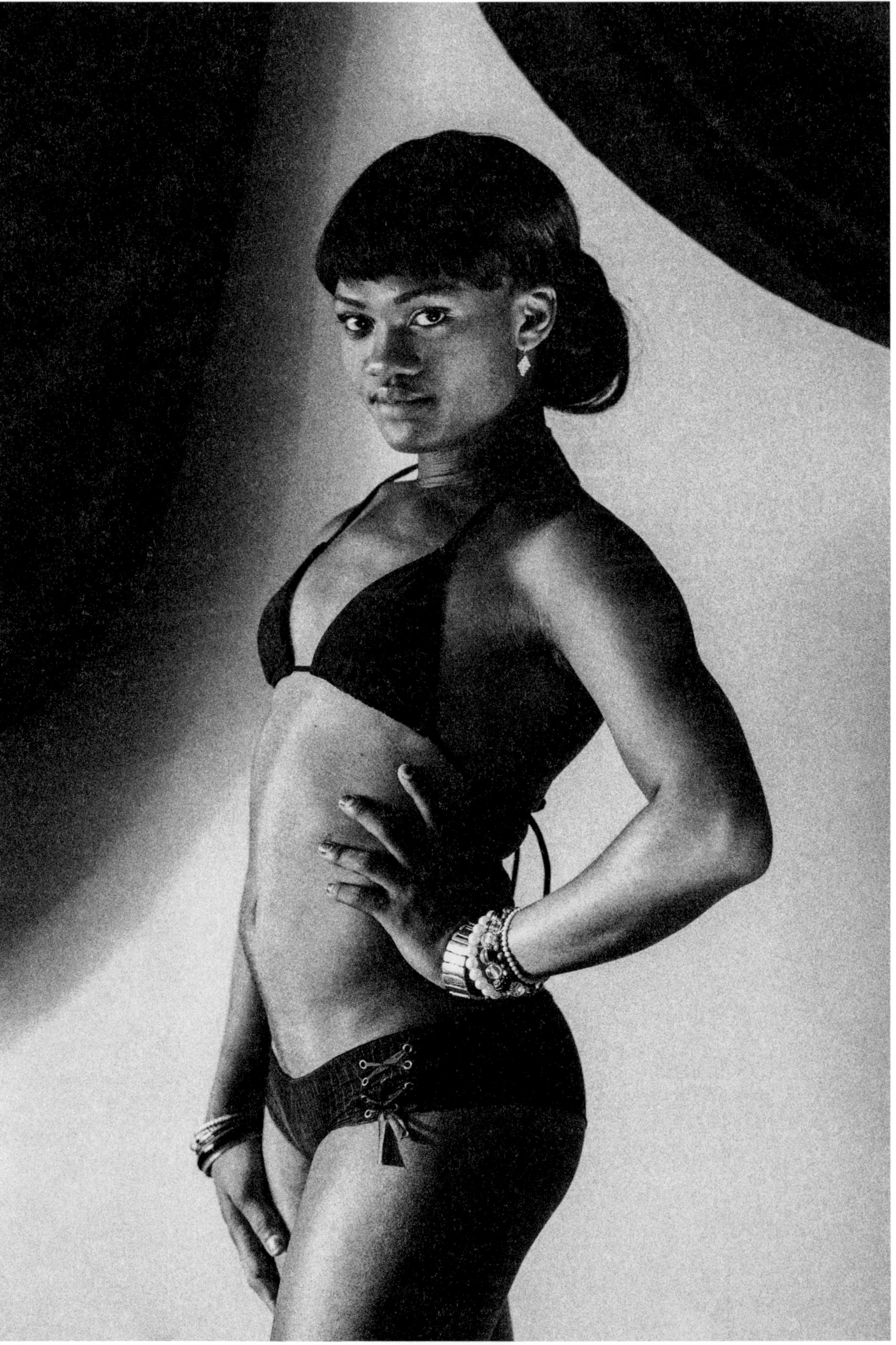

Queering Space through Photography: Zanele Muholi's Colour Portraits

Yasufumi Nakamori

Queering Space through Photography: Zanele Muholi's Colour Portraits

Yasufumi Nakamori

Zanele Muholi's remarkable colour portraits are worth investigating in regard to a number of factors. First, the artist and participants often chose public locations for the photo-shoots, in light of both the recent history and current conditions of South Africa. Secondly, the act of photographing a Black LGBTQIA+ cohort in public space constitutes a core aspect of Muholi's activism through photography. Thirdly, the decision to make the images colour, thus distinguishing the impact of the photography, gives a sense of naturalism and reality to the people and places depicted, helping to convey immediacy and nuance, and making the work more clearly rooted in the present.

Some of the portraits from *Brave Beauties* (portraits of transgender women and beauty queens) and many from *Beulahs* (portraits of gay and gender-non-conforming men), as well as the work titled *Miss D'vine*, were photographed in colour in a public space, mostly outdoor. In contrast, for the artist's well-known *Faces and Phases* series, portraits of South African Black lesbians and transgender women were made in various locations, including private indoor spaces and semi-private settings in outdoor areas. These images are presented in black and white, and retain formal elements of traditional portrait photography, revealing the upper body, or the body above the knee, with natural light in contrapposto. Participants are rendered in a dignified fashion, presented like icons, in deep black and white contrast. Muholi and the participant exchange intense, direct looks, jointly engaged in 'returning the colonizing gaze and responding actively to heteronormative and patriarchal constructions of Black queer bodies, genders and sexuality'.[1] With some collaborative elements, Muholi directs their poses and gazes, and focuses on producing images that reflect them in the best light.[2] On the other hand, in their colour portraits, the exchange of gazes between participant and photographer varies and is often loose. As a part of collaboration, Muholi gives the participant freedom to pose in public and outdoor environments that are often significant to the history and people of South Africa. Each participant's expression in each photograph differs based on the chosen place and the mood of the photo-shoot. Muholi and the participant are aware that a location may not necessarily be safe or suitable for a shoot because of the public nature of the space. With this in mind, images are made while Muholi and the participant are in a dialogue.[3] During the photo-shoots, Muholi has also had someone, like their nephew, to watch out for them against curious onlookers, so that they can accomplish the shoot without interruption.[4]

Locations for such photo-shoots have included a Durban beach, Constitution Hill in Johannesburg, and mostly working-class inner-city suburbs such as Hillbrow and Yeoville. Muholi's use of colour adds complexities and realism to the locations and brings a viewer's attention to details of the participants and the environments. Muholi characterises as 'queering space' their collaborative shooting of, and with, a participant in a public space where LGBTQIA+ citizens are not expected, or where Black individuals were prohibited during the apartheid era, or in a location that signifies the legal achievements of the Black South African LGBTQIA+ community. For the photographer, this act is key to their activism, challenging prejudice against the LGBTQIA+ community, in particular transgender and gender-non-conforming individuals whom Muholi has photographed.

Despite the fact that apartheid was dismantled around 1994, one can still find strong remnants of the system in every corner of South African society. Accessibility to certain types of public space – a remote scenic beach, for example – is even today not equal to all, often available only to wealthy white residents and visitors, due to enormous differences in economic statuses and therefore resources among the people of South Africa, traceable back to apartheid-era legislation.[5]

During apartheid, beaches were strictly subject to the daily practice of segregation of public facilities and social events, under which the most distant and undesirable beaches were allotted to those classified as Black, Indian and coloured.[6] Exceptionally, in Durban, in 1982, a beach designed for multiracial visitors was allocated just north of white-only beaches, which caused much local controversy.[7] Beach space for a transgender population, moreover, was extremely limited at best, or non-existent.[8]

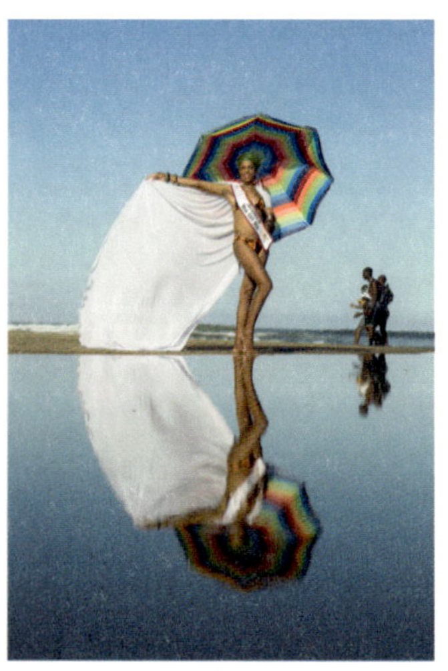

I.

Against this historical background, a portrait of Mellisa Mbambo symbolises the abolition of apartheid, centering the beauty queen, in a bikini, on a Durban beach (left). A transgender woman, who won the Miss Gay South Africa 2017 contest, she strikes a pose with a beauty pageant sash across her body and a rainbow parasol in her left hand. On a clear day with a blue sky, Mbambo dominates the public beach once prohibited to Black, Indian and coloured people. Frontally facing, she marches on triumphantly, paying no attention to the people walking behind her. Muholi's lens, shuttered from a distance, has transformed and queered the once-segregated beach and turned it into a central stage for Mbambo, who celebrates her beauty and transgender identity. Muholi's choice to present the image in colour makes it distinctly vibrant and contemporary, and accentuates the natural beauty of the beach.

However, the photograph does not offer the kind of artistic intensity and density that Muholi's black and white portraits do. In this regard, it is important to note that Muholi initially became accustomed to seeing photography in black and white – fine art, and particularly documentary photography that unfolds the recent history of South Africa – through their formal training and viewing of works by others, particularly South African photographers and photojournalists.[9] Colours in their photography are Muholi's conscious selection, and they are part of a photographic vocabulary that seems experimental and still developing, given that Muholi's primary photographic practice still lies in black and white.

In urban settings like Johannesburg's working-class neighbourhoods, Muholi photographed members of the Black LGBTQIA+ community in colour. Muholi themself once lived not far from Yeoville, one such neighbourhood. *Muzi Khumalo I, Yeoville, Johannesburg, 2006* is an outdoor portrait of an effeminate gay man named Muzi Khumalo (opposite). In this work, Khumalo stands straight and still on a seemingly bleak patch of land in populated Yeoville. The slender body in a yellow floral top and maroon pants, with a matching pair of sandals and a colourful beaded necklace, stands out against the background. Shot as if an ordinary moment in daily life, with the participant gazing straight at Muholi, the portrait suggests Khumalo's resilience and will to be seen in society.

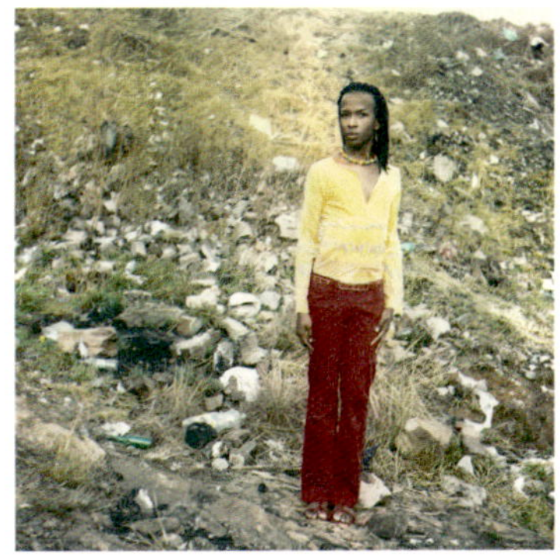

II.

This picture makes a stark contrast with *Miss D'vine I* and *II* (pp.108 and 109), photographed in an area just further up from where Khumalo was photographed. In the pictures of the two sequences, Miss D'vine, a well-known drag queen, is photographed in a pair of red high heels. First, she sits with her legs out to one side in a scanty Zulu maiden garment made of beads. Then she stands up in a black mini dress, revealing her perfectly proportioned and toned body, making a dynamic impression against a cloudless blue sky. While arguably *Miss D'vine I* shows the participant's vulnerability, *Miss D'vine II* signifies her strength. The vibrant colours make the work exceptionally vivid, create a sense of urgency, and emphasize the public nature of the environments where the photo-shoots took place. With these acts in a field in Yeoville, Muholi, together with Khumalo and Miss D'vine, transformed what was otherwise an ordinary space in the midst of a populated neighbourhood into a queer space.

The most significant public location for Muholi's photo-shoots is Constitution Hill. This important site symbolises South Africa's journey to democracy. A former prison and military fort that bears testament to the nation's turbulent past, it houses the Constitutional Court, which exists to uphold the rights of all citizens, including LGBTQIA+ individuals. Among the prisoners kept there were Nelson Mandela and Mahatma Gandhi, but the prison also confined numerous ordinary people during its 100-year history: men and women of all races, creeds and ages.[10] In the context of South Africa's LGBTQIA+ community, the Constitutional Court played a crucial role in advancing rights; for example, issuing a series of decisions that culminated in the legalisation of same-sex marriage by the Civil Union Act, 2006, based on the Bill of Rights in the Constitution of the Republic of South Africa, 1996. The constitution prohibits discrimination based on sexual orientation. However, not only have rights for the LGBTQIA+ community frequently been violated, but many individuals have also been subject to heinous hate crimes.

In this significant public space, *Stanley I, 2006* shows Stanley Mabena, a gay man, revealing his chest with a scar near his left nipple – the evidence of physical violence against him (p.106). Confronted by a camera, he looks away. His facial expression – pained and troubled, as evinced by numerous vertical lines in his forehead – serves to make the viewer concerned and curious about Mabena's personal narrative. Colours play a crucial role in conveying the scar and the participant's nuanced expressions and gestures against the ambiguous exterior background.

The composition of the 2006 colour portrait *Too Beulahs* (a gay South African slang word for 'beauties'), also shot at Constitution Hill, symbolises a still-existing division between LGBTQIA+ individuals and South African society (p.104). Featuring two effeminate young men with slender bodies, standing behind a barbed-wire fence, where their hands were placed – separating Muholi from the participants, who look away from the photographer – the image suggests a distinct visual structure symbolising the division (as if they were imprisoned). The photograph acts as a metaphor for persistent discrimination based on race and LGBTQIA+ status. Here, too, with Muholi's use of colours, the participants – particularly in the tones and contours of their bodies – are distinguished from the airy background, clearly marking their presence in the public space in the present time.

Through their photography-based activism, Muholi challenges and critiques the South African notion and reality of public space, space meant to be shared by and safe for everyone, in relation to the LGBTQIA+ community. In queering public space, Muholi and their participants collude in a collaborative act of protest, reflecting and contesting current situations surrounding LGBTQIA+ individuals, including discriminations and hate crimes. Muholi's colour photographs do not offer a simple aesthetic value, but instead provide viewers with a hint at the complex and raw environments, physical and societal, that Muholi and the participants occupy.

But Muholi doesn't stop there. The visual activist has photographed in colour the LGBTQIA+ community in various cities, particularly at Gay Pride events in South Africa, including Johannesburg, Cape Town, Durban and beyond. Most recently, Muholi photographed Yaya Mavundla, a South African transgender woman, in the June 2019 World Pride to celebrate the fifty-year anniversary of the Stonewall riots in New York City. Here, Yaya is pictured as an active and present participant in the celebrations. In a colour photograph that conveys the fresh green and sense of heat and excitement of an early summer morning, Muholi captured a moment of their activism by occupying the public space with other queer individuals, and celebrated the achievements of the LGBTQIA+ movement in their spirit of international solidarity.

III.

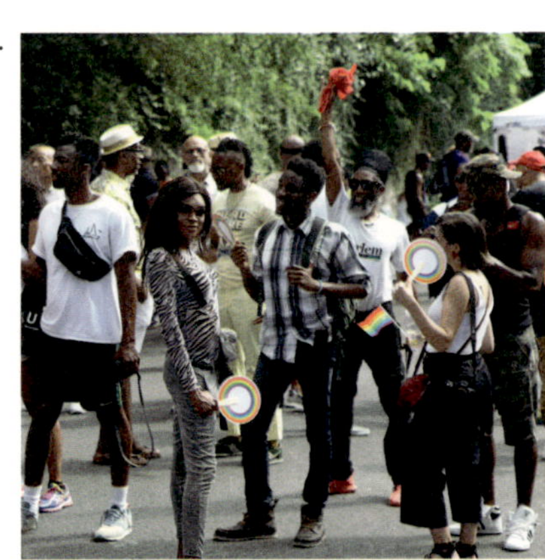

I. Zanele Muholi, Mellisa Mbambo, Durban
South Beach, 2017

II. Zanele Muholi, Muzi Khumalo I, Yeoville,
Johannesburg, 2006

III. Zanele Muholi, Yaya in Harlem, 2019

Queering Public Space

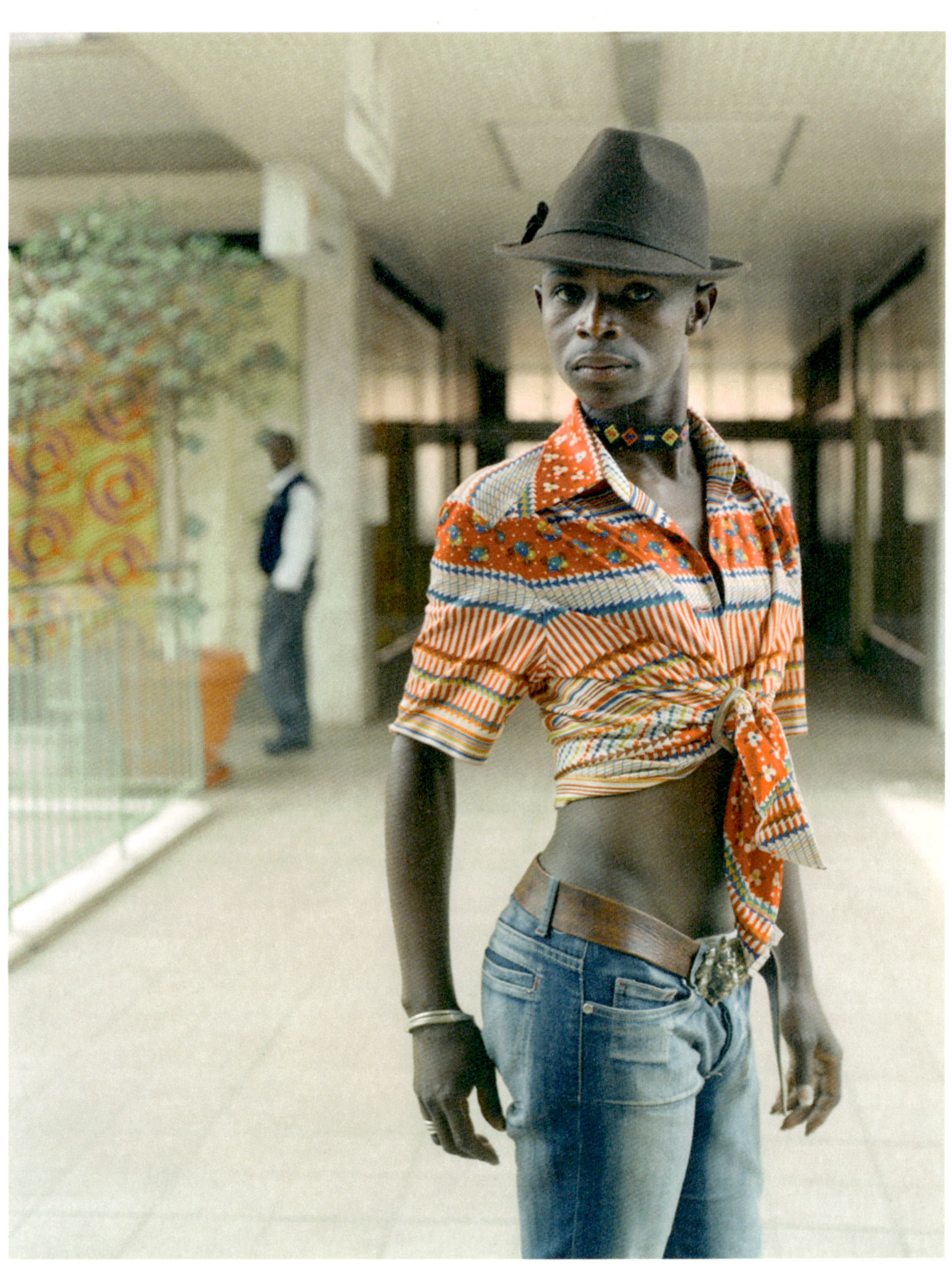

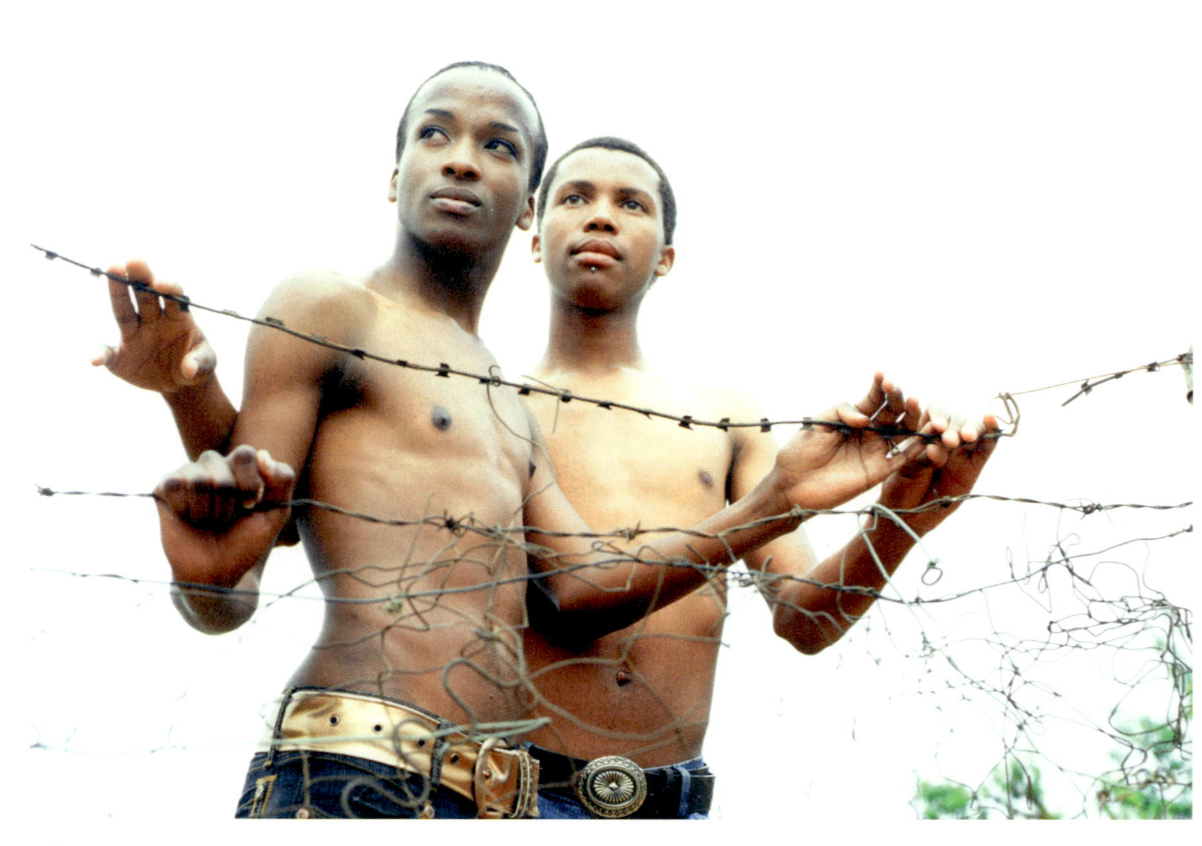

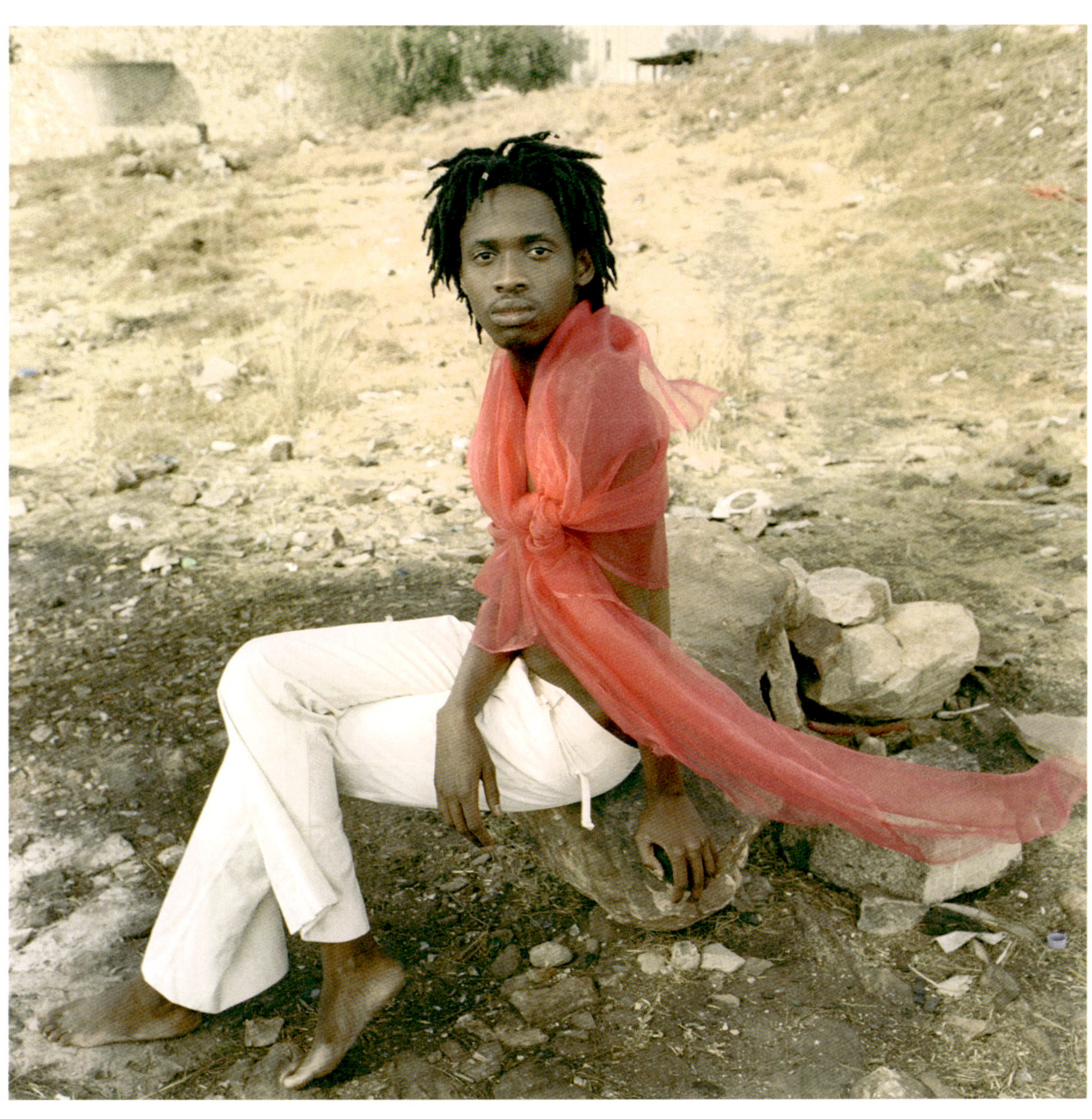

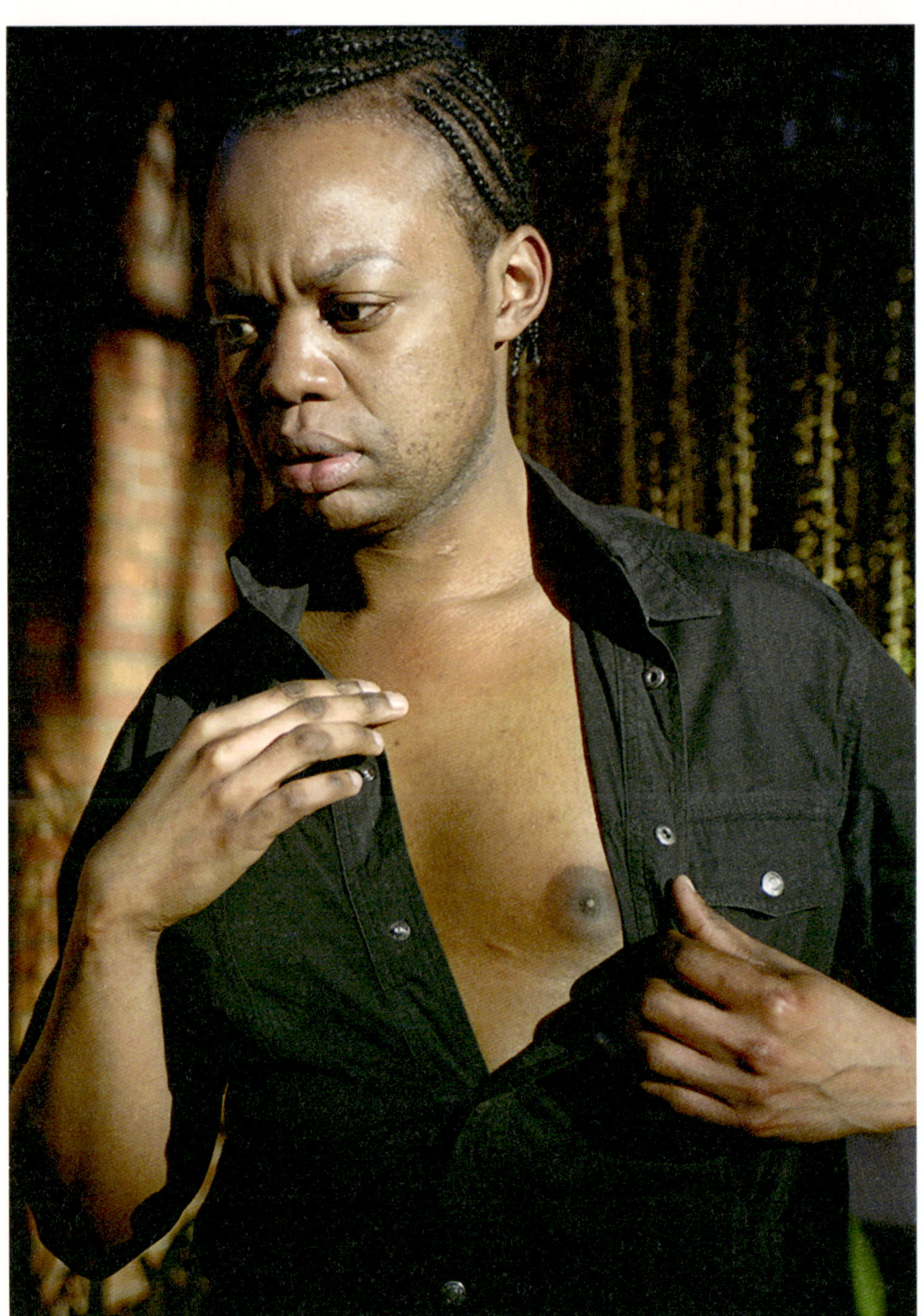

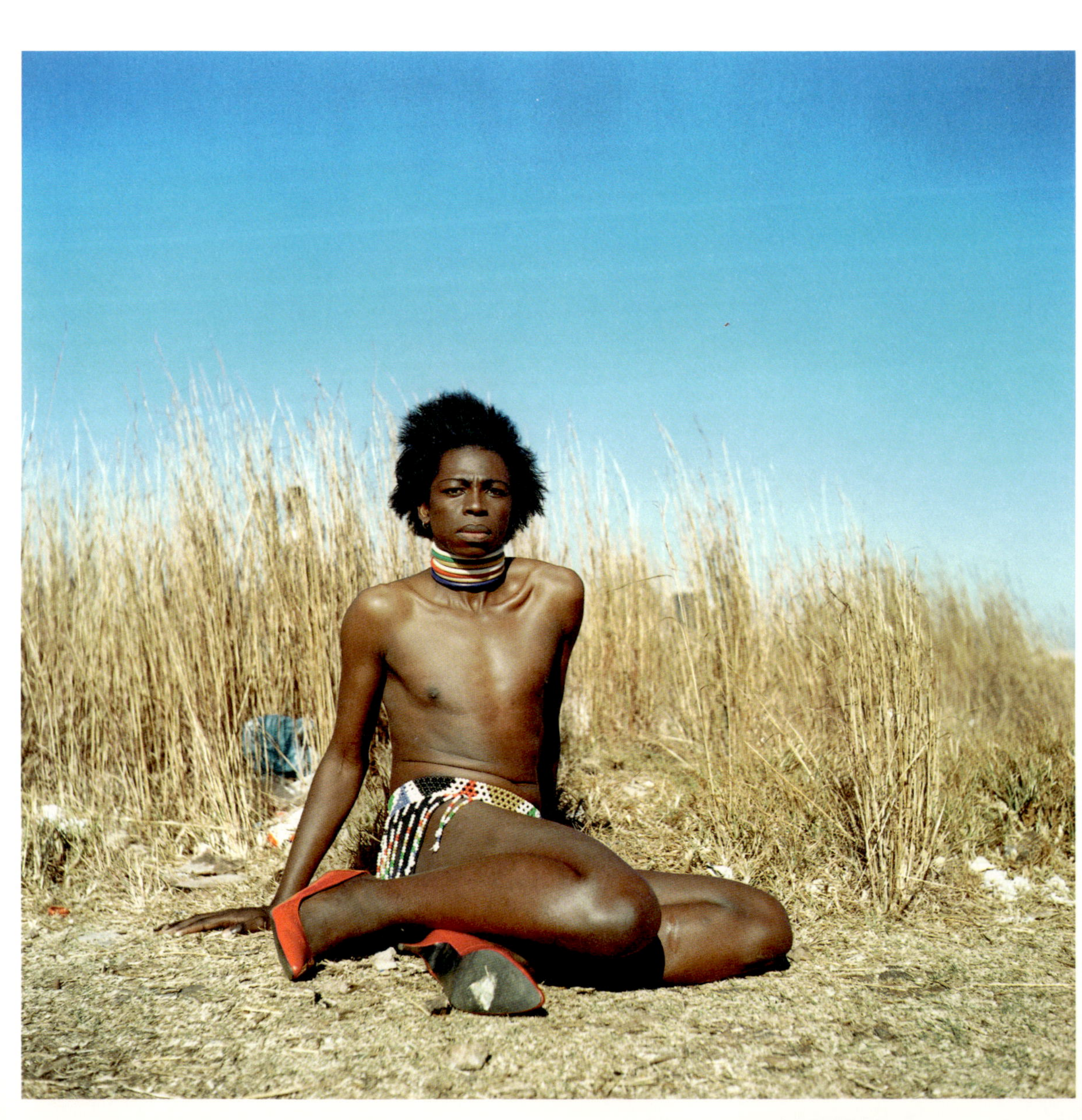

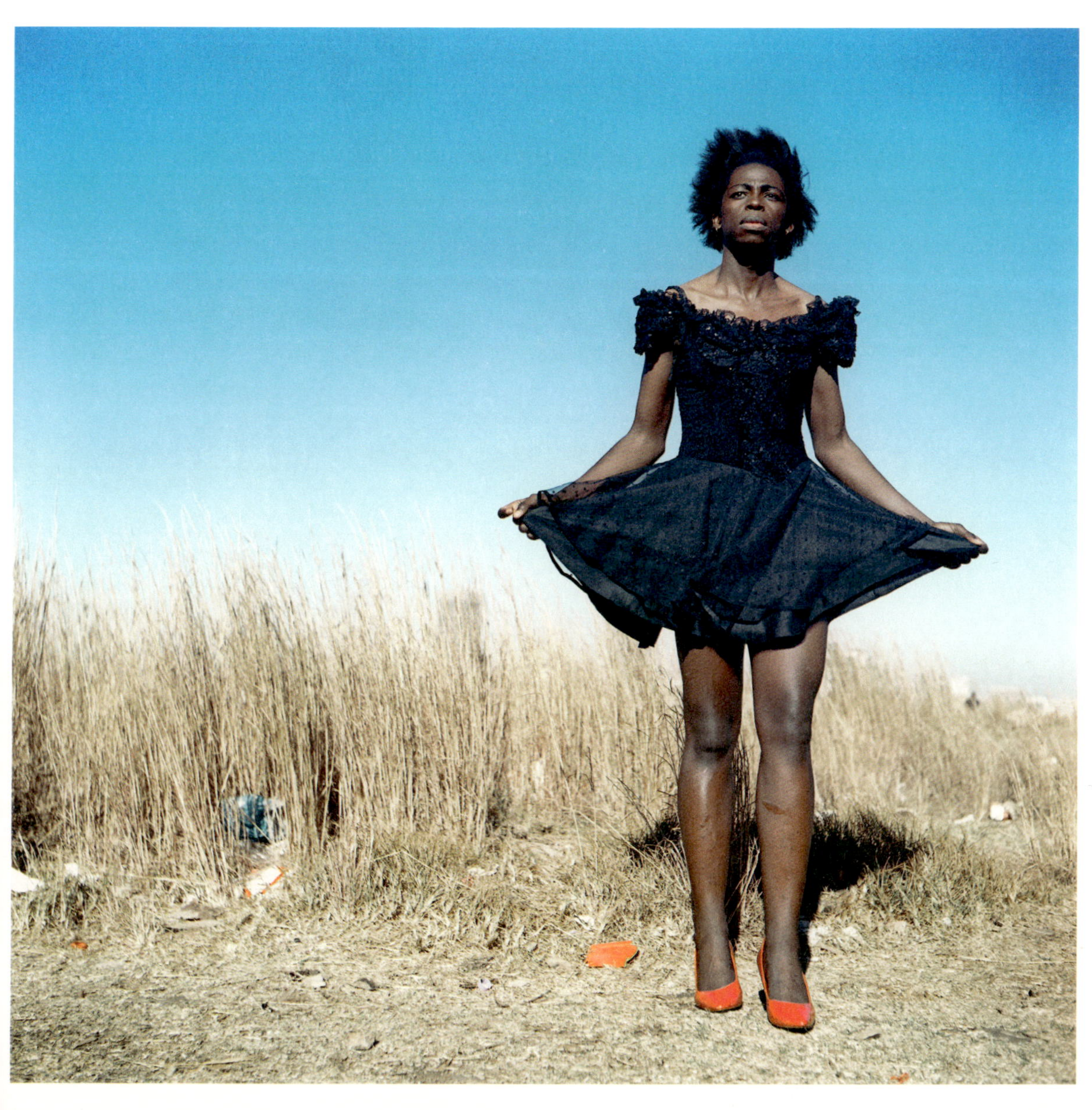

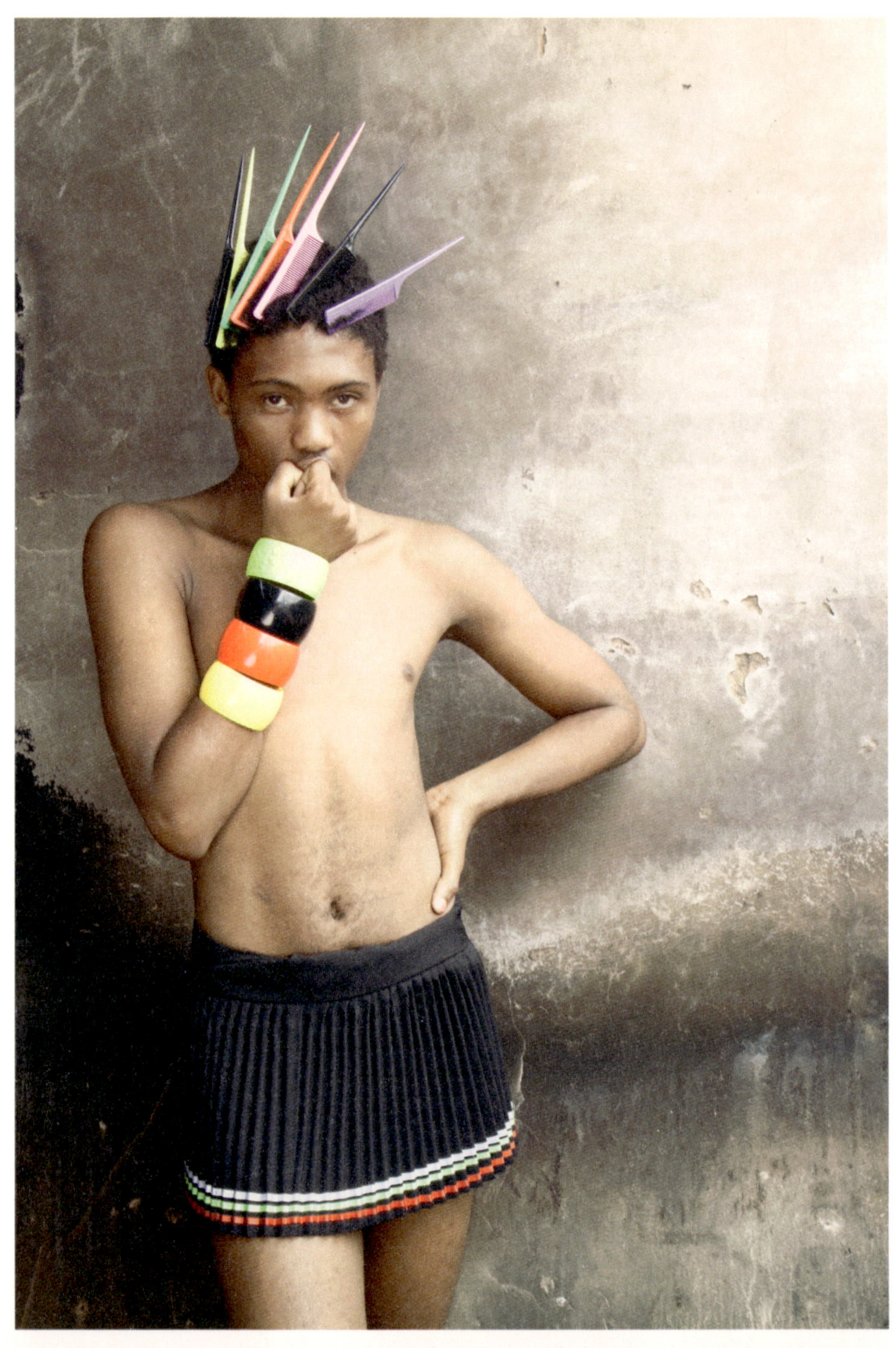

See Anew:
Religion, Marriage and Funerals

Sindiwe Magona

See Anew:
Religion, Marriage and Funerals

Sindiwe Magona

'See anew' proclaim Zanele Muholi's photographs. The beauty, boldness and honesty with which they render queer lives prises wide open the eyes of the beholder to the reality of the existence of difference. Ignorance and denial are confronted head on; bigotry is shamed.

Freedom of sexual orientation is guaranteed under the constitution of South Africa. However, African lesbians live precarious lives: often rejected by family; discriminated against by society; denied, despised and abused. They are under assault from so-called or self-proclaimed African traditionalists who bank on weak to almost non-existent police protection of queer individuals.[1] Meanwhile, the Church is still debating the rightness or otherwise of embracing homosexuality even as we enter the second quarter of the twenty-first century.

The misconception that homosexuality is 'un-African' plays a role here. Much scholarly research has focused on this topic, but the central thesis that underpins the misconception is that homosexuality was a colonial import to Africa. The truth is that binary notions of gender and sexual relationships were enforced by colonial powers. As Donna Smith, former director of Forum for the Empowerment of Women, explains, 'some people believe homosexuality is an idea brought [to Africa] by the white man. But it has always been here. What the white man brought was homophobia clothed in religious doctrines that we did not have before.'[2]

In fact, it was religious missionaries who imported homophobia to Africa. Missionaries used homosexuality as proof of Africa's primitivism and need for reform and saving. The bible became the first and only word on African morality, changing African sexuality to the missionary position of heteronormativity.

Today, the Catholic Church does not have an official position on homosexuality itself, does not permit gay marriages, and only to some extent tolerates civil unions provided that the concerned remain faithful. Yet, the question can legitimately be asked: 'We, Christians, always profess "God is beyond human comprehension!" Then we adamantly claim: "God did not create this!" How do we suddenly become so all-knowing about God and all His intent when it comes to human sexuality?'

Instead of waiting on a satisfying response from the Church, some members of the queer community in South Africa are taking matters into their own hands. Lesbians are no longer waiting for approval but going ahead with worship of the God they know loves them just as they are. After all, belief in the existence of a higher being can be an integral aspect of all human life.

Pastor Zenzi Zungu, together with his late wife, established Victory Ministries Church International (VMCI) in 2011. Their mission was to 'give hope to the hopeless and voice to the voiceless through preaching the Gospel of Jesus Christ irrespective of gender, race and socioeconomic [status]'.[3]

Pastor Tebogo Moema co-founded the Hope and Unity Metropolitan Christian Church (HUMCC) as a place of 'hope and spiritual renewal' and a safe space for LGBTQIA+ religious people. Since its founding, he believes it has saved many from 'self-loathing and condemnation'. Today the mission seeks to 'direct the church to establish a cohesive society by foregrounding inclusivity'.[4]

Zanele Muholi is a member of VMCI and documents many of the activities of the congregation through their lens. People need to see themselves in the arts – books, film, theatre; in short, in the story – and so Muholi and their team document significant events in the lives of the queer community, many of which intertwine with the church. Muholi and team act as the official photographers of these moments of joy and sorrow. In July 2013, Muholi documented the funeral of Duduzile Zozo who was brutally raped and murdered in the township of Thokoza, in the Gauteng East Rand, in June 2013. Duduzile Zozo was a victim of that senseless oxymoron, 'corrective rape'. What kind of mind juxtaposes two such diametrically opposed binaries? Her rapist and murderer was sentenced to thirty years in prison in 2014.

Muholi also turns the lens on moments of joy. In 2013, together with collaborators, Muholi took video footage and photographs of the wedding of Ayanda Magoloza and Nhlanhla Moremi.[5] This marriage, like any in the queer community, did not take place in a church, as same-sex unions are prohibited. Instead, the happy couple exchanged their vows at Kwanele Park in Katlehong. Even though such weddings do not take place in church, pastors can find ways of offering queer couples support, and Magoloza and Moremi's union was blessed by Pastor Tebogo Moema. Another wedding Muholi and team documented, that of Ziningi and Delisile Ndlela, was blessed by Pastor Zenzi Zungu.[6]

I.

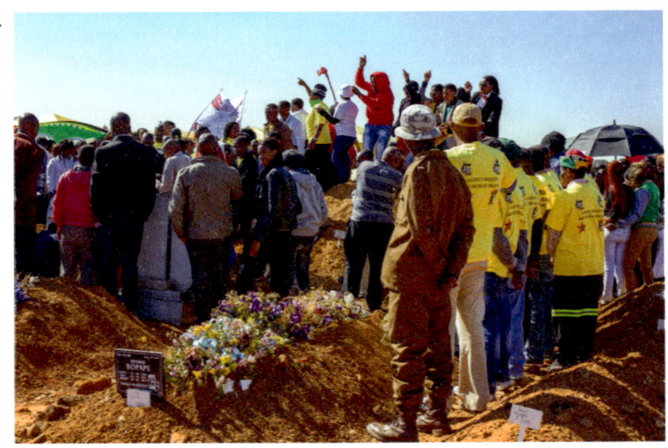

II.

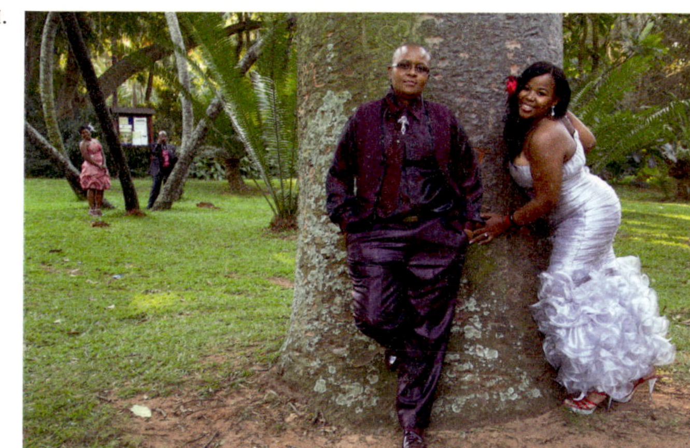

These images of marriages and funerals take on different lives. They exist in the form of art shown in Muholi's exhibitions, displayed online and printed in publications, but they also of course hold a place in the personal lives of the participants. For documentation of funerals, the images act as evidence and comfort in times of need. For moments of joy, they act as precious memories given to the participants and can take pride of place on mantelpieces and in wedding albums.

These images are part and parcel of Muholi's archival work, which serves an important function as evidence of queer life. It is through this documentation that Muholi's work will not only survive but also ensure the survival of queerness. The coming generations of queer individuals will have a weapon to use in their defence. Why, they may not even need any defence. Unlike their ancestors, the present generation may never need to whisper their same-sex love but instead shout it from the mountaintops!

III.

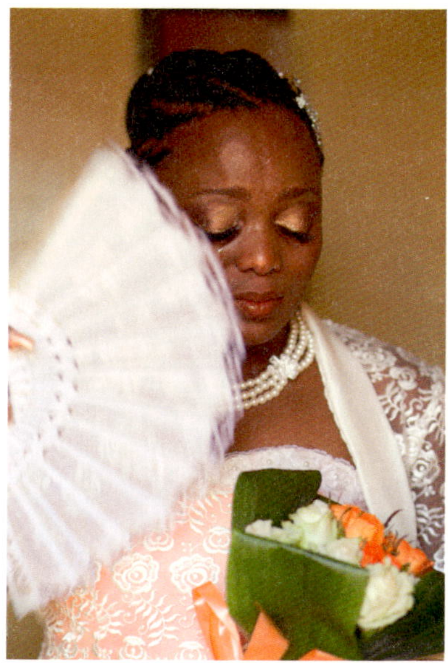

I. Duduzile Zozo's funeral, Thokoza, July 2013

II. Ziningi and Delisile Ndlela's wedding VI,
Chesterville, Durban, 15 June 2013

III. Ayanda Magoloza and Nhlanhla Moremi's wedding,
Kwanele South, Katlehong, 9 November 2013

The Skin They Live In

Elvira Dyangani Ose

The activist's hand lingers a second, just long enough to hide their genitalia in what is one of their first self-portrait images. The composition of *Mirror, 2005* (below) is somewhat puzzling, framed by an indistinct shadow that almost surrounds the four edges of the picture. We are compelled to sustain our looking, our glance becoming complicit with the gaze that Zanele Muholi returns. Their face remains hidden behind the camera, unreadable, while we inhabit the space that they are in. The viewer's position is between their legs, in the dizzying vortex created by their reflection in the mirror, which is the vanishing point of the camera, and the space where the light that will make the photograph possible is captured. We are also framed by the activist's body; somewhere between our desire to remain an unwanted voyeur and our impulse to surrender to their challenging appeal – one that avoids any modernist mannerism or heteronormative determination, whether that was expected by the subject portrayed, the photographer or the beholder.

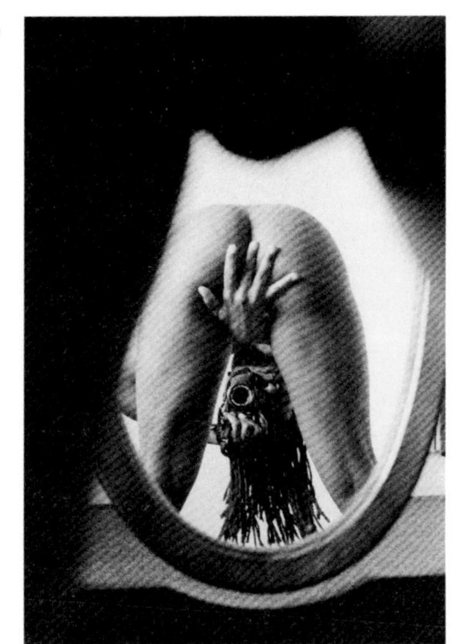

At the time of first seeing this work, I recall myself wondering how much Muholi would have known about the importance of trompe l'oeil, and the lineage of artists she was about to join with that seemingly naïve, yet sophisticated proposition – Édouard Manet, Jeff Wall and Carrie Mae Weems, to name but a few that come immediately to mind. For Muholi's *Mirror* as trompe l'oeil is an illusion with the capacity to challenge both the beholder and the discipline of photography itself. In essence, it constitutes a type of blank slate that offers up opportunities for self-reflection and critique – a critique which, in Muholi's case, is also a statement of intent that includes the viewer, whether they have agreed to that self-reflexive exercise or not. The escapism proposed by *Mirror*'s trompe l'oeil is one in which we are trapped. Distancing itself from the articulation of performativity of the space between figures that one would observe in, say, Manet's *A Bar at the Folies-Bergère* 1882 or Jeff Wall's *Picture for Women* 1979, *Mirror* contains a critical commentary on the history of modern portraiture, the like of Carrie Mae Weems's series *Framed by*

Modernism (1996), and even more so *Not Manet's Type* (1997). In those bodies of work, Weems gives agency to Manet's models, and challenges the artist's questioning of his sitters' subjecthood, as she takes on dual roles – both in front of, and behind, the camera. Even though in Weems's practice her body usually stands in for something larger than herself as photographer, her reflection in the mirror in her *Not Manet's Type* series and its annotations offer us a clue, as a means of confession, that places the artist's body, her womanhood, her agency, at the centre of this enquiry.

STANDING ON SHAKEY GROUND
I POSED MYSELF FOR CRITICAL STUDY
BUT WAS NO LONGER CERTAIN
OF THE QUESTIONS TO ASK

IT WAS CLEAR I WAS NOT MANET'S TYPE
PICASSO – WHO HAD A WAY WITH WOMEN –
ONLY USED ME & DUCHAMP NEVER
EVEN CONSIDERED ME

BUT IT COULD HAVE BEEN WORSE
IMAGINE MY FATE HAD
DE KOONING GOTTEN
HOLD OF ME

I KNEW, NOT FROM MEMORY,
BUT FROM HOPE, THAT THERE WERE OTHER
MODELS BY WHICH TO LIVE

I TOOK A TIP FROM FRIDA
WHO FROM HER BED PAINTED INCESSANTLY – BEAUTIFULLY
WHILE DIEGO SCALED THE SCAFFOLDS
TO THE TOP OF THE WORLD

II.

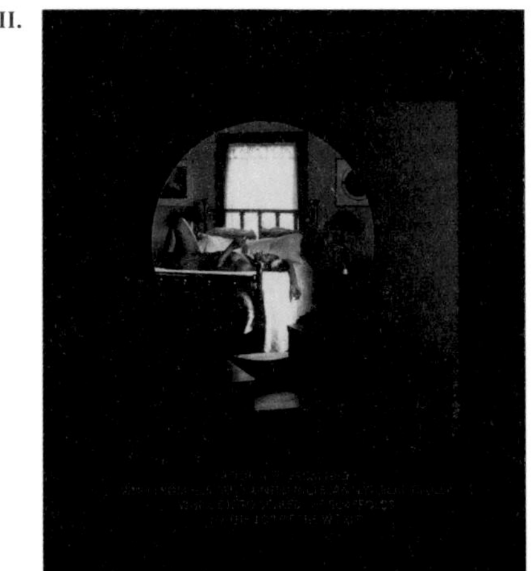

Weems, who begins her meditative journey in the first of the five images that constitute the series, offering only her back to the viewer, reveals herself – her face and her body – and the intimacy of her environment, as our gaze moves from one image to the other. These beautiful images are powerfully charged with a political agenda that avoids any form of condescendence. She never looks at the viewer; she does not have to. 'He' is not even the witness of her self-discovery. Photography is.

Zanele Muholi's seemingly mischievous disregard for historical revision takes us a step even further. Away from references to possible historical sources, we focus instead on the ambiguity of space that we and they inhabit, contracting our attention to the place of the photograph – both the photograph taken and the environment – and its capacity to move beyond previous archetypes to embrace or, better yet, embody the myriad opportunities of its present-ness. Using a similar formula for empowerment and self-representation as Weems's artworks, Muholi's *Mirror*, and the portraiture it initiates, articulates notions of beauty, visibility and storytelling – poignant political tools that extend Weems's critique of the patriarchal historical imagery of Black women, incorporating a Black LGBTQIA+ activist agenda that goes beyond the realm of art and photography. Their self-declaration as an activist, rather than an artist, is a clear indication of Muholi's insistence that what really matters occurs far beyond the art world; that photography is a vehicle of exposure, a platform to raise the collective voice, and an instrument they use to define themself and their communities beyond a limited area of public reach.

Perhaps more than in previous bodies of works, in *Somnyama Ngonyama, Hail the Dark Lioness* (2012–ongoing), Muholi returns to some of the predicaments of *Mirror*, but expressing a previously unprecedented rage, soliloquy and subtlety born of the mastery they have achieved in a career now spanning almost two decades. If in *Mirror* the lack of reference to class, identity or gender, and the concealment of their face, left race as the only distinctive signifier in an otherwise ambiguous space, in most of the vast series of portraits that comprise *Somnyama Ngonyama*, Muholi is looking straight at us – at history, at racial theory, at mainstream media, at popular culture; at art, photography, and the museum – challenging us and those institutions of performativity and display, unambiguously. In this series of black and white self-portraits that have been imagined, if not taken, daily over a long period of time, Muholi offers us a response to moments of their recent past – moments of conflict, and of rest; moments of sadness and outrage – together with decisive, imaginative and revealing challenges to historical understandings of blackness. They do so visually, using a thicker, glossier pitch black – the darkest that a silver gelatin technique provides. And conceptually, in doing so, they restore the agency of the Black female subject through an ingenious exercise whose ultimate aim is to enact their agency and disarticulate racist imageries and historical archetypes displayed in mainstream media and multiple other exhibition platforms. These images are more than an allusion to historical portraiture. They offer up the possibility of Muholi's own disappearance into the absolute blackness that they are always represented by; a consciousness of blackness that once imprisoned them through an imposed narrative from the West – and the art world – and that drove them to find a liberated path in which they are no longer a subject themself, and where black is no longer a mechanism to escape insurgency, but is insurgency itself, freedom itself; selfhood. Not only theirs, but ours too – at its fullest.

The series is as much a proclamation of the Black subject's agency as it is a disavowal
of the framework in which the process of de-canonisation and re-appropriation of
that agency has been exercised. For *Somnyama Ngonyama* utilises an expanded notion
of what constitutes its framework, which for the first time moves beyond the partic-
ularities of the LGBTQIA+ struggle to embrace the violence and the silencing mecha-
nisms inflicted onto Black subjects everywhere, historically and in the present.
As 'Black' subjects, they include non-human species, nature, the objects which
Muholi demands we liberate from any form of historical objecthood: trees, stools,
pins, pneumatic tyres; objects misplaced from their daily use and no longer determined by their original function. Conjured here, they become part of the process
of alchemy that Muholi invokes, which prevents us from perceiving them as only
adornments or props.

That appears to be their intention in *Bona, Charlottesville, 2015*, in which Muholi is
seen lying down in a sumptuous bed, looking at their reflection in a mirror (p.123).
Appropriating certain modernist mannerisms, *Bona* is one of the few images in the
series in which we are not being stared at. And yet it would be a mistake to believe
that we are invited into the scene. The atmosphere of a recognised beauty is an
escapist trickery. Muholi, who is seen holding the mirror over their belly, their hair
styled in a sculptural set of tresses, looks at their reflection sideways, as if about
to tilt their head to the left, which would indicate they had caught us – their
unwanted voyeur – observing them from the back of the room. 'Who are you?'
they seem to ask. 'How dare you?'

Since seeing most of the images from this series for the first time at their exhibition
at Autograph, London, in 2017, I could not help but identify them as a victorious
counter-narrative to two other stories of blackness of a very different nature: the
depiction of Josephine Baker in Paul Colin's *Le Tumulte Noir* portfolio of lithographs
from 1929, as well as other photographs of the Parisian artist; and the image of
Grace Jones created together with her partner of many years, Jean-Paul Goude –
particularly in the way in which the music video for 'Slave to the Rhythm' offers us
a glimpse into the making of some of Goude's legendary shots and collages of the
singer, actress, activist and icon. Jones has also challenged her viewers on more than
one occasion. Her path to self-discovery and freedom was only ever hers to take.
As in Muholi's daring challenge in *Bona*, the introduction to Jones's famous musical
hit announces: 'Rhythm is both the song's manacle and its demonic charge. It is the
original breath. It is the whisper of unremitting demand. "What do you still want
of me?"'

I. Zanele Muholi, Mirror, 2005

II. Carrie Mae Weems, I Took a Tip from
Frida (Not Manet's Type series), 1997

Somnyama Ngonyama

2012–
ongoing

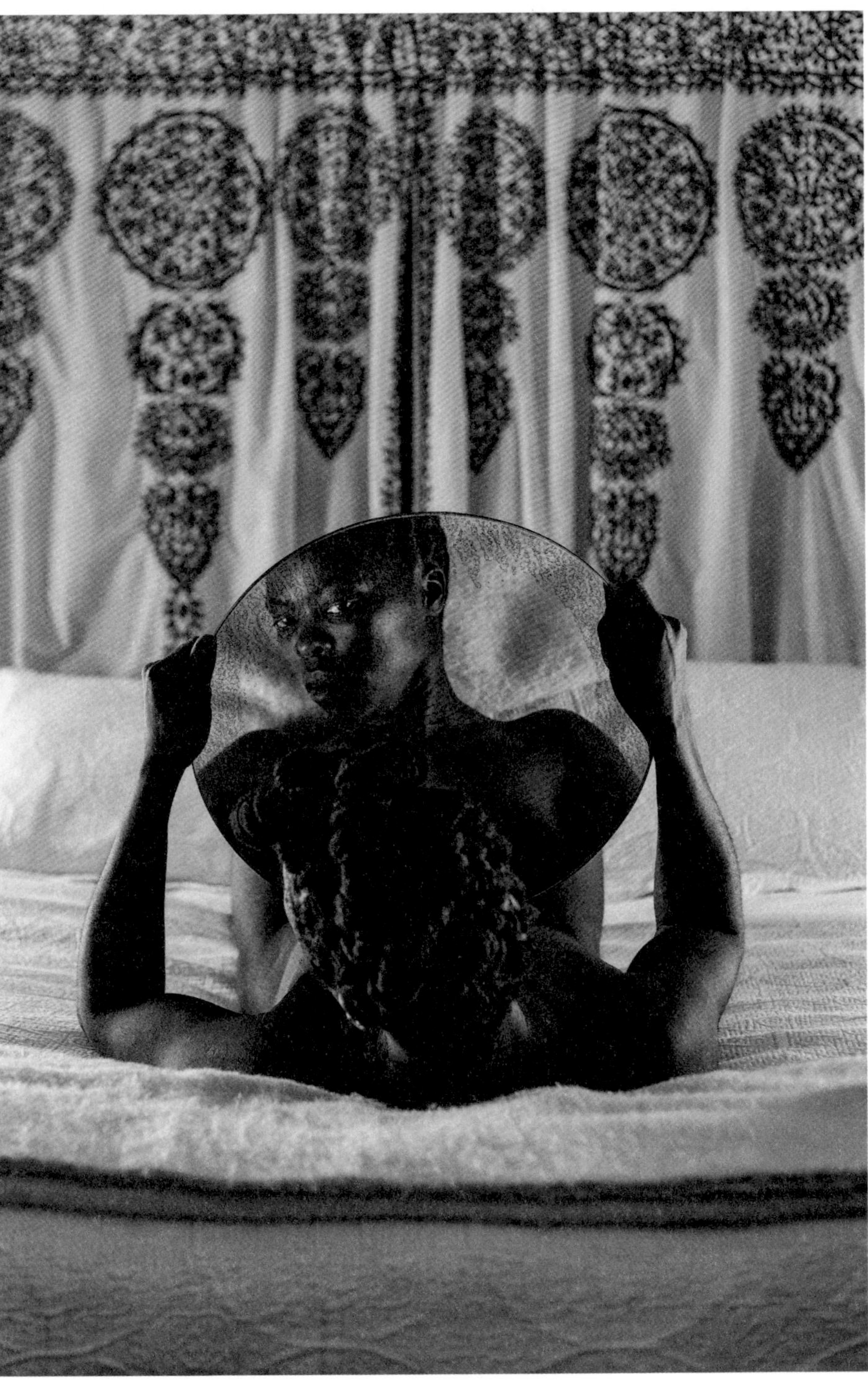

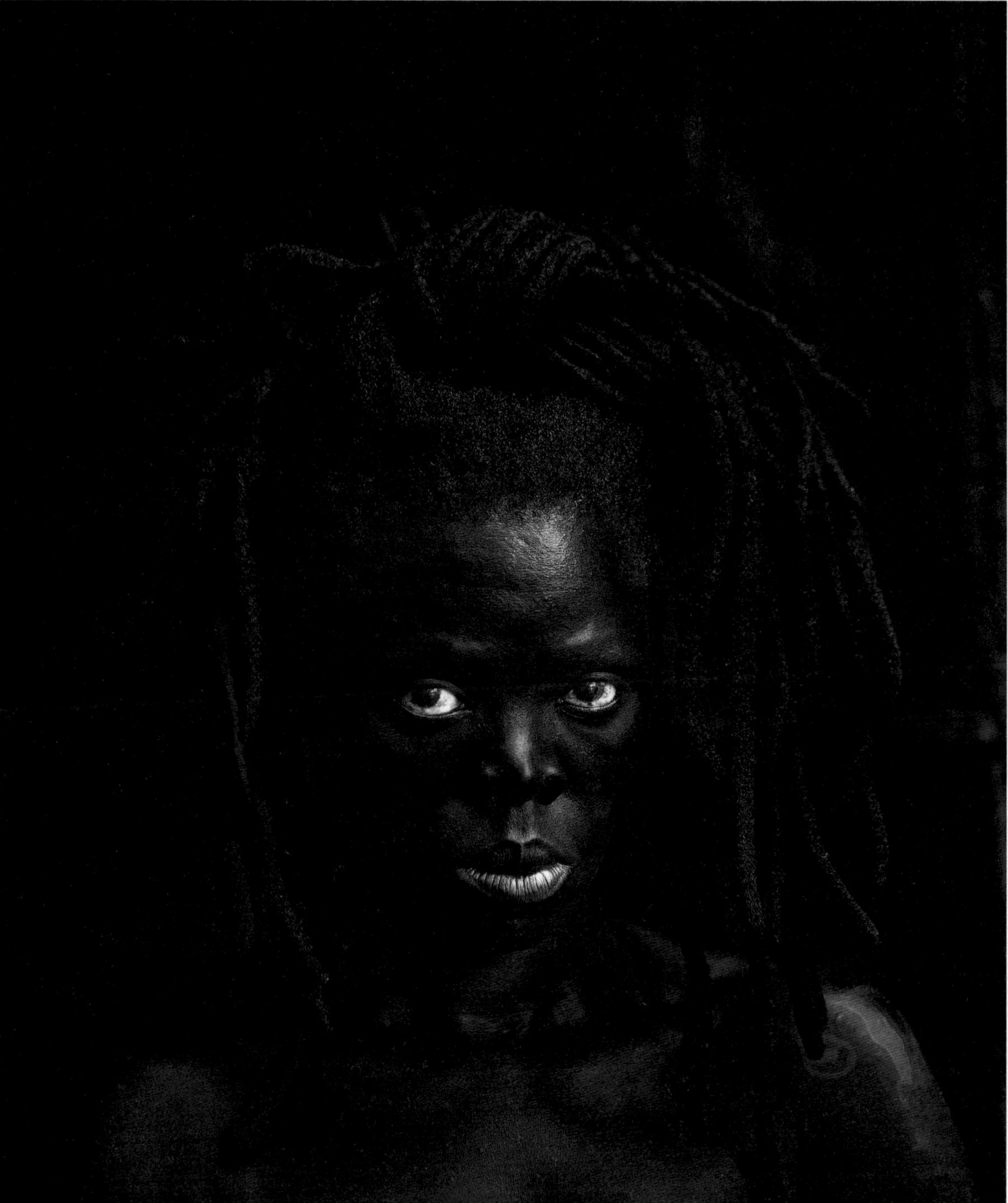

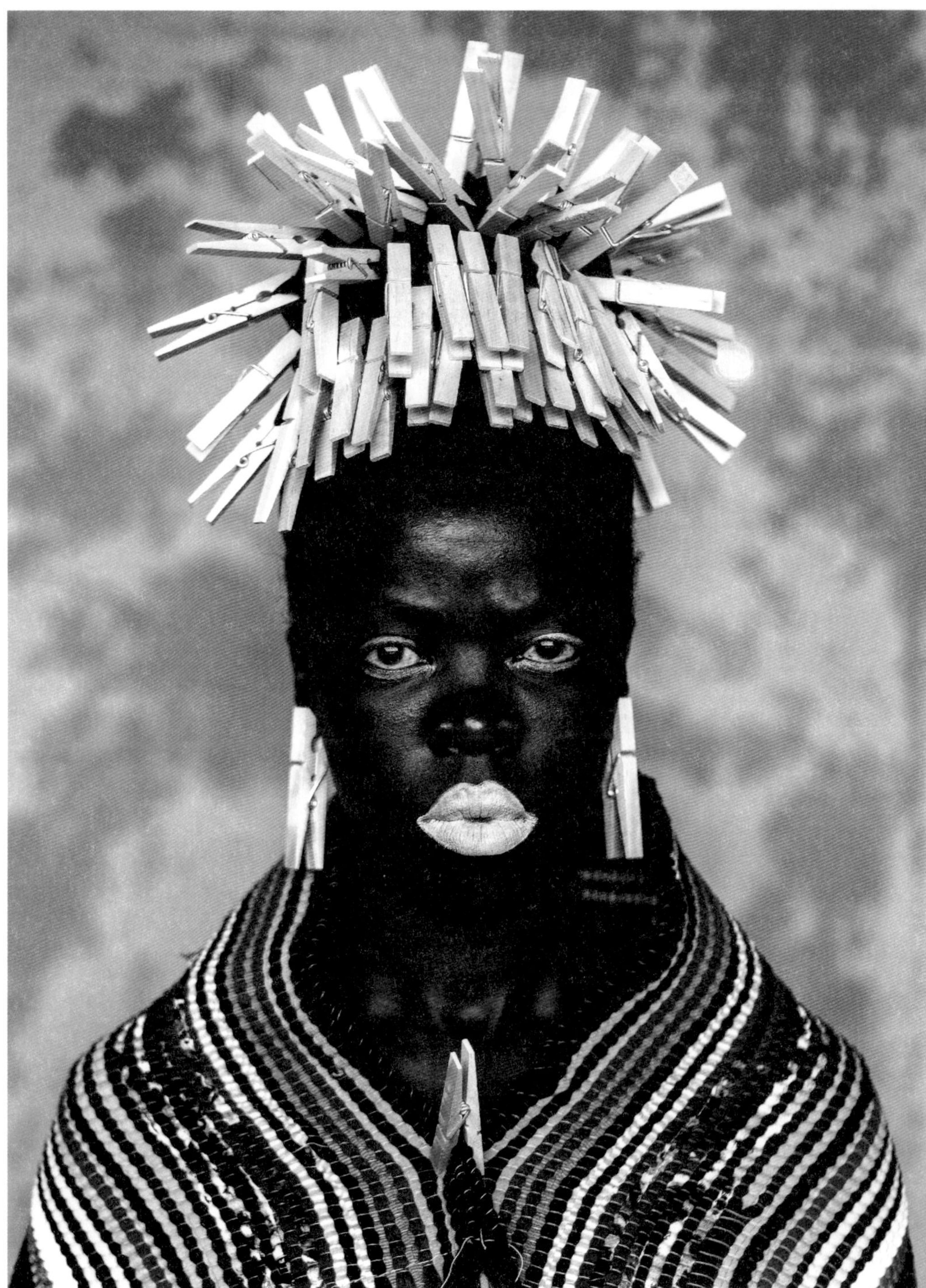

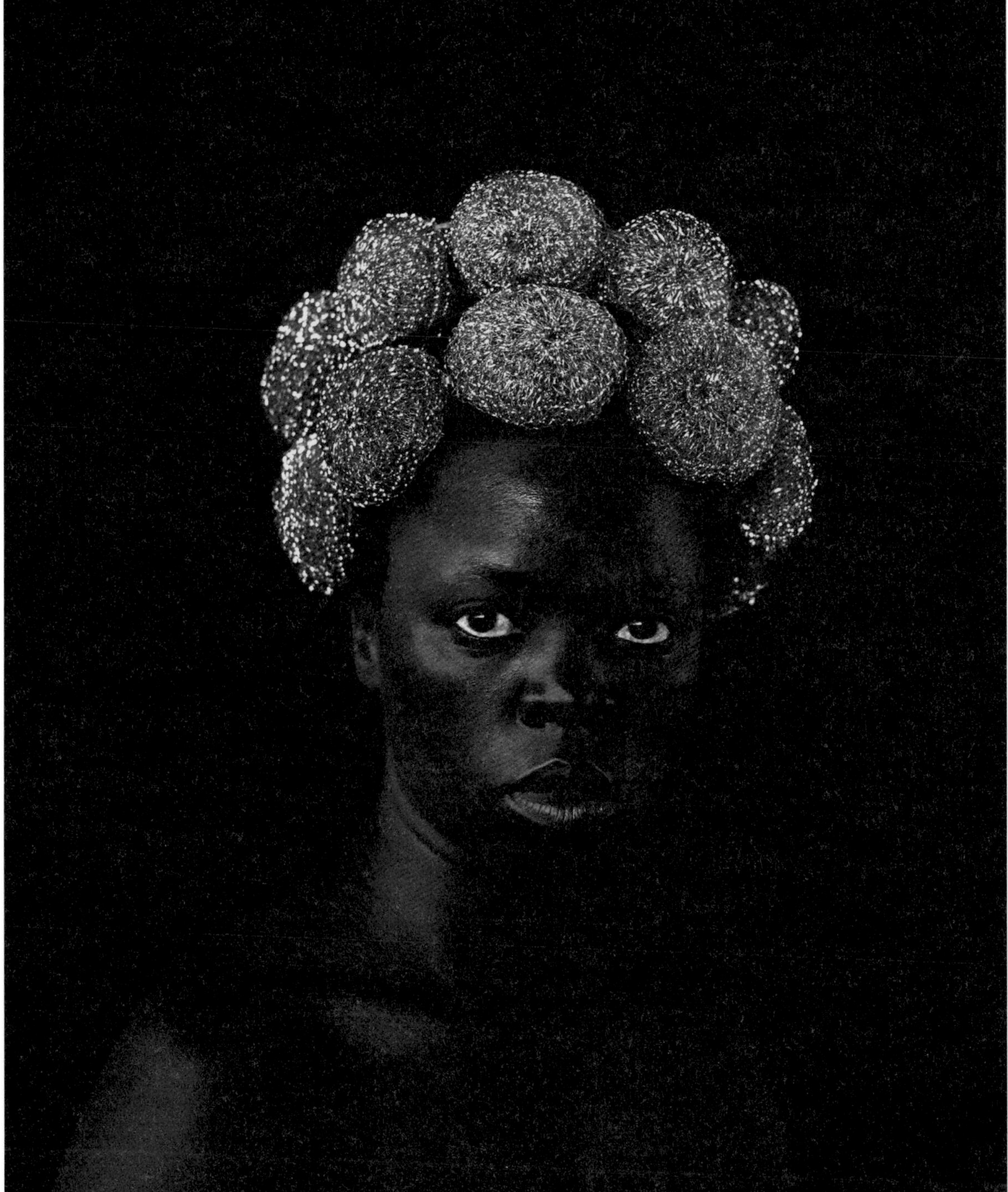

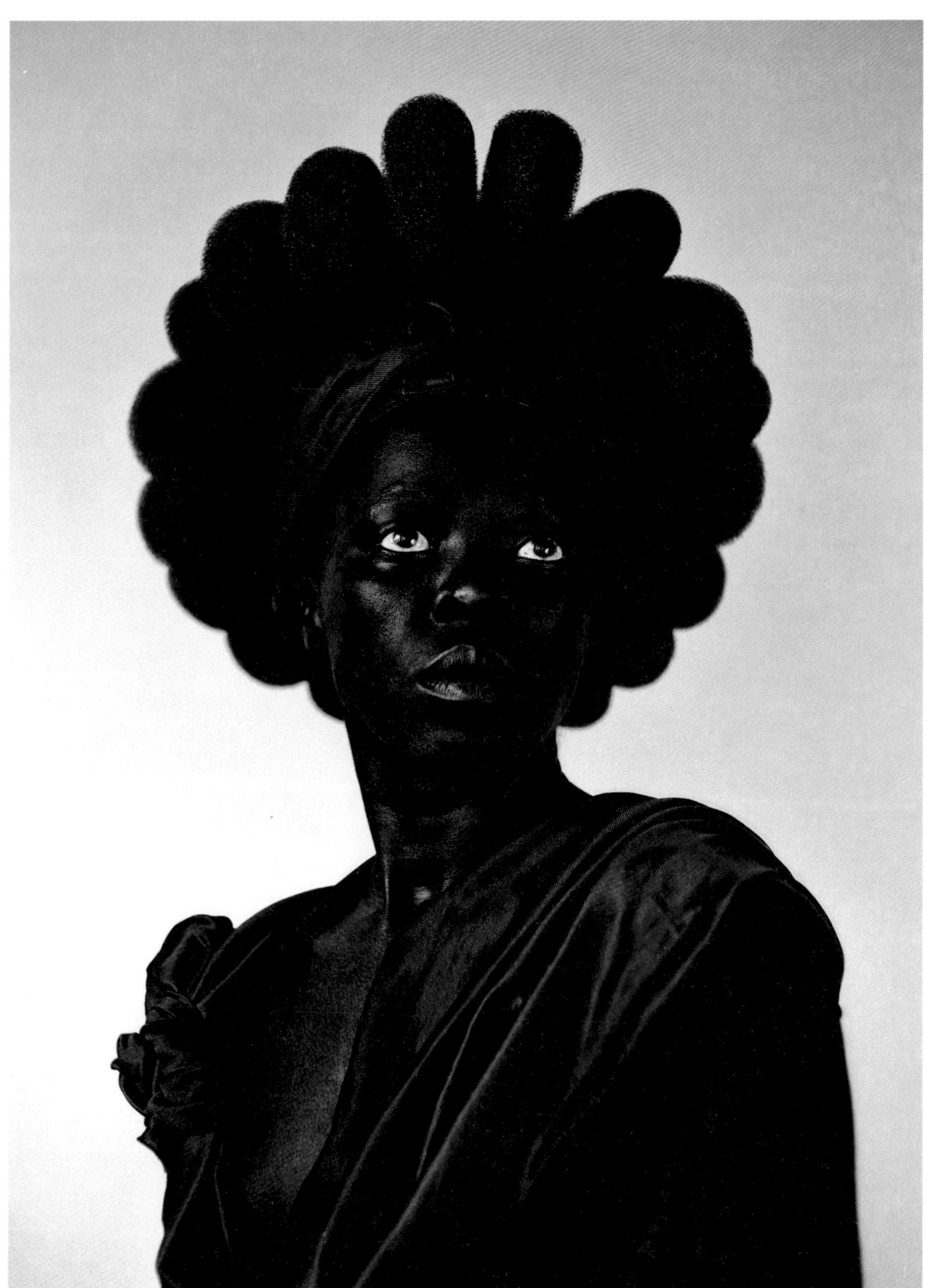

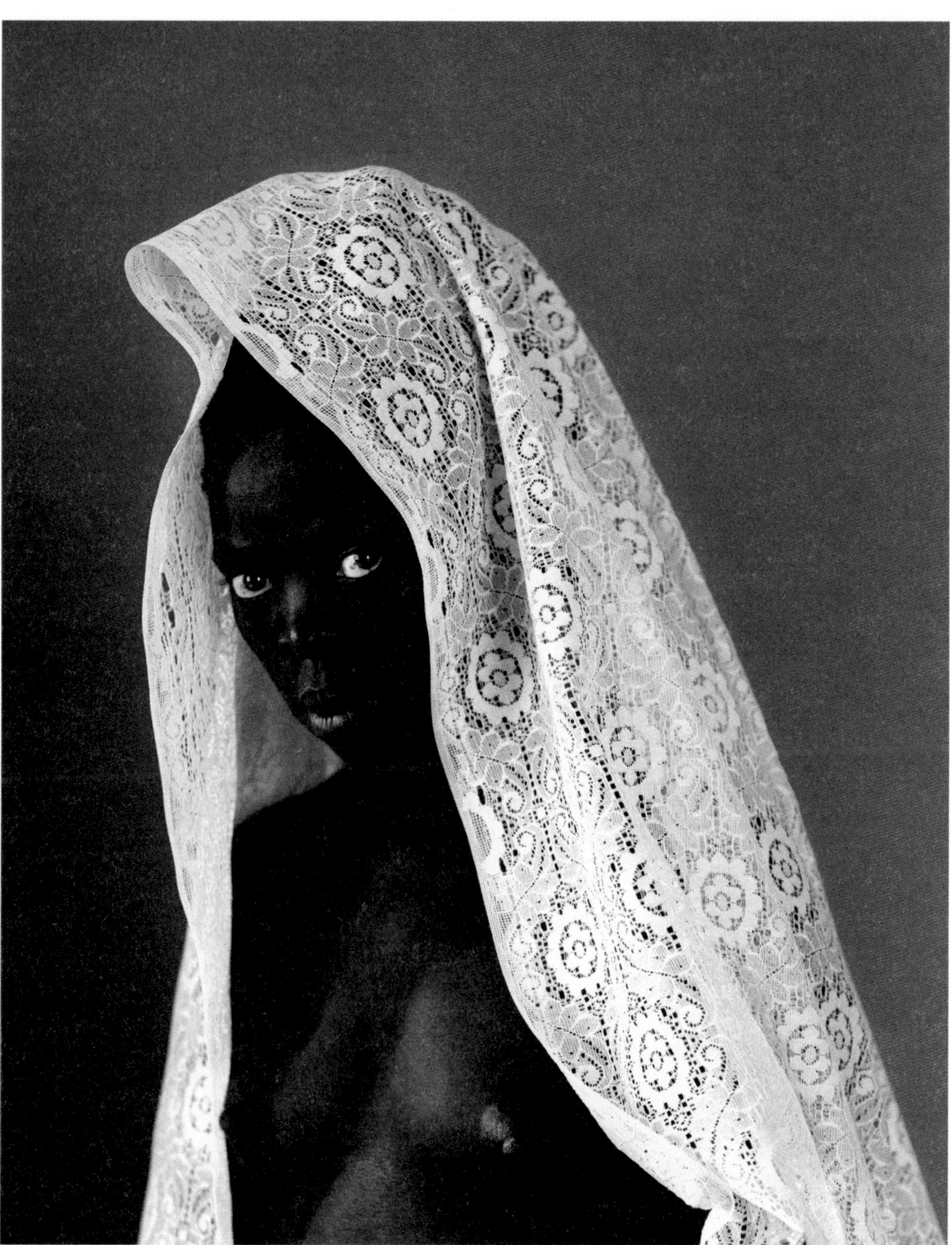

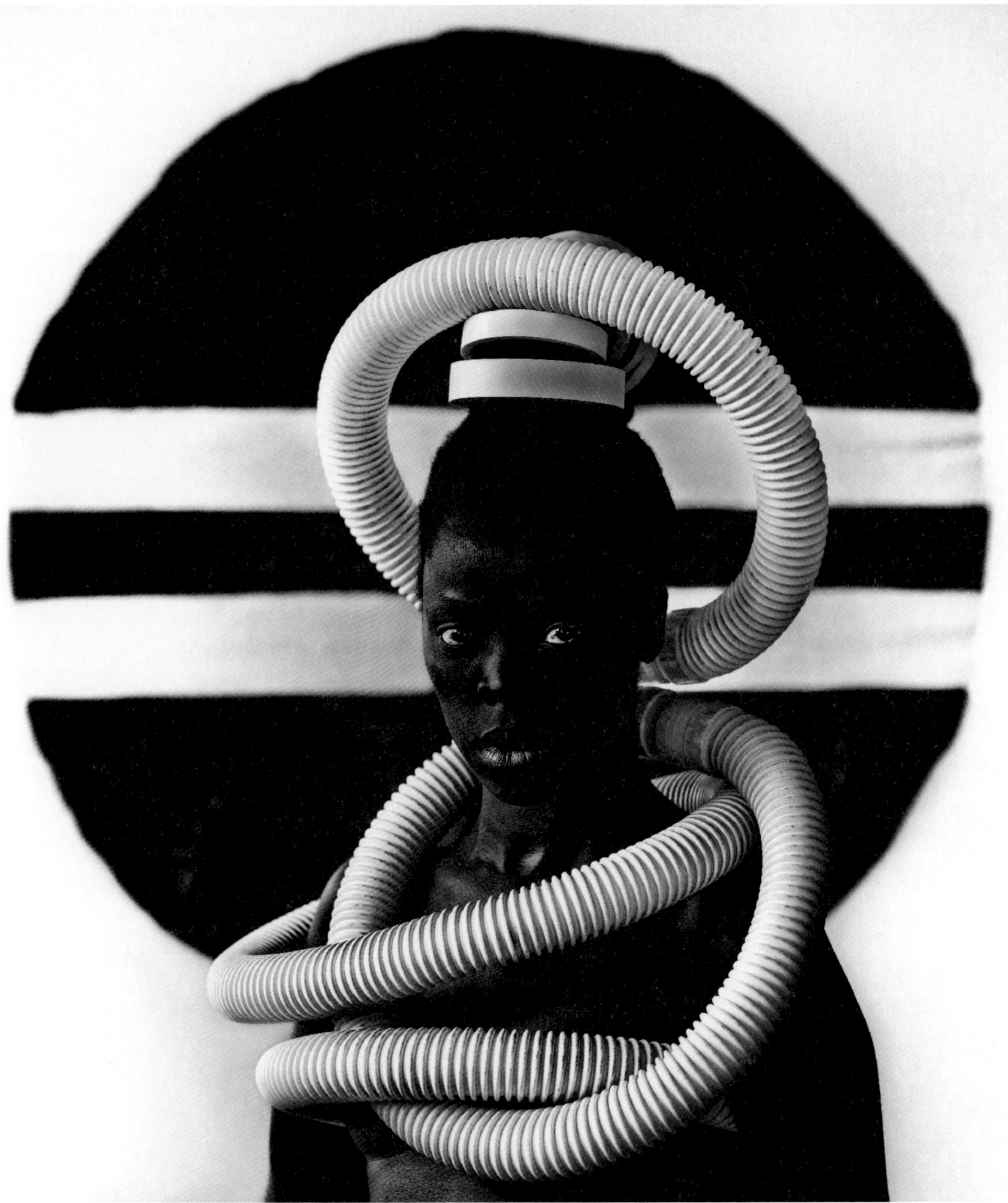

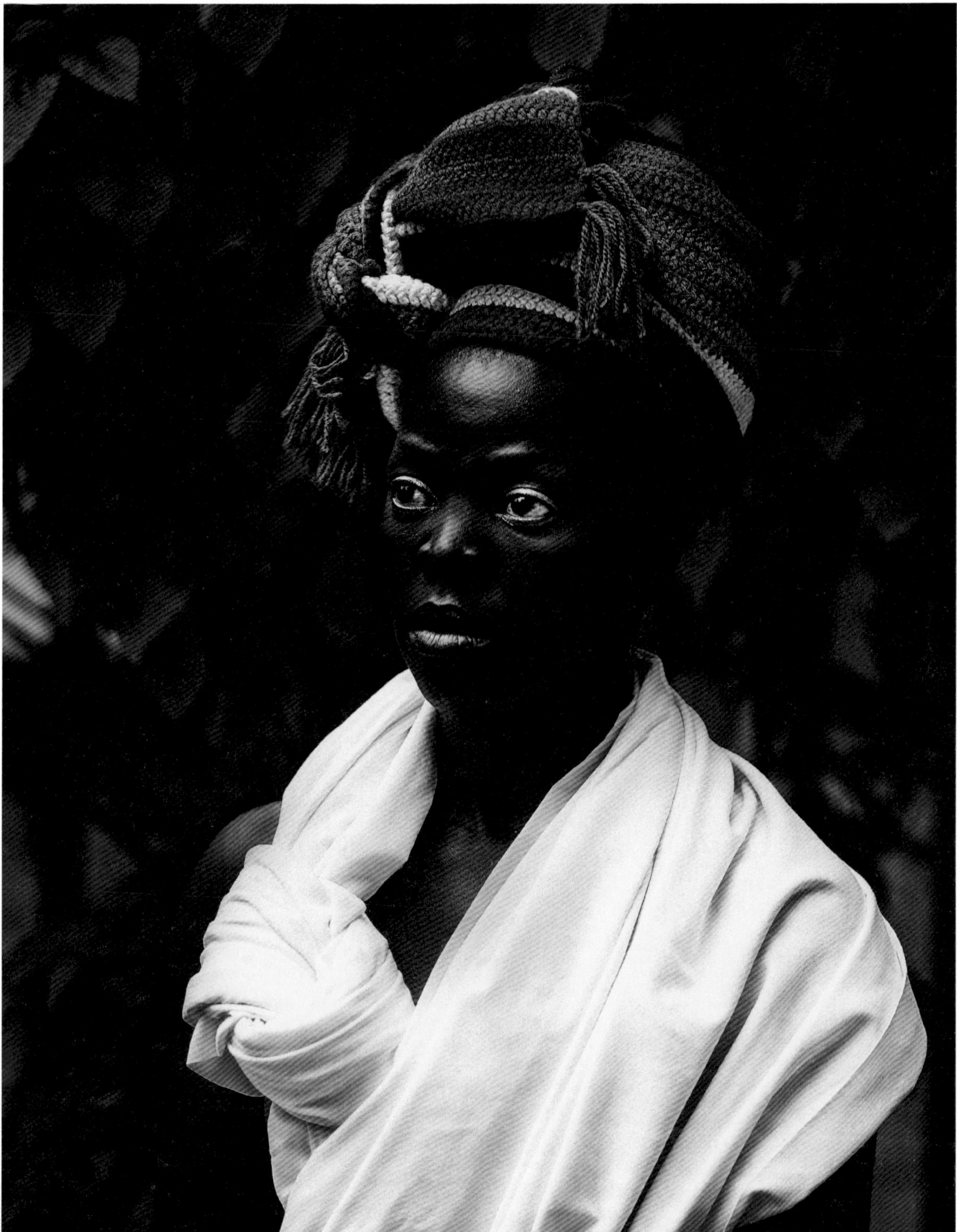

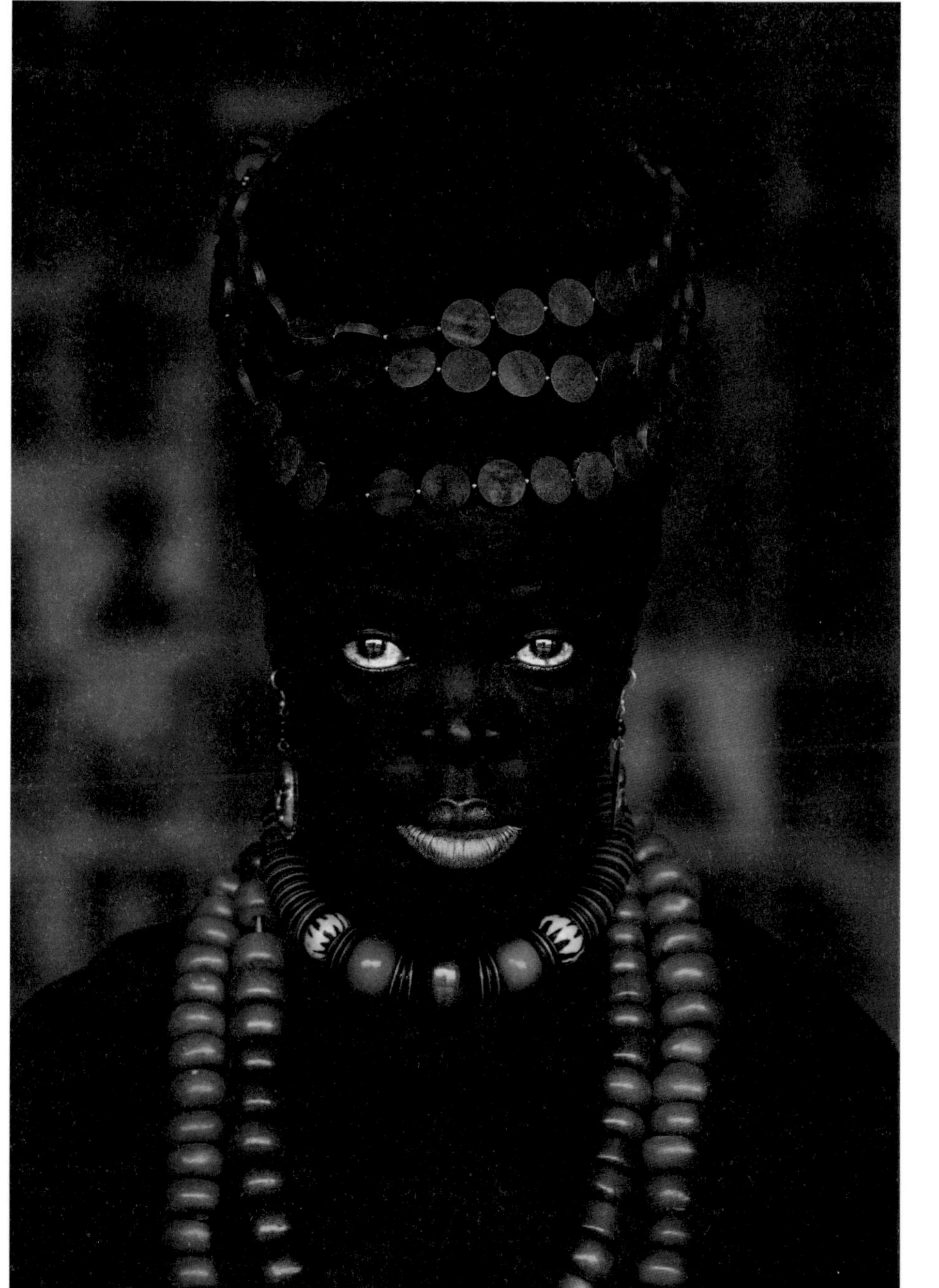

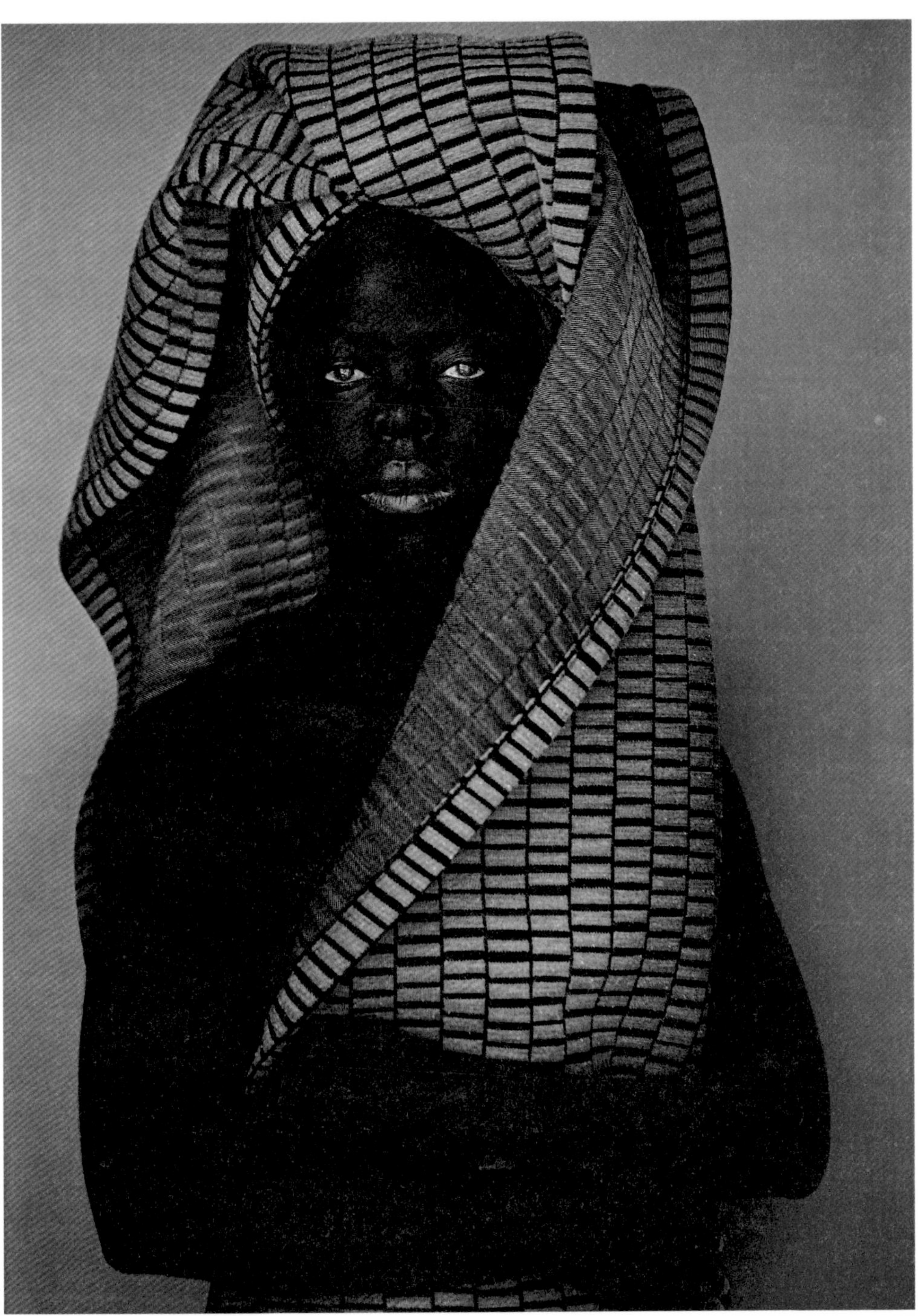

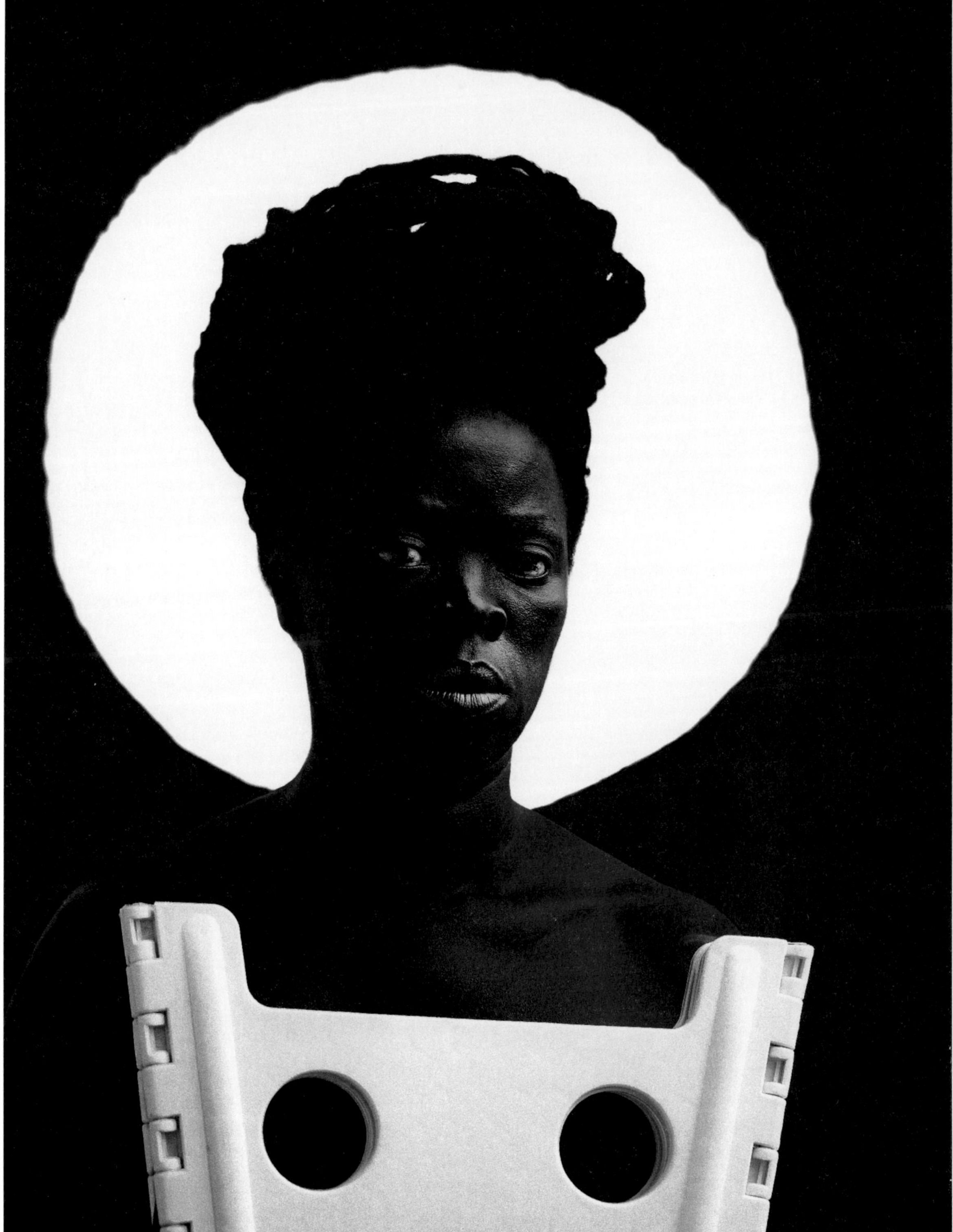

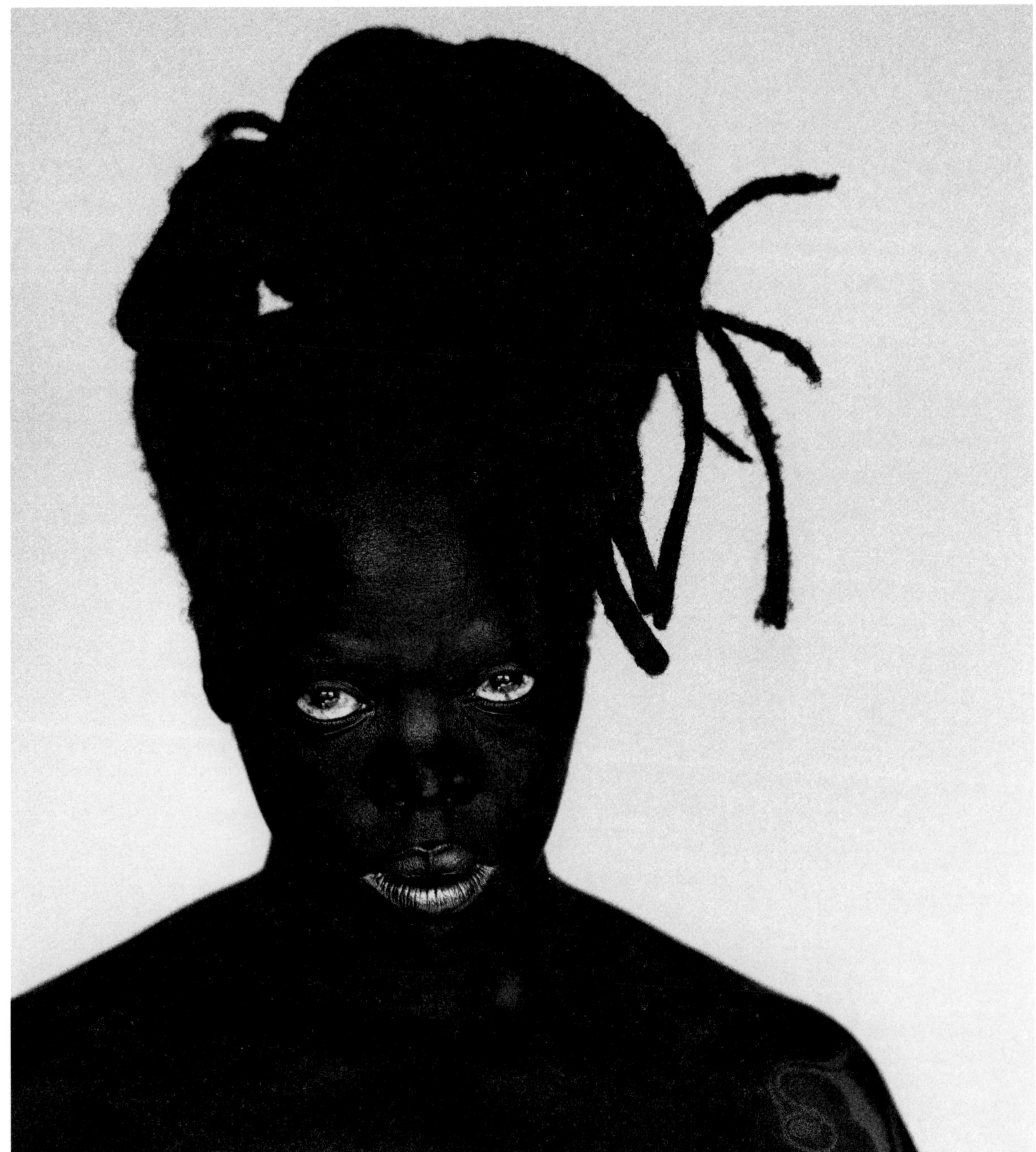

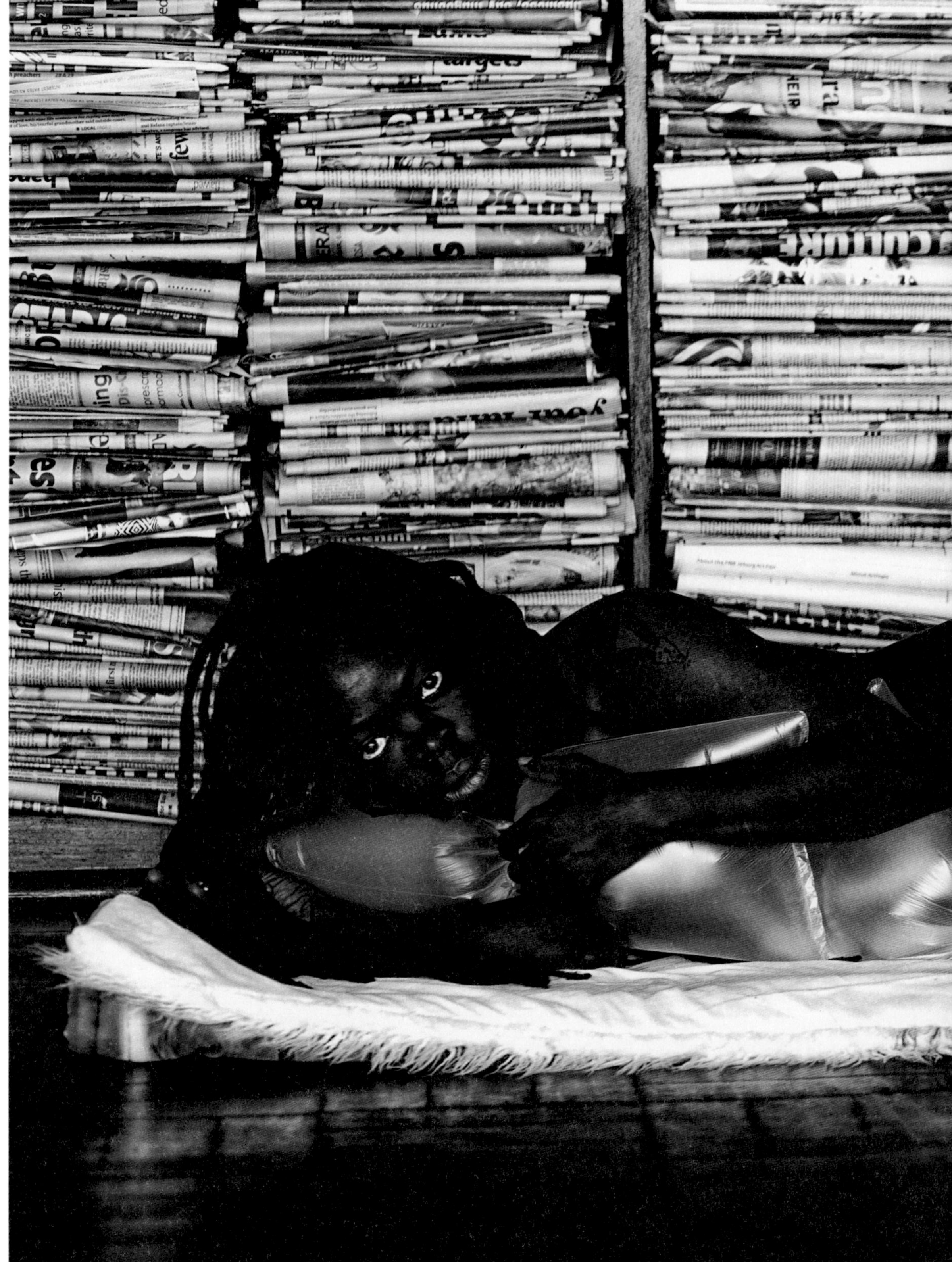

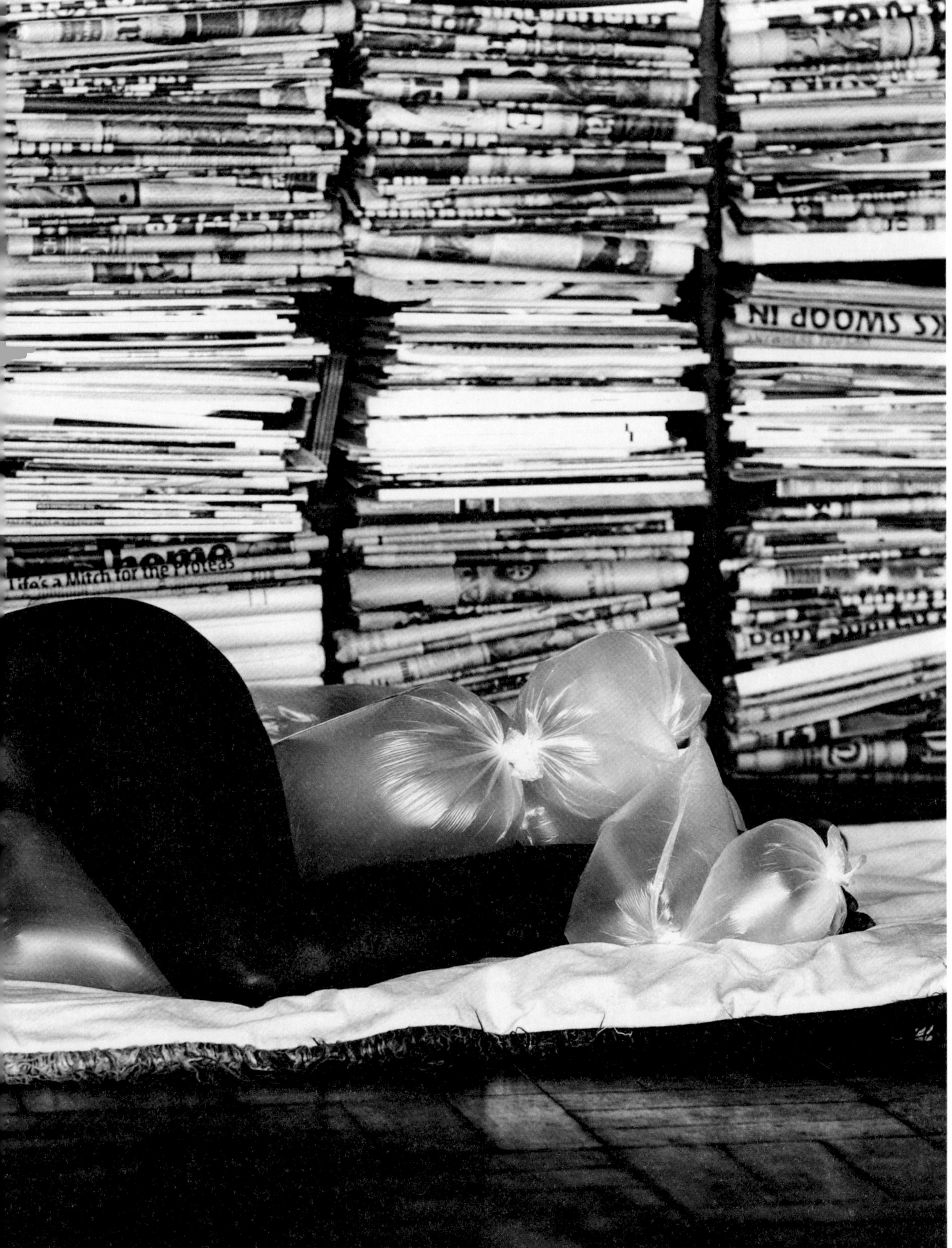

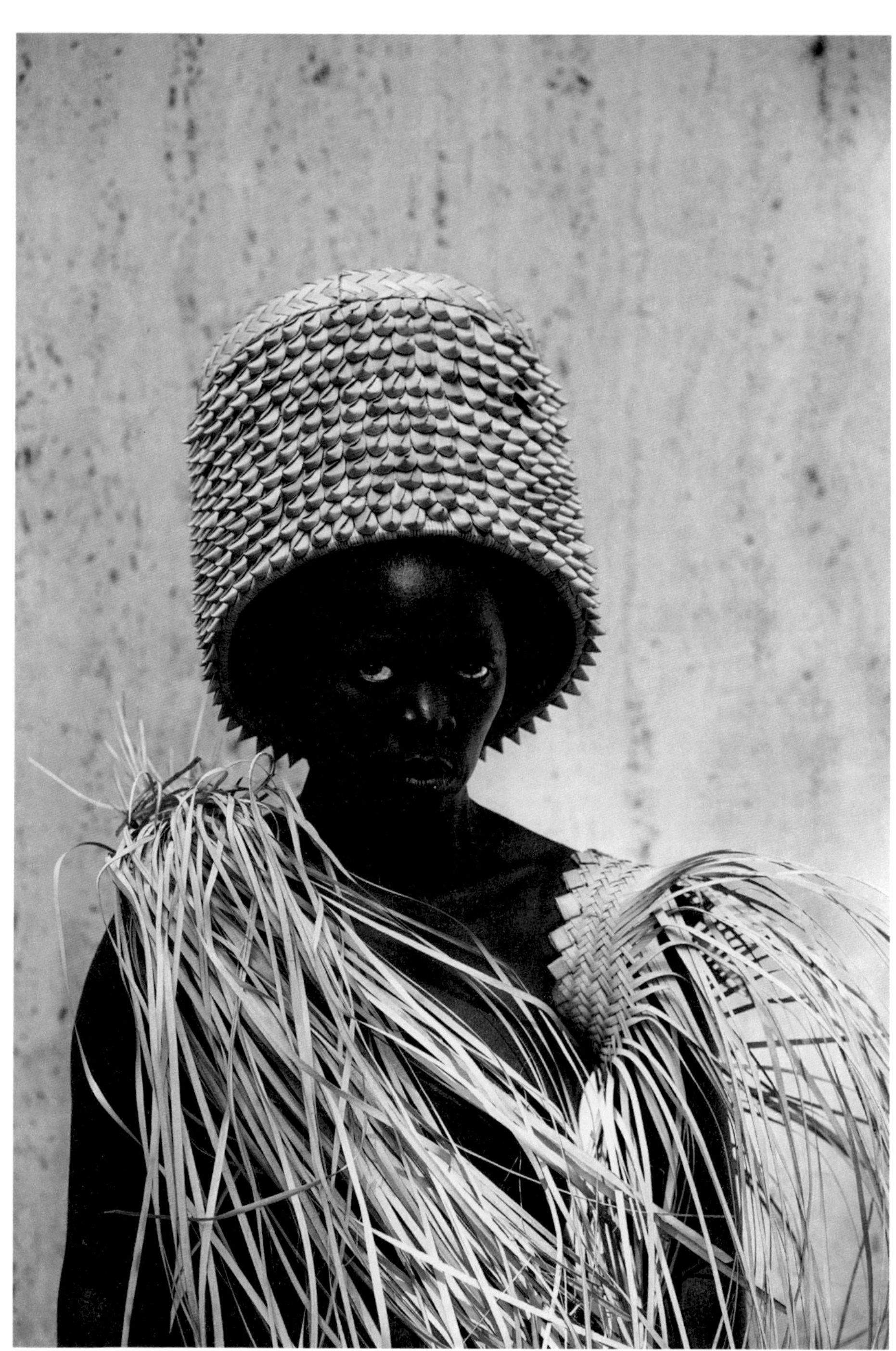

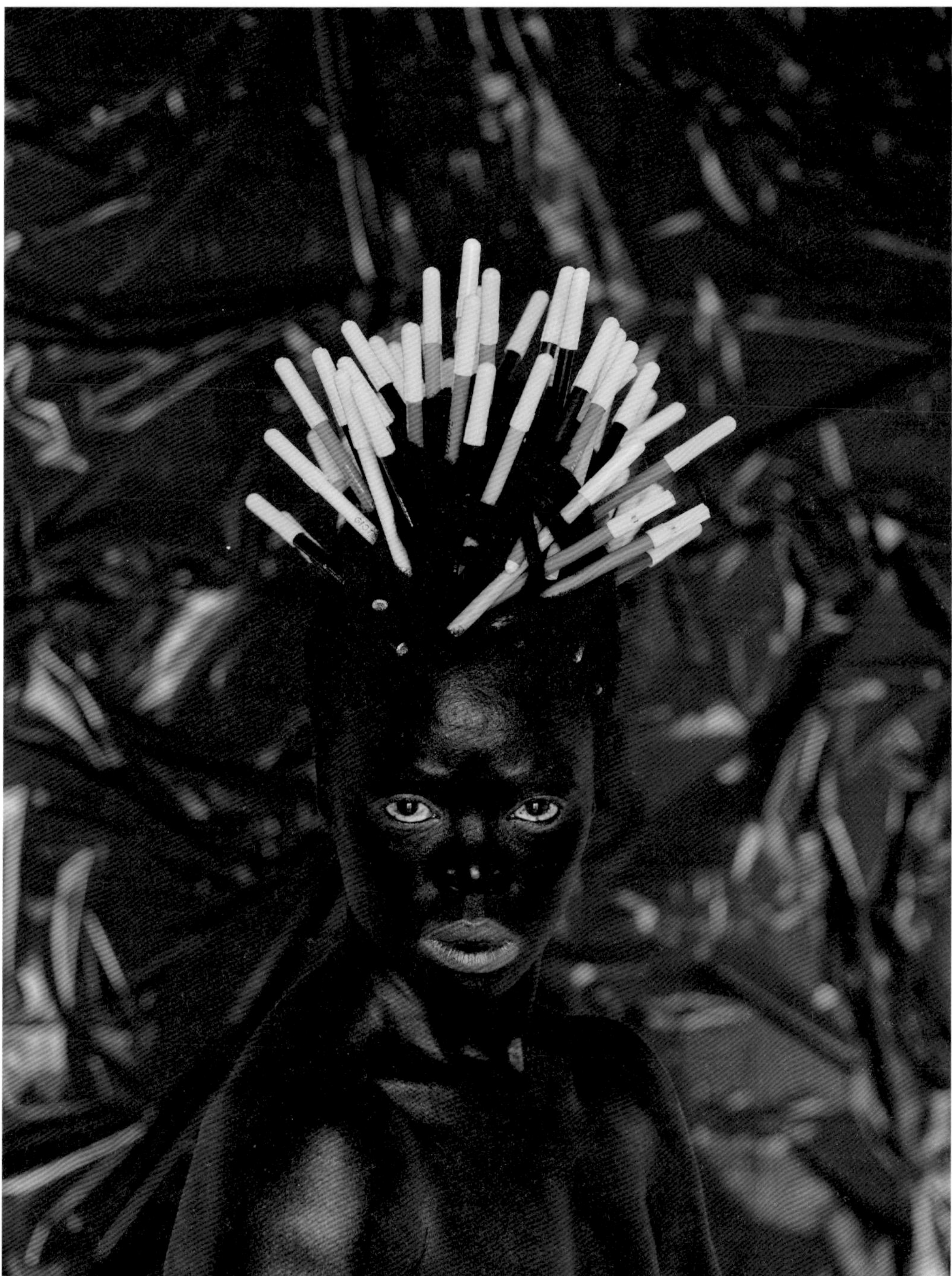

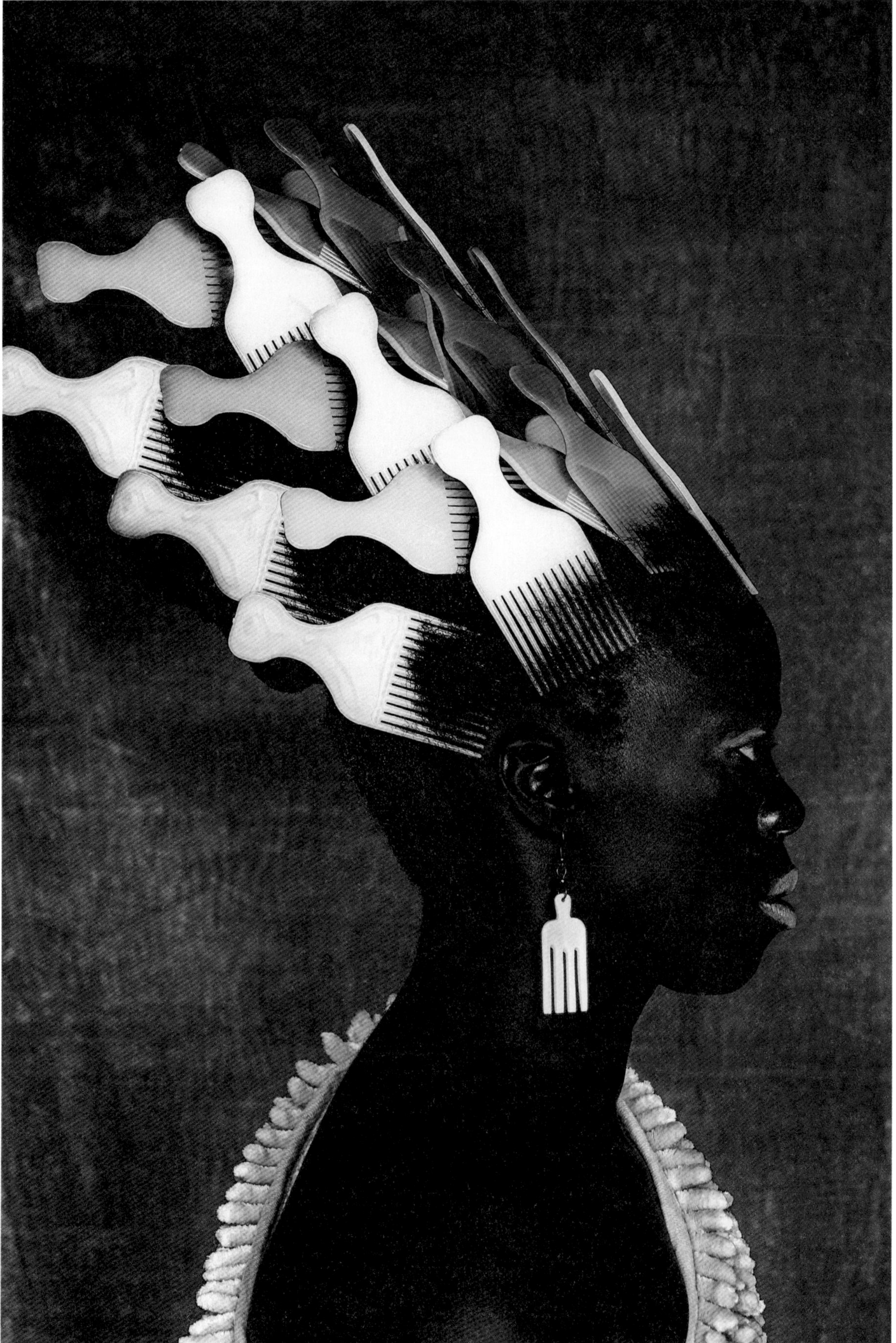

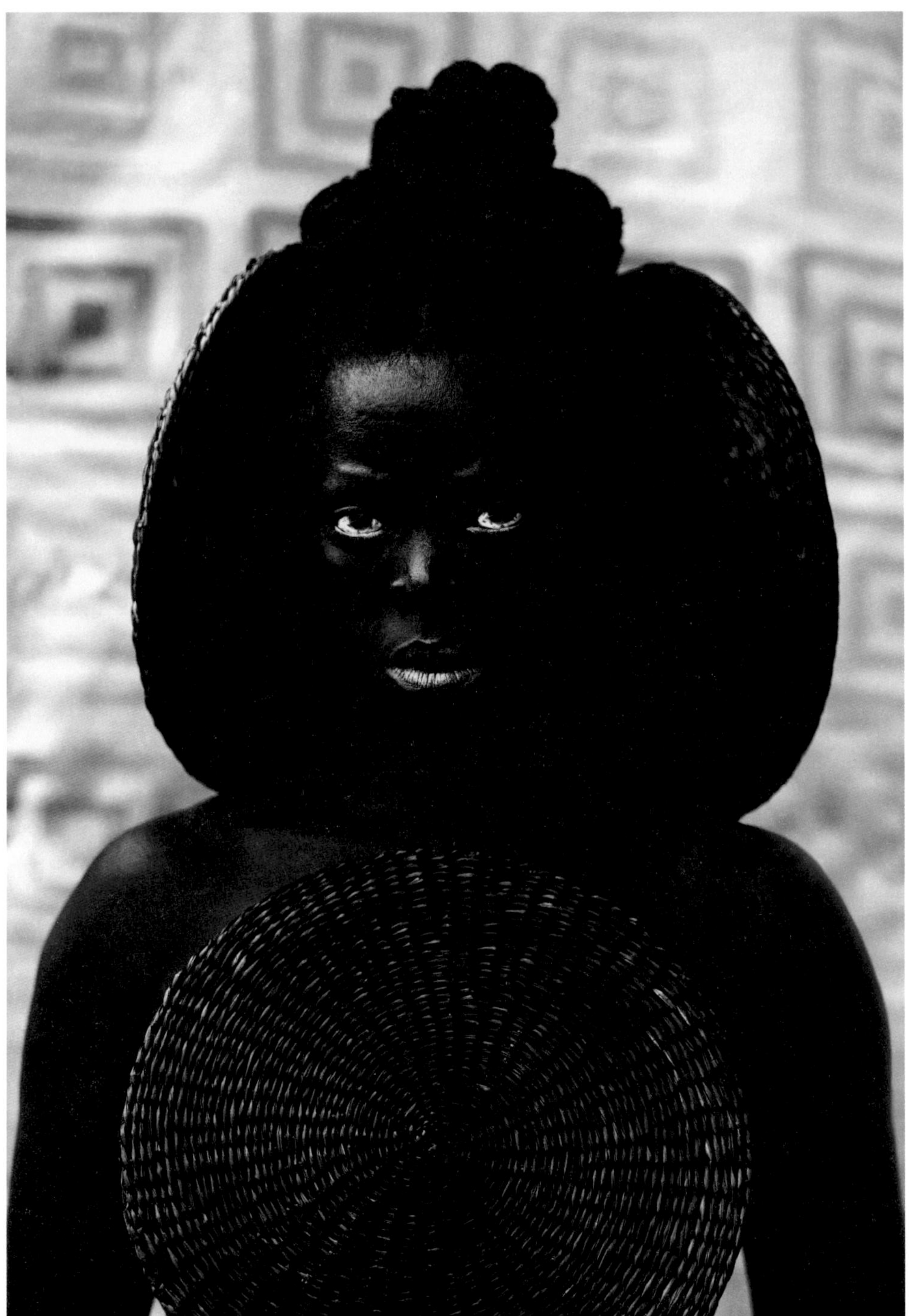

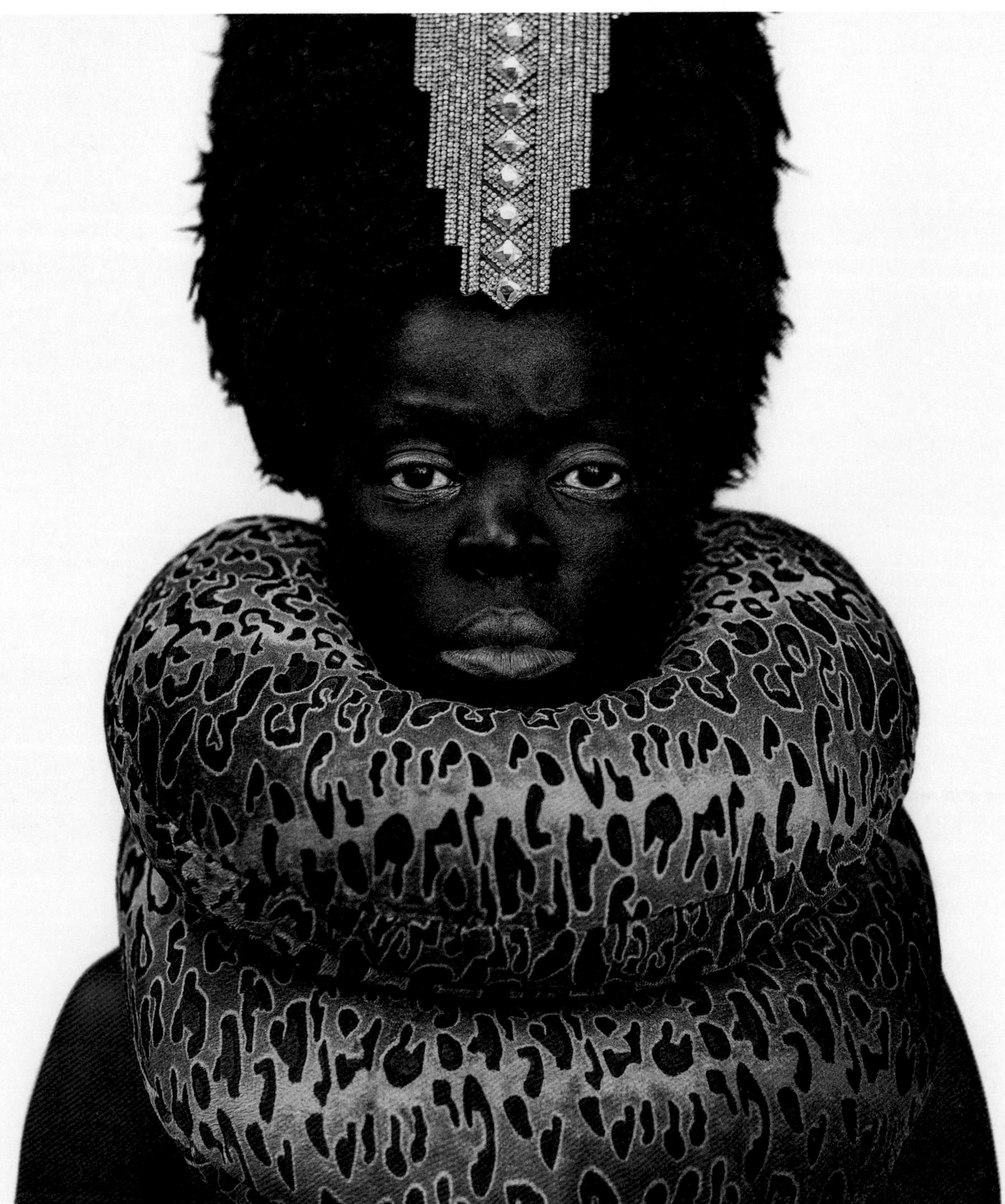

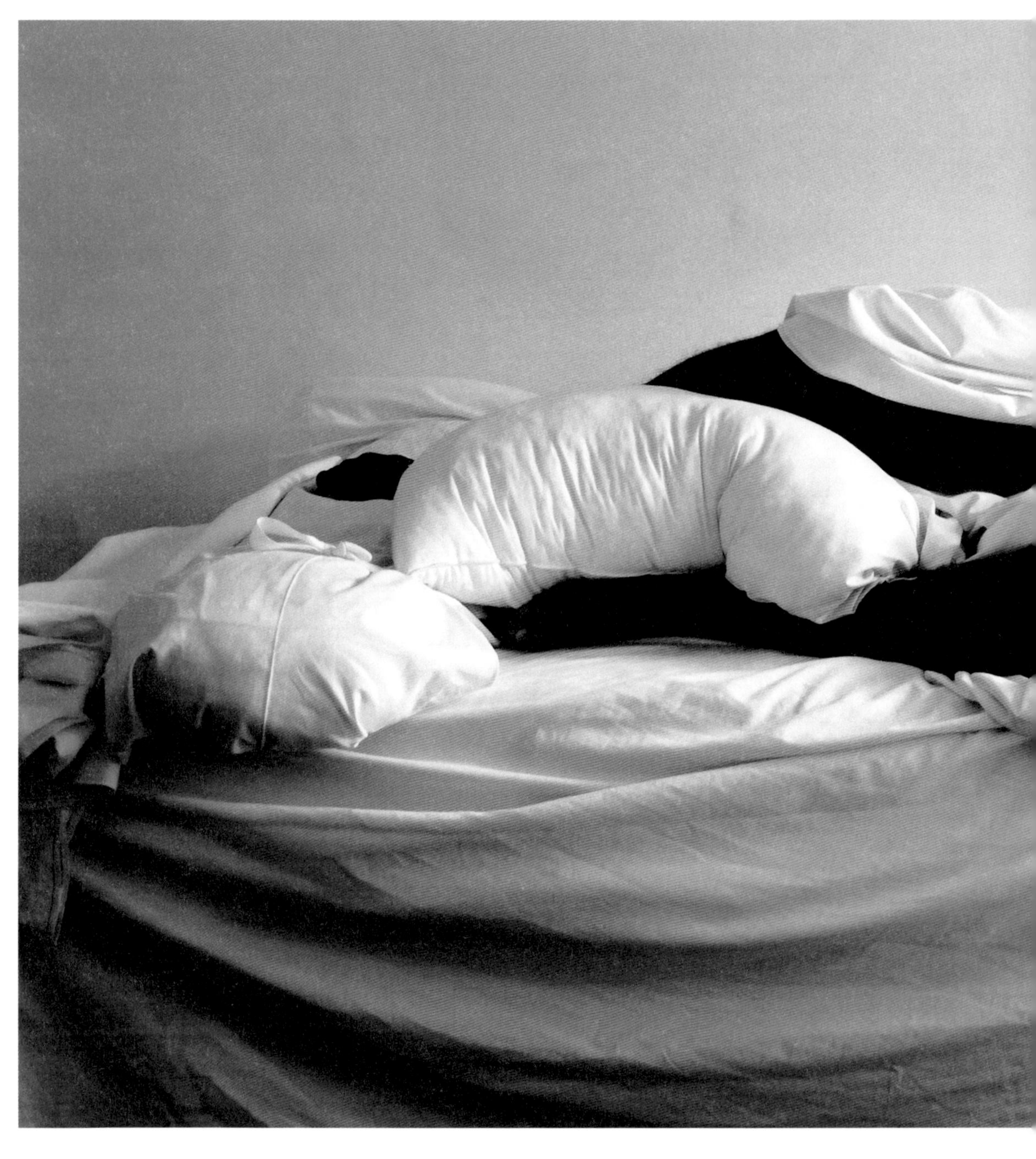

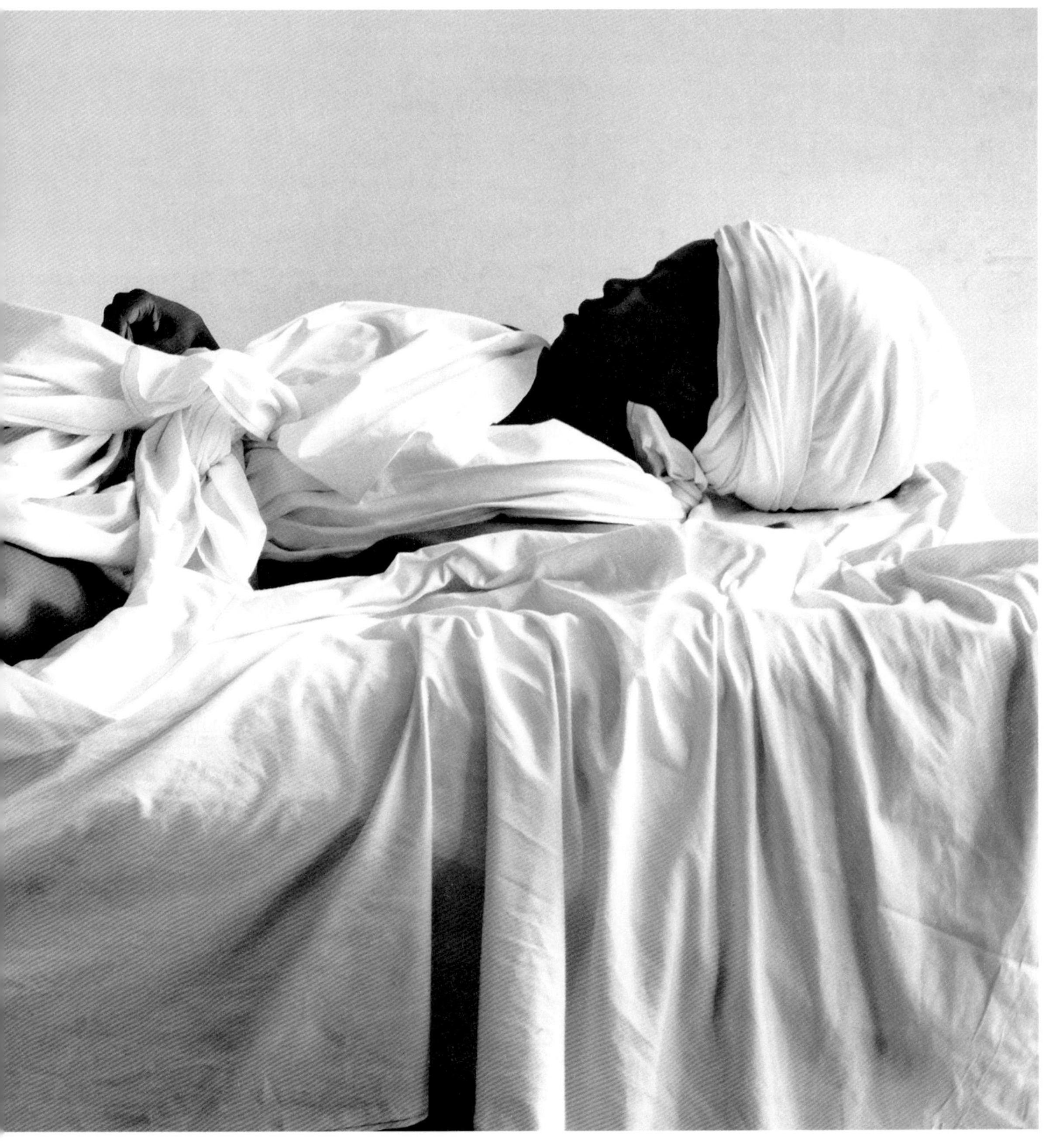

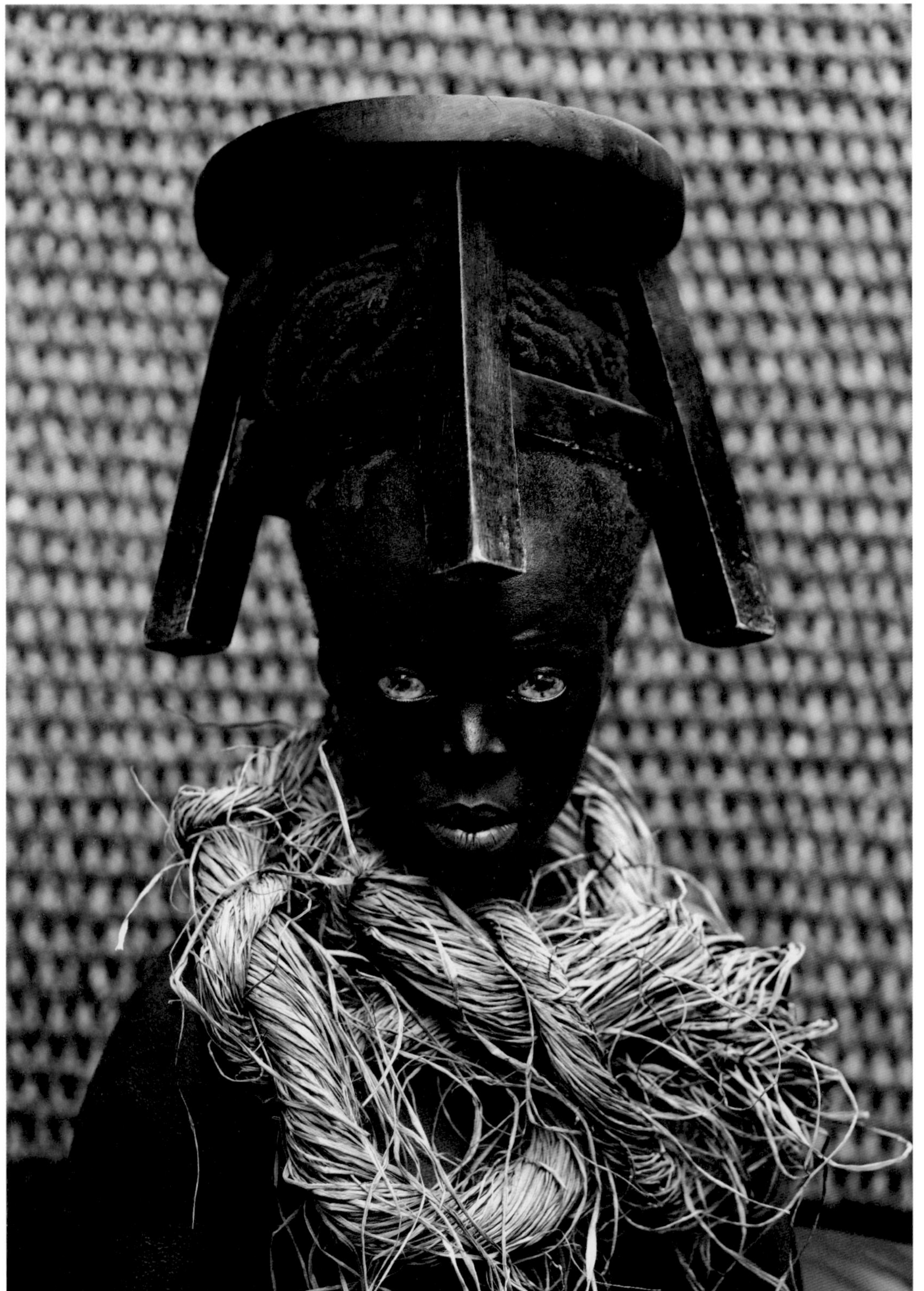

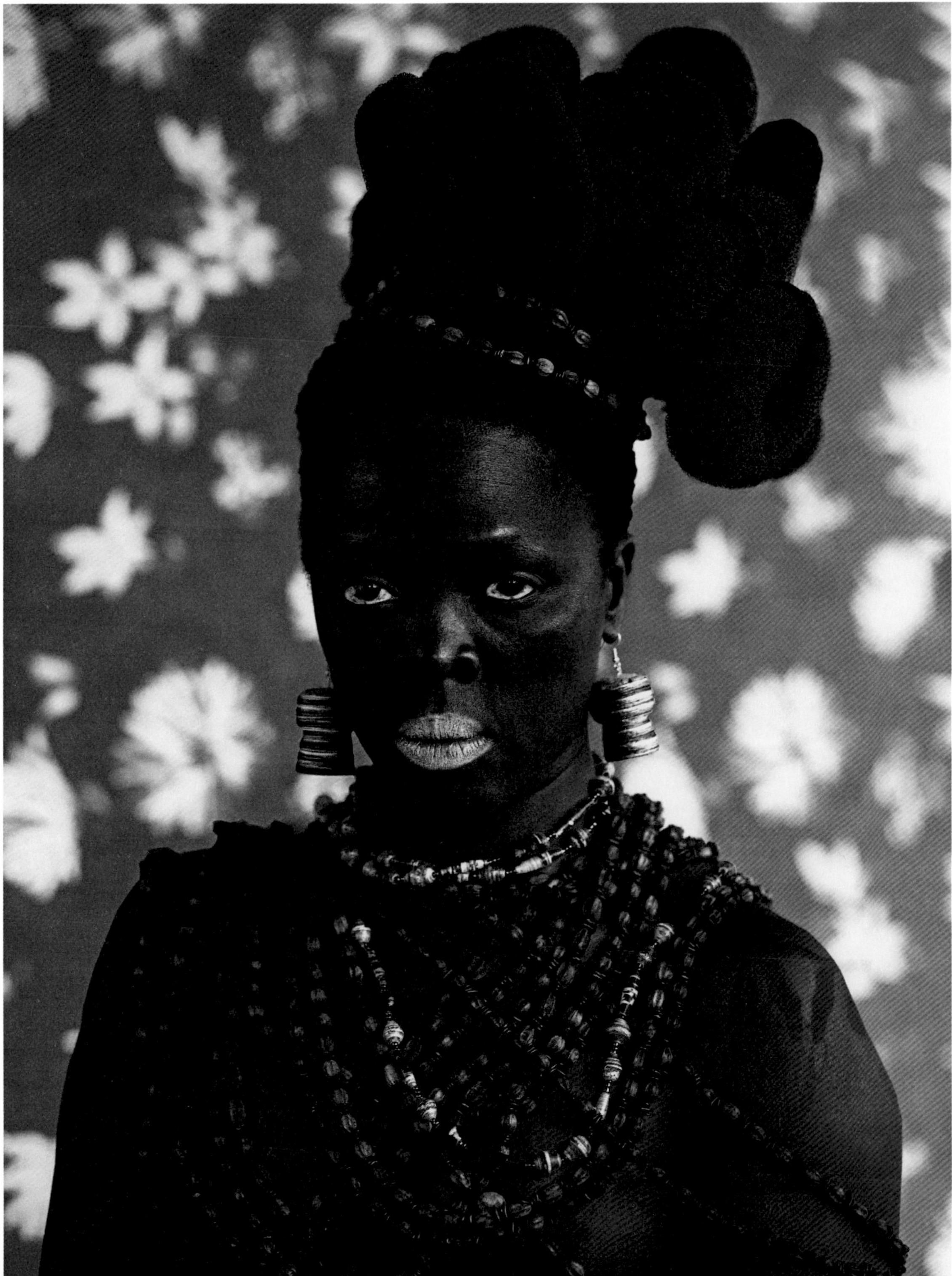

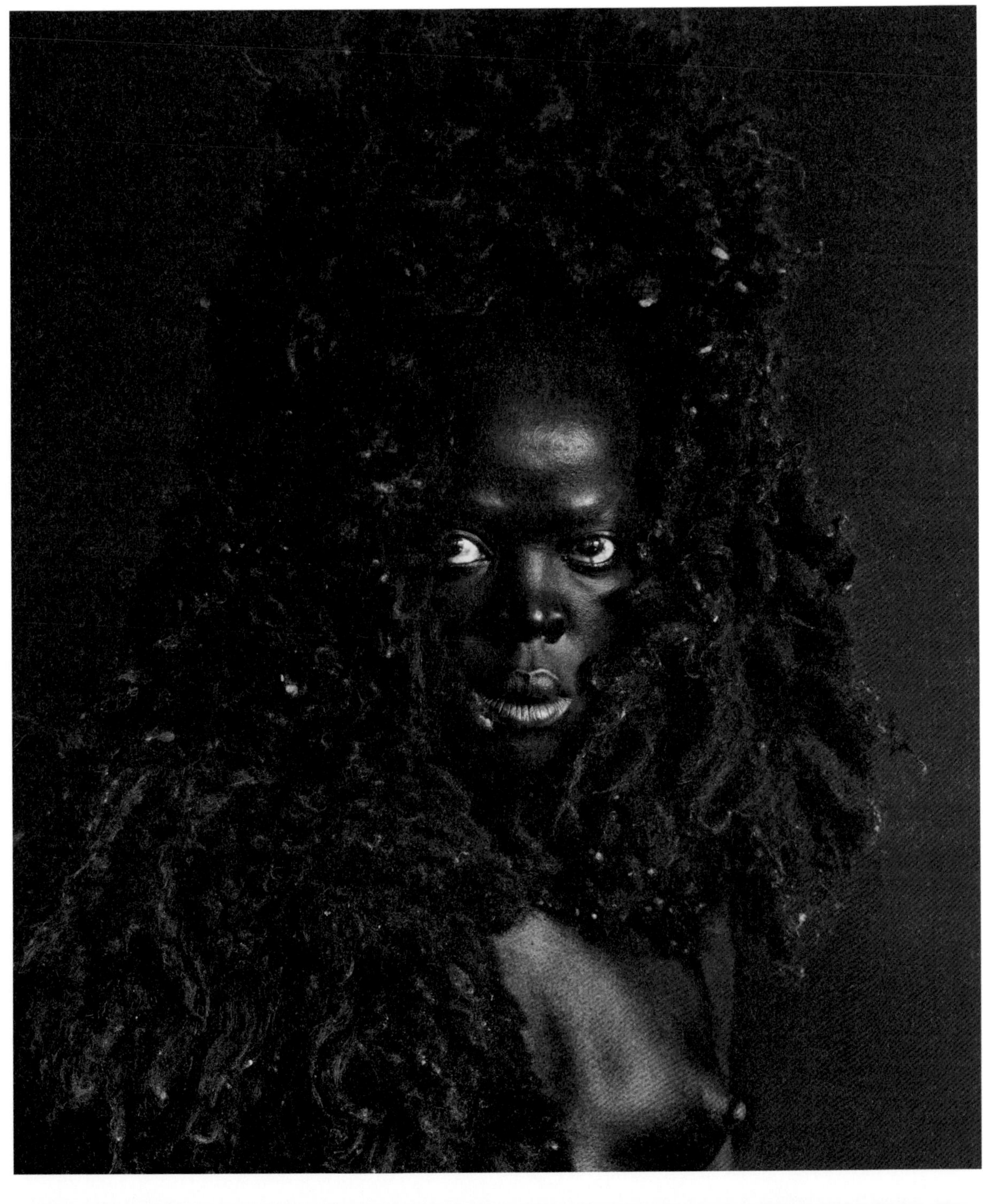

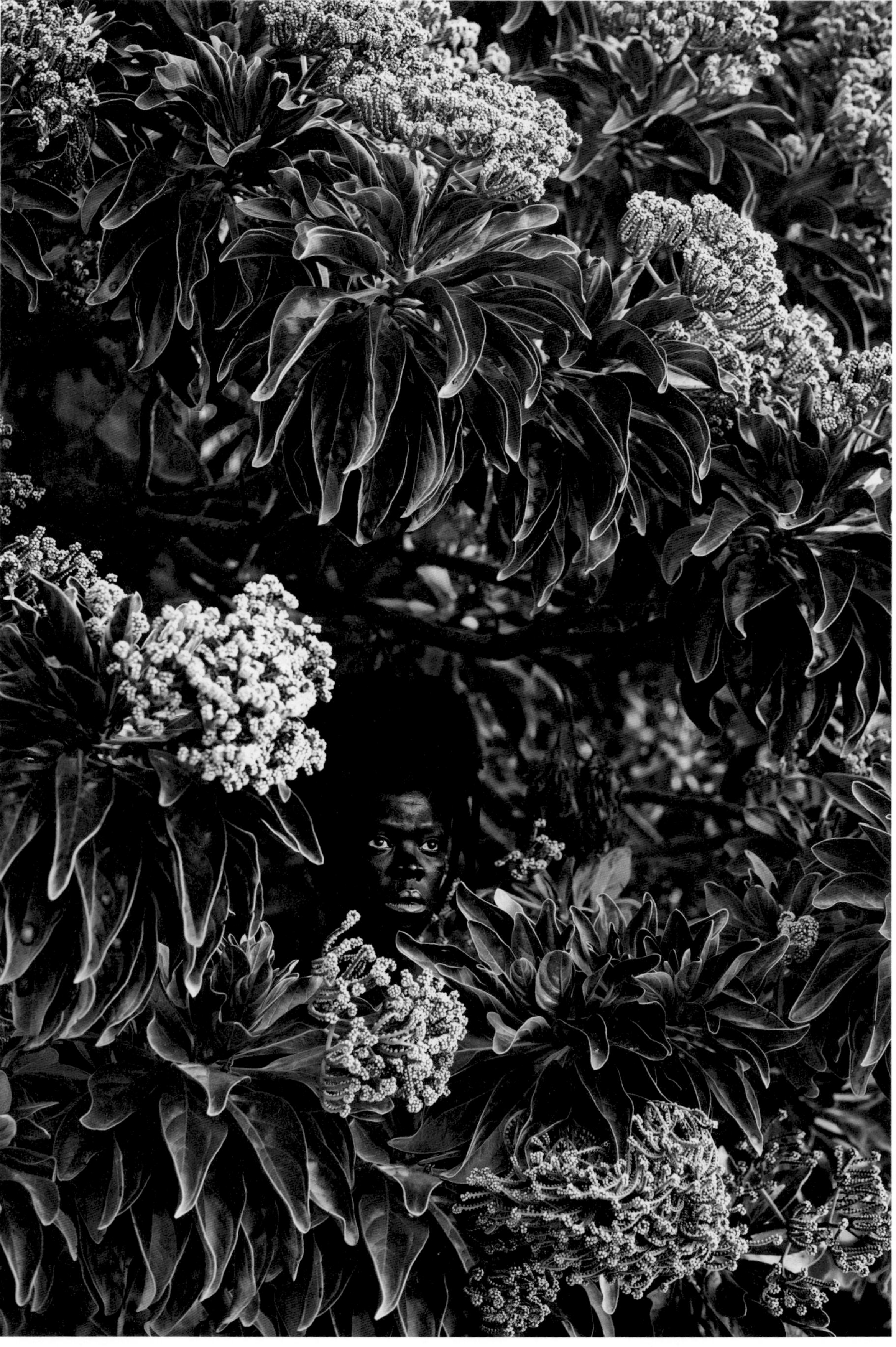

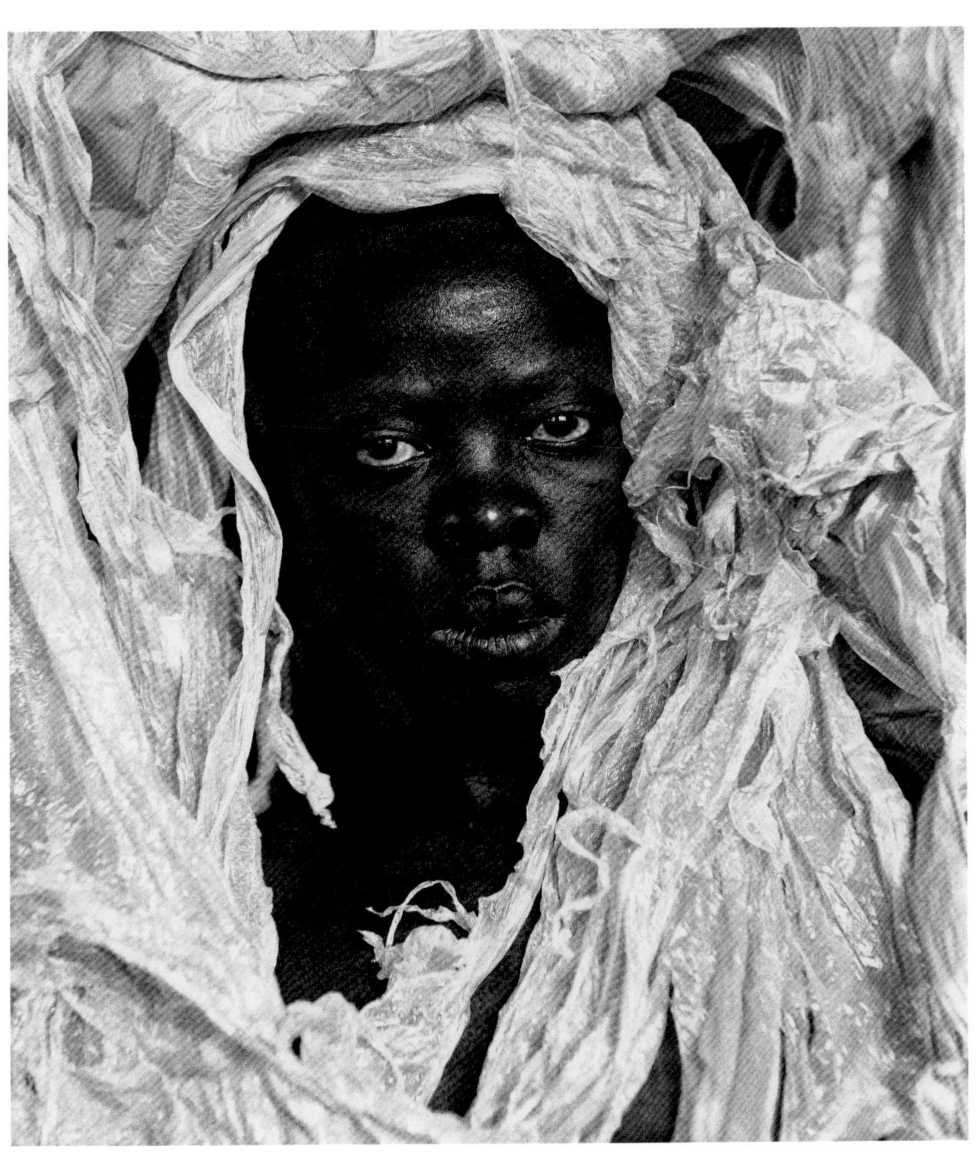

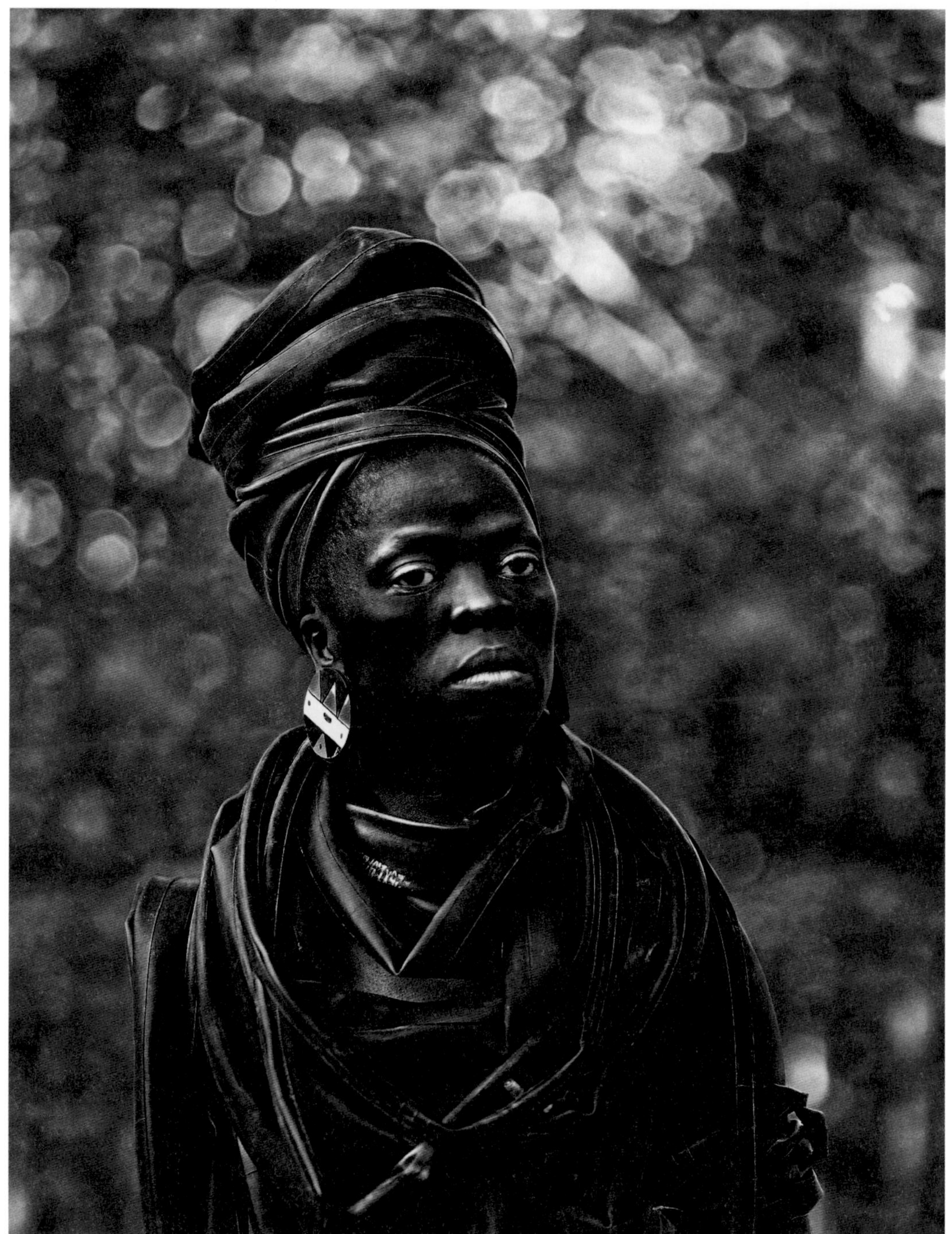

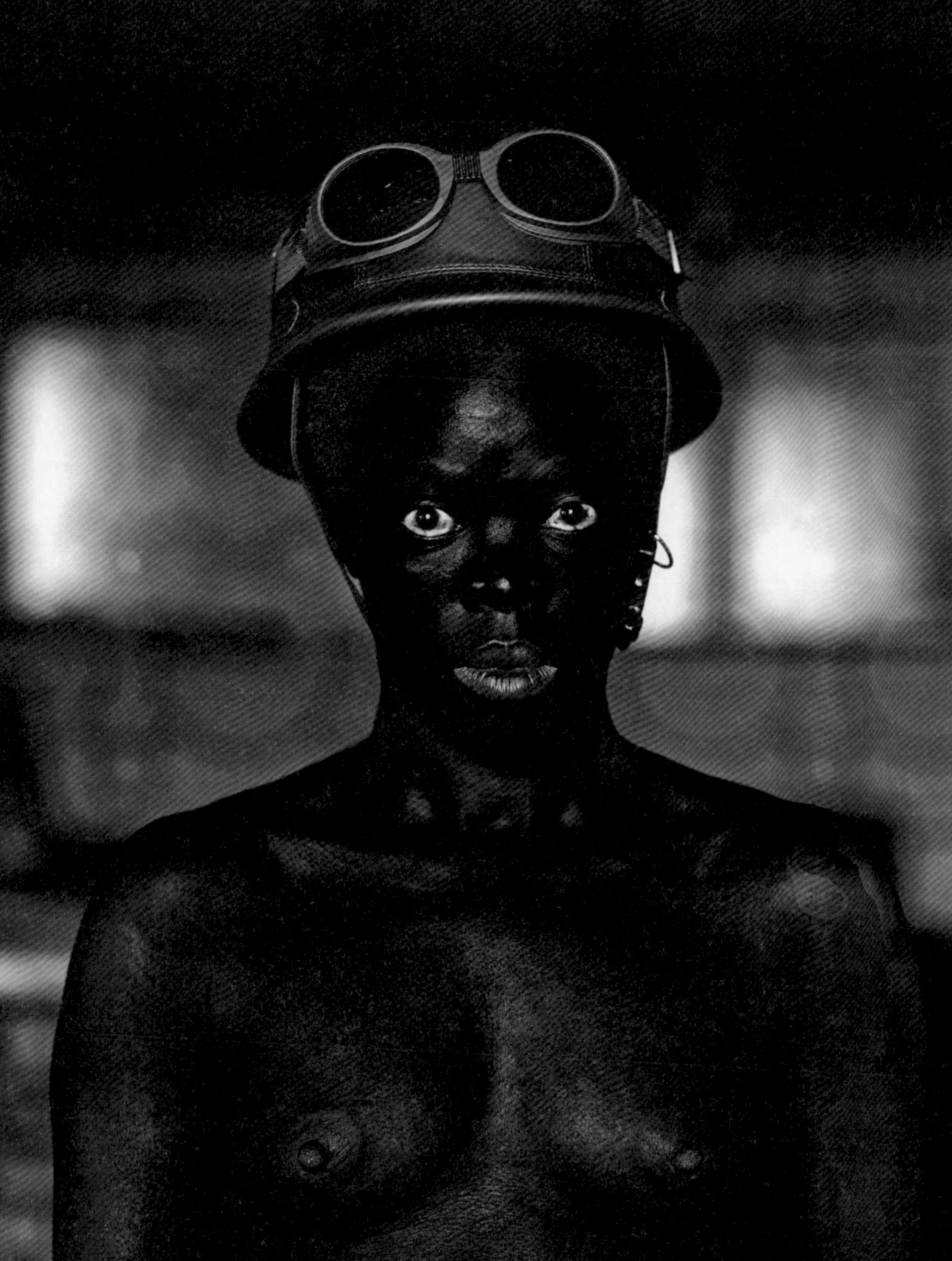

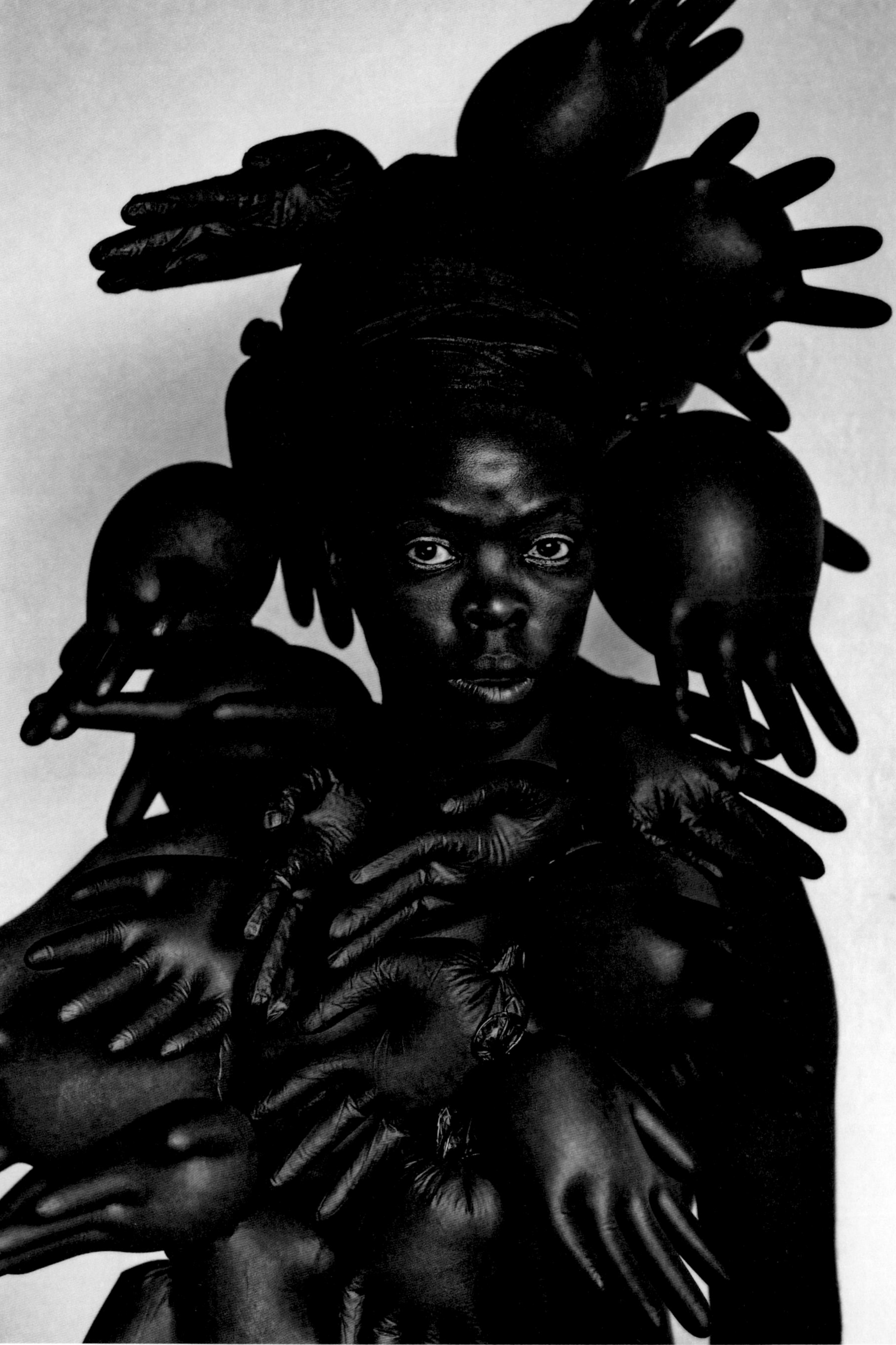

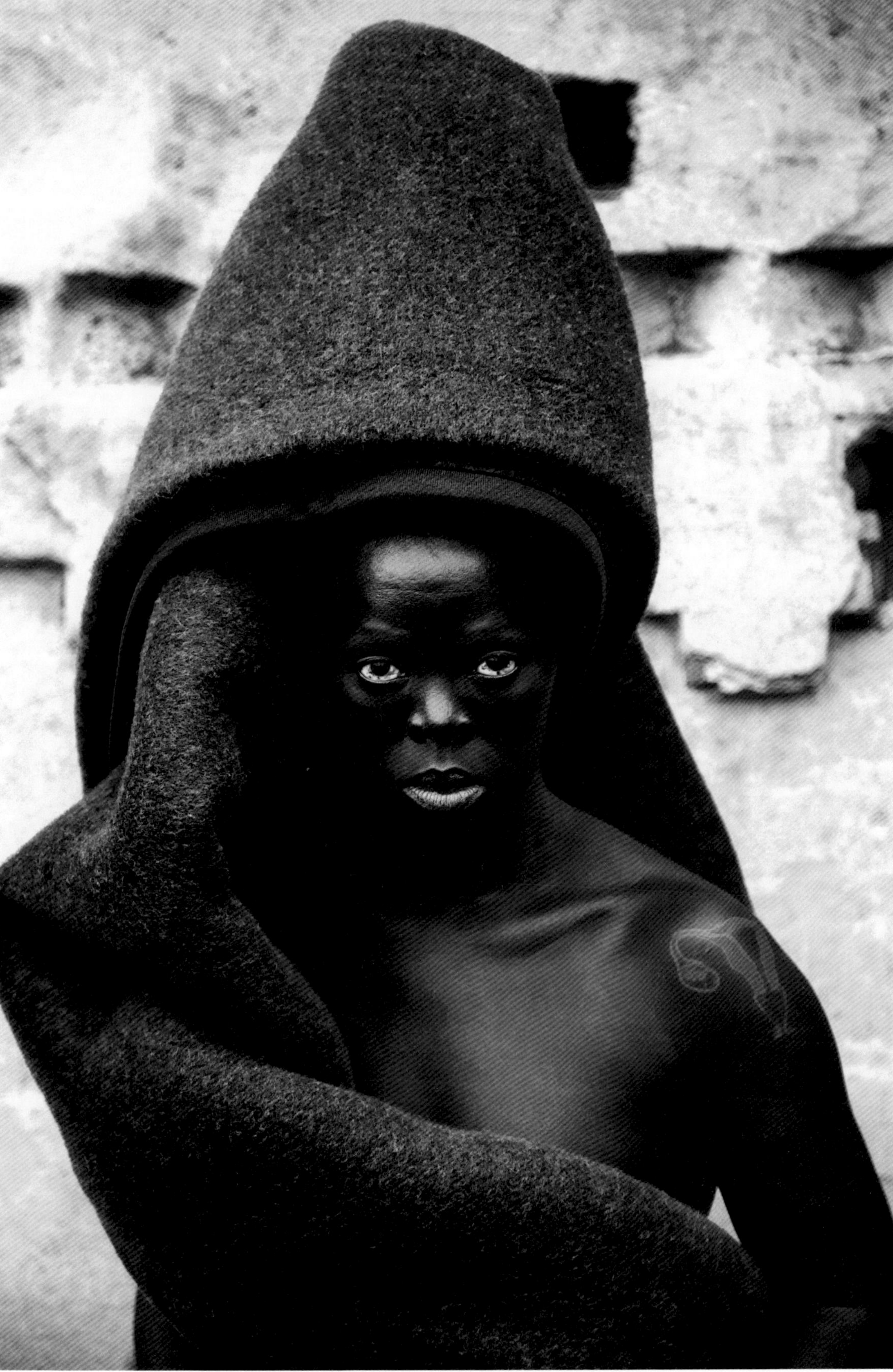

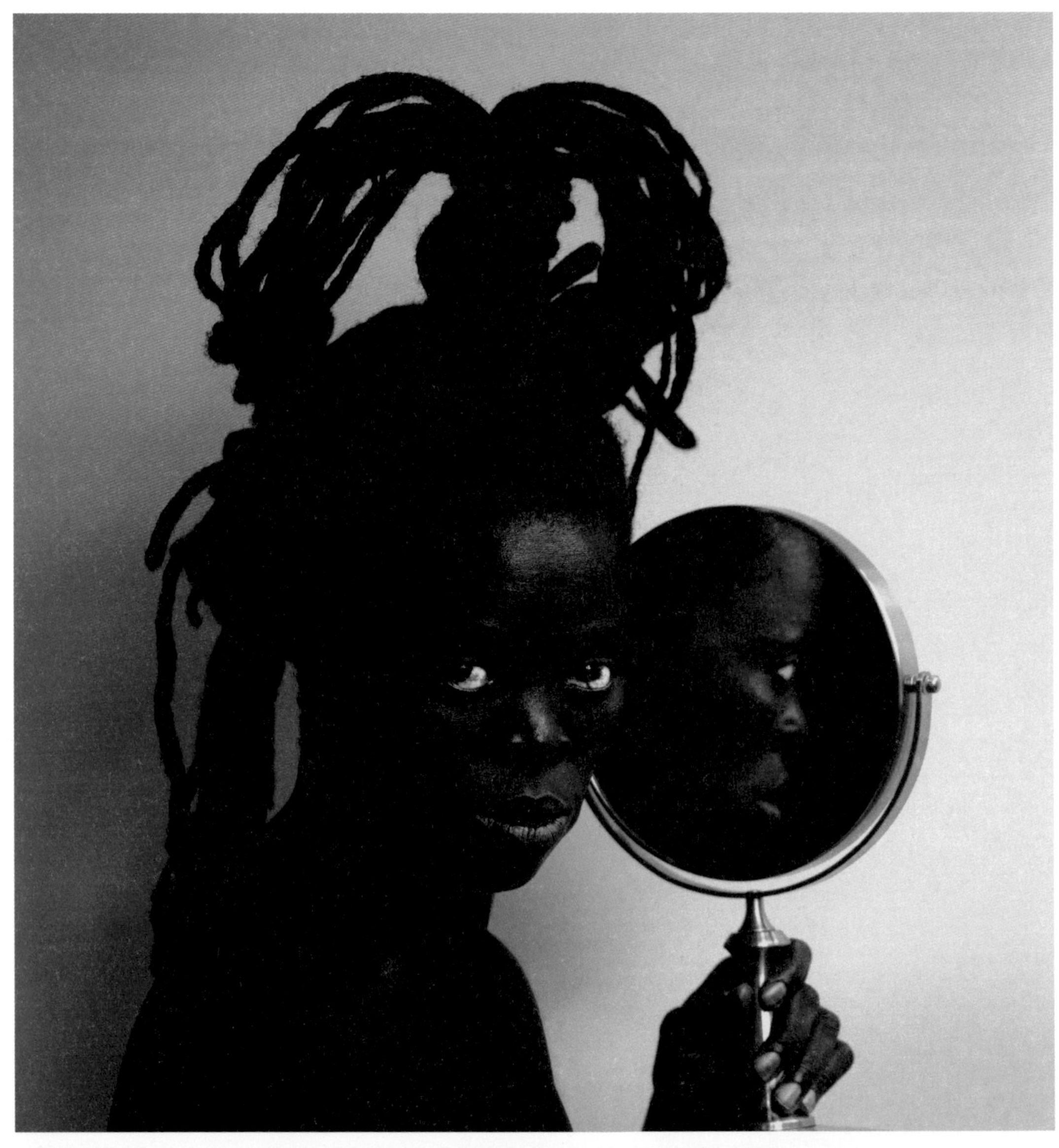

Another Approach is Possible

Sarah Allen

Another Approach is Possible

Sarah Allen

From the moment they picked up a camera Zanele Muholi was already resisting and transgressing. They were resistant as much to their cultural norm, which proffers men as the sole documentarians of family life, as to the notion that anyone other than themself be the narrator of *their* story, the archiver of *their* history. They often say 'another approach is possible'. That approach can be defined as one of resistance. Over the past decades they have re-visioned Black queer life in South Africa, resisting the status quo in all its guises. They have done so by telling the story they know best – their own.

Muholi was born in Umlazi, Durban, and an awareness of their beginnings, never the sum total of their being but roots that inform the journey, has never dissipated – a child born at the height of apartheid, a factory worker, a hairdresser, the youngest daughter of a dedicated mother who laboured tirelessly as a domestic worker to support her family, and then, an emergent visual activist who, dissatisfied with the image repertoire prescribed to them, set out to create a new one.

They took part in the first multiracial and democratic vote in 1994, which brought Nelson Mandela to power, and watched as a new democracy ushered in the first constitution in the world to outlaw discrimination based on sexual orientation. Yet Muholi observed a deep chasm between the appearance of democracy and the reality. They bore witness to the rise of homophobic hate crimes and documented the funerals and scenes related to them. Questions began to crystallise. How do those pushed to the social, economic and cultural margins access all the good of South Africa's constitution? Why do some of South Africa's citizens have to settle for 'protection by paper alone'?

Propelled by such questions, as well as the need to visualise their own lived reality, and an awareness that in order to change that reality one must expose it, Muholi began to document hate crimes with an unflinching eye. In 2002, as part of their work with the Forum for the Empowerment of Women, they journeyed to various townships in the province of Gauteng, listening to and recording 47 cases. Muholi took portraits of those they interviewed, individuals whose state of 'hyper-visibility', as Pumla Dineo Gqola describes it, had rendered them targets for homophobic vio-lence.[1] These images formed the nucleus of what would become Muholi's first series, *Only Half the Picture*.

From this very first series Muholi encountered a dilemma. How to represent a survivor of trauma without reproducing their victimhood? How to raise conscious-ness while resisting a dominant stereotype? How to subvert a narrative of pain – one that left an indelible mark on them, having come of age during the anti-apartheid struggle? One of the first steps in addressing this was to picture another side of queer life; to show that joy and love existed alongside trauma. And so images which reveal the varied meanings of queer intimacy freed from a heteronormative vision punctuate *Only Half the Picture* and become the main focus in *Being*, one of the series that followed.

To further challenge what we would presume to know about Black queer lives Muholi told an inclusive and varied story. To do so they asked those they photographed to share their own experiences, through their own eyes. In *Faces and Phases* the testimonies of Black lesbians, transgender persons and gender-non-conforming individuals are spotlighted; they present themselves not as queer 'types' but as multifaceted individuals with agency, proudly subverting the camera's power dynamic by returning its gaze. 'Don't see my gender, just see me as a person', states Yaya Mavundla, a trans woman from Muholi's *Brave Beauties* series (see pp.90 and 100). In Muholi's photography there are no subjects, but participants – those who actively participate in a collaborative process, some becoming friends, co-producers and comrades.

For Muholi's participants, seeing their individual portraits has been personally healing and in some cases transformative. When seen together, the body of work performs an act of collective healing for a community in need of visual validation in a critical post-apartheid moment. When Muholi needed to heal themself of their own wounds, both personal and collective, it was the medium of self-portraiture that provided the most potent salve. In *Somnyama Ngonyama*, Muholi exorcises painful racisms both past and present, so that they might inch closer to an unburdened reflection of themself. A significant number of works are titled in isiZulu, as much a gesture of pride in the beauty and nuance of their mother tongue as an act of redress to apartheid's history of linguistic oppression.

I.

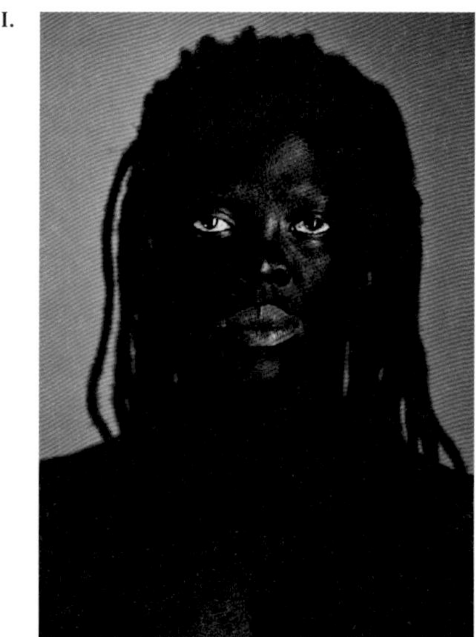

As Muholi's practice has developed, it has found influence in dialogue with visual histories and literature of the past. It has solidified in resistance to anthropological imagery such as Alfred Martin Duggan-Cronin's study, *The Bantu Tribes of South Africa*: those portraits, in Muholi's words, of 'somebody – some *body* which in the end equated to nobody'.[2] It forms a counter-archive for its own people in its own time, in a similar manner to the work of W.E.B. Du Bois. It is the visual evidence to support research which deals with Black representation, which dismantles the notion of homosexuality as 'un-African'.[3] It intervenes in established canons, finding influence in publications such as *Viewfinders: Black Women Photographers* by Jeanne Moutoussamy-Ashe. It is channelled through the writings of bell hooks, whose 'oppositional gaze' Muholi seeks to activate in *Somnyama Ngonyama*, and it is roused by the urgency of Sindiwe Magona's refrain in her poem 'Please, Take Photographs'.[4]

The road Muholi has claimed for themself is not treated as a luxury, and the title of 'visual activist' is worn with a sincere sense of responsibility. This flows simultane-ously back to the community from which it emerged, and outward to prick the con-sciousness of the resistant or unknowing: the politician who promotes homophobia, transphobia or racism as a means to uphold conservative values, the Western viewer whose unconscious bias has gone unchecked, the young man for whom patriarchal tradition so orders his life that he ceases to recognise it, or simply a person who has never seen an image which offered the nuanced complexity of a Black queer human being.

Muholi's work over the past decades has proved that another approach is possible. They have not only created an archive and written a visual document for their country, but they have re-written the common understandings of how activism and art can coexist as a brave new form of resistance. Today Muholi's mission 'to *queer* to *blacken* to *open* and to *occupy* spaces'[5] is as strong as ever, and their commitment still palpable.

1. Zanele Muholi, Mfana, London, 2014

Zanele Muholi and Katarina Pierre:
A Conversation

Zanele Muholi and Katarina Pierre:
A Conversation

ZANELE MUHOLI   At a time when I was going through an emotionally challenging period, the camera offered me an opportunity to heal. I needed to find self-healing, and photography became a form of therapy. But it was also a response: I realised that there were few images that spoke to me, that showed people like me, that document-ed my immediate and close community – Black lesbian, gay, bisexual, trans, queer, intersex and gender-non-conforming persons. I did not see us represented. Since then, photography has become a lifelong mission for self-expression for me. And series such as *Somnyama Ngonyama* and *Faces and Phases* are ongoing because they form part of my daily experience, they are part of who I am – and they have also connected to different constitutional moments for me as a photographer.

KP   South Africa has a strong tradition of activist photography: for example, collectives like Afrapix and photographers like Cedric Nunn, Santu Mofokeng, Omar Badsha and David Goldblatt. You studied at the Market Photo Workhop, which has strong links to the political photography of the 1980s. Do you feel connected to this history of activism? What is your relationship with the past?

ZM   In response to your first point: David Goldblatt, the founder of Market Photo Workshop in Johannesburg, helped me a lot when I started out in photography. He was a mentor who opened doors and was a great advocate of my early practice. And many of the photographers you mention have done important work for South African photography to be appreciated globally, and as part of the struggle for visibility and justice.

In relation to the past: it is important to recognise that our past history of struggle has shaped the present moment. As citizens of South Africa especially, we cannot forget the brutalities of apartheid; it has shaped our consciousness as a nation, hence our work is deeply connected to this history of activism. To me, *Somnyama Ngonyama* is one way of reckoning with this past – to address its politics of race, racism and colonialism – and it is also a way of addressing a past that still informs the present. My artistic practice offers me the opportunity to not only work creatively through these politics of the past, but also to directly link them to the present; to connect these dots. Photography for me is always first and foremost a tool of activism, driven by the idea of social change.

KP   Would you like to comment or expand on the fact that photography in the past, and still today, is a highly gendered and male-dominated field?

ZM   We need diverse voices in every arena, creative or otherwise, whether in relation to gender, race, sexuality or class. There is no denying that there is still much work to be done in order to create a balance and undo gender imparity – photography and art included. It is an ongoing process. The same question applies to many countries all over the world and is especially relevant when it comes to marginalised groups –

Black people, women, and those from LGBTQIA+ backgrounds. Whose voices are heard? Who is given access, and offered opportunities? Who produces the work we see in public spaces from galleries to museums and screen industries, or the books we are taught in school or at university? It is a crucial, ongoing project of decolonisation. South Africa has been at the forefront of this movement.

KP   **Your photographic practice ranges from documentary photography to a more theatrical or performative use of photography in your series *Somnyama Ngonyama*. Could you say something about your different modes of working? And how you think photography can affect our lives in terms of politics of representation and self-representation?**

ZM   I don't like to use the word 'performative' because I am not performing the self, and I am not performing for the camera, even though others might perceive it that way. I am responding to real experiences. In *Somnyama Ngonyama*, I am using different materials that viewers can relate to if they take the time to read the images carefully and think about what these objects might mean. For example, the scouring pads and clothes pegs I use in the images that represent tributes to my mother, Bester Muholi, speak to domestic workers, labour and servitude. These self-portraits are still documentary images to me, as they relate to mundanity and real life. In *Faces and Phases*, which constitutes an archive of Black lesbian, transgender and non-binary individuals, I wanted to ensure that we are counted as citizens and recognised as economic contributors in South Africa. I see them as closely related modes of working – whether I am facing the camera myself or directing the camera towards my participants. I have always been part of my visual project, and in 2012 I began *Somnyama Ngonyama*; it is a continuous journey of self-discovery and self-expression. The camera is a constant presence in my life. And now after fourteen years, *Faces and Phases* is an archive numbering several hundred portraits documenting the Black LGBTQI community in order to positively affect the politics of visibility in South Africa, and beyond. This work is done to ensure that the next generation will be able to draw on a diverse – and queer – archive of images for visual reference: a document to see themselves in and feel represented.

KP   **Could you speak about the challenges of documenting your own community, and your preference for the term 'participants' as opposed to 'subjects'?**

ZM   Firstly, it is very important to understand that these portraits are made from an insider's point of view. I hardly ever photograph strangers, though this is not to say that I won't do so if the opportunity presents itself. People in my projects are individuals I am familiar with; they form part of my wider community; many are friends, or friends of friends. They are participants because they partake in the process of creating these portraits. We each contribute differently to the process, but we are in this process together. I do not like, and have never used or related to, the term 'subject'. Photography to me is supposed to be a collaborative act. Oftentimes

I am both behind and in front of the camera. There is an intimacy, a familiarity and importantly a trust, which is shared. Trust is the biggest concern. It is my responsibility to ensure a positive representation that honours who they are as persons, as individuals. It is important to remember that people's lives also change over time – not all do, but some – and yet their photograph remains in perpetuity. The question then is, how does one ensure that participants are still comfortable with their image, say, fifteen years later? Their lives might have moved on, they might be identifying differently, married or transitioned. It can be difficult. Feelings and moods change: there are the 'phases' that point to the future, and the 'faces' that are captured in the moment, there and then, in the present.

KP   Could you explain why it has taken so long for the Black queer community to emerge from their position of invisibility when the South African constitution was the first in the world to guarantee the rights of LGBTQ in 1996?

ZM   To begin with, the constitution is still young. It takes time for a society to be ready. Even today, inequalities, discrimination, xenophobia, displacement, and the threat of violence against particular communities of people are still prevalent in South Africa. I started photographing Black LGBTQIA+ consciously in the early 2000s and have been working on positively affecting politics of visibility ever since. But people needed to be ready; we must not forget the high risk we face. Hate crimes and gender-based violence are still systematically present in our country. To be visible means to take great risks. A lot of lives have been lost, and continue to be lost, due to queerphobia, homophobia, transphobia and other forms of discrimination. The constitution is on paper; the violence and danger are real.

KP   You describe yourself as a visual activist and a self-defined community worker. As I understand it, there are many different ways you support your community...

ZM   Support comes in different ways. There is emotional support to empower, and financial support to study, especially in photography. Over the years I have supported participants in my series to attend classes at Market Photo Workshop, if they are interested. This is one way of me giving back to the community that shapes my career. It is a way of fostering the spirit of exchange in the hope that others will later continue the work I have started to build our visual legacies for the future. I have founded mobile schools of photography – part of an ongoing collaborative educational project called Photo XP – to equip younger generations with photographic skills and the tools to help them feel comfortable with documenting their own lives as well as those around them. These projects are often led by collaborators and participants in my series, who are now creative practitioners in their own right. We distribute cameras, we teach, and I also commission emerging artists to produce and exhibit their work, and offer scholarships and travel grants as part of my philanthropic work.

KP Could you talk about what 'visual activism' means to you? And how your community work influences your artistic practice?

ZM Visual activism is a mode of survival. There are real, urgent issues at hand. People are violated, people are killed, and people are denied access to spaces. My community is directly connected to all the work I do: so, for me to have a show, being invited to exhibit my work at a gallery or museum, as a Black queer person, means that I have the opportunity to also mobilise members of the community to share that space and see themselves in it. It has taken a long time for us to see ourselves portrayed in a positive way. That struggle was real for me from the start, and continues to be. Hence, I termed my practice 'visual activism', to say: I will use visuals to promote a political agenda that ensure visibility beyond our borders. It is a community-based activism that transcends time and space, beyond national boundaries.

KP What questions preoccupy you the most right now?

ZM There are so many questions that keep me awake at night and preoccupy my mind. How to empower people by the work we do? How to ensure all participants are represented and their views heard? How to work towards a democracy where, as citizens, all of our rights are protected, regardless of sexual orientation, gender or ethnicity? How can I do more to help others, and take care of the self/myself at the same time? How can I stay positive in the face of all the trauma and turmoil and worrying political movements and backlashes; the rise of hate crimes, troubling ideologies, oppressive regimes and continuous attacks on our liberties? Wherever possible, I try to channel these questions into *Somnyama Ngonyama*.

KP You have also developed a writing practice. What is the relationship between your photographs and your texts?

ZM I have written texts in the past, artistic statements to contextualise my practice or process situations in relation to my practice, but I have not written much lately. I have been focused on visual production and developing my activism. For me, language is primarily about my mother tongue, and the desire to incorporate Zulu language into the work and the vernacular I am developing. For instance, the image titles in *Somnyama Ngonyama* are always in Zulu, unless they are individual names or made-up phrases. This is one way for me to engage the written word, and to express things in a tongue that is resolutely African, and my own. I would like to be able to link our own language to what we produce, to bring our mother tongues into conversation with photography. Right now we have visuals, but we don't have a written language yet to interpret, express and cite these visuals for scholarly review and journals, etc. I do hope to write again in the future.

KP Your work is courageous and daring in challenging hierarchies of power, gender,

sexuality and race/ethnicity. Are you ever scared? And what do you find the most challenging part of your work?

ZM I am scared. There is a lot of risk, and a lot of responsibility. It can be a very lonely space, too. People might be there with you, but you are not necessarily in the same phase, sharing the same concerns or anxieties. There are often no boundaries between your life, your activism and your practice. It can be, at times, overwhelming and isolating. Working with people is always challenging, because of the great responsibility that comes with such collaborations and exposures – there are matters of safety, of care... Another big challenge is sustainability, and legacy. How do we make sure that all the documentation is preserved, and will continue to live beyond us?

KP **Do you have people or role models that have inspired you in either your personal or professional life?**

ZM Above anyone else, my late mother, Bester Muholi – all my work in *Somnyama Ngonyama* is a tribute to her, inspired by her strength, her courage and her resilience. In general, women serve as my role models, those powerful, beautiful women who make ends meet, survive and nurture others under difficult circumstances, regardless of traumas or harsh experiences they face on a daily basis. I think of individuals such as Sindiwe Magona, the South African writer: she speaks to me in many ways. I am inspired by the courage of my fellow artists, writers, teachers, and other cultural producers and activists.

KP **What can people do to support your community and activist work?**

ZM More than ever we need emotional support in order to sustain and regain the strength needed to carry on with what we are doing. There is so much trauma and depression within the community, and not enough help psychologically. Open forums for skills development and the sharing of knowledge are also crucial, offering spaces, advocacy and networks of access.

KP **Do you think we can transform society through artistic practices?**

ZM I have to believe that art can make a difference ... but of course my response is only a partial 'yes'. If you are living in a society with constraints, without a democracy, or where freedom of expression is not guaranteed, the circumstances are different. The stakes are higher when artists and media producers are persecuted by the government and their lives are at risk, their voices routinely silenced – as opposed to a democratic society, where people are free to express themselves. If I didn't believe that art can be used to raise awareness and institute some level of social change, what would be left to fuel the work I do? We must have hope ... and continue to believe, and produce.

CHRONOLOGY

Fluid gender roles and same-sex relationships exist across Africa. For example, the legal marriage between two women is practised in approximately 40 pre-colonial societies across Africa and continues to be practised in some today.

In South Africa, the Modjadji, or Rain Queen – the hereditary queen of the Balobedu, a people of the Limpopo Province – is not permitted to have a male husband but can take several wives.[1]

The long course of South African history takes a decisive turn in the middle of the seventeenth century when the Dutch East India Company establishes a base at present-day Cape Town. This is an act of conquest, for the Dutch do not find an empty land.

For millennia the region of initial European settlement has been occupied by hunter-gatherer and pastoral peoples, the Khoesan. The small outpost very quickly develops into an extensive settler colony, one built on notions of white supremacy, the violent exploitation of imported slaves, and the reduction of Khoesan people to the status of near slaves.

A new phase of conquest emerges during the last third of the eighteenth century when the expanding colony comes up against more densely settled Bantu-speaking agro-pastoralists. Over the next century, as competition over land and resources intensifies, Africans and Europeans are pitted against each other in frequent and bitter warfare. European missionaries are integral to the colonial project. Although their primary aim is to win converts to Christianity, their actions are complex and contradictory. There are those who goad colonial authorities into annexing territories, while others frequently intervene to protect Africans against the excesses of white settlers. But almost all assault African traditions and customs, including ones as fundamental as rainmaking rituals and marriage. Very few separate the task of capturing souls from that of seeking to transform African life in its entirety.

The tide turns decisively against indigenous societies when Britain conquers the region at the end of the eighteenth century. Time after time, and especially after the rediscovery of diamonds and gold in the South African interior, British arms come down on the side of white settlers, defeating once-powerful African kingdoms and incorporating their members into the colonial economy as cheap labourers. British rule culminates in the South African War (1899–1902), the ultimate consequence of which is the consolidation of power in the hands of white settlers.

Legislators very quickly formalise earlier centuries of conquest and dispossession, passing a body of laws underpinned by the ideology of racial segregation and aimed at restricting African rights and land-ownership. As increasing numbers of Africans find ways to resist segregationist policies, Afrikaner nationalists turn to apartheid, a substantially more rigid and violent system of discrimination that blights the lives of the African majority for the ensuing decades.[2]

1948   The National Party comes to power and formalises apartheid.

Daniel François Malan becomes prime minister.

The African National Congress Women's League is formed, replacing the Bantu Women's League in the Eastern Cape.

1949   The Prohibition of Mixed Marriages Act forbids marriages between white people and people from all other racial groups.

1950   The Immorality Amendment Act amends the 1927 act and prohibits extramarital sexual relations between white people and all non-whites. The Immorality Act, 1927, prohibited extramarital (heterosexual) sexual conduct between Black and white people.

The Group Areas Act formally segregates races.

1952   The Natives (Abolition of Passes and Co-ordination of Documents) Act, commonly known as the Pass Law, requires all Black people over the age of 16 to carry pass books.

1953   The Bantu Education Act enforces racially separated educational facilities and creates a curriculum that reduces quality and resources for the education of Black people.

The multiracial anti-apartheid women's organisation, the Federation of South African Women (FEDSAW), is formed and officially launches on 17 April 1954.

1954   J.G. Strijdom becomes prime minister.

1956   Nelson Mandela and 155 others are arrested and tried for high treason. They are acquitted in 1961.[3]

Lillian Masediba Matabane Ngoyi becomes the first woman to be elected to the executive of the African National Congress (ANC).

The Women's March to Pretoria, in which an estimated 20,000 women protest the introduction in 1952 of apartheid pass laws to Black women, takes place.[4]

1957   The Immorality Act, later renamed the Sexual Offences Act, 1957, repeals the 1927 and 1950 acts and intensifies prohibitions against interracial sexual relationships.

1958   Hendrik Verwoerd becomes prime minister.

1959   The Promotion of Bantu Self-Government Act is passed. Black people are classified into ethnic groups, for whom a so-called 'homeland' will be established.

1960   A march by Pan Africanist Congress (PAC) supporters to the police station in Sharpeville on 21 March – in protest against the pass laws and calling for a minimum monthly wage of £35 – is turned into a massacre when police fire at the protestors, killing 69 people and injuring 180 others. The event becomes known as the Sharpeville Massacre.[5]

The government declares a State of Emergency on 30 March.

1960s   International pressure against the apartheid regime begins.

1961   South Africa is constituted as a Republic after a referendum in 1960 and withdraws from the Commonwealth.

1963–4   The Rivonia Trial tries ten leaders of the ANC for 221 acts of sabotage designed to overthrow the apartheid system. The trials lead to the sentence of life imprisonment for Nelson Mandela, Walter Sisulu, Govan Mbeki, Elias Motsoaledi, Andrew Mlangeni and Denis Goldberg.

1964–77   Winnie Mandela spends more than 15 months in prisons around South Africa and 10 months in solitary confinement.[6]

1966   Balthazar Johannes Vorster becomes prime minister.

Police raid a private gay party in Forest Town, Johannesburg – an event which contributed to a proposal in parliament for amendments to the Immorality Act that would extend the ban on male gay sex to make all forms of homosexuality (including lesbian activity) illegal.[7]

1968   **The Homosexual Law Reform Fund is formed in an attempt to block the proposed amendments to the Immorality Act. It is the first organised gay resistance in South Africa. The movement is moderate, middle-class and exclusively white. The fund is successful in staving off the most repressive aspects of the proposals.[8]**

1969   The Immorality Amendment Act amends the Immorality Act of 1957. The amendment introduces or expands a number of offences. It includes the first explicit mention of homosexuality by the apartheid government.

1969–87   **Male and female soldiers in the South African Defence Forces are forced to submit to 'curing' their homosexuality under a medical torture programme. The Aversion Project report, published in 2001, estimates 900 individuals were given gender reassignment surgery as part of this programme over the period 1971–89.[9]**

1970 The Bantu Homelands Citizenship Act makes Black
South Africans citizens of their designated 'homelands'.
The act is designed to strip Black South Africans of
their South African citizenship, replacing it with citizenship of the 'homeland' to which they are assigned.
More than 3.5 million South Africans are forcibly
resettled.[10]

1972 Zanele Muholi is born on 19 July in Umlazi, a township
in Durban, KwaZulu-Natal, to mother Bester Muholi
and father Ashwell Tanji Banda Muholi.

1974 The Afrikaans Medium Decree mandates the use of
Afrikaans and English as languages of instruction,
beginning with the last year of primary school in Black
schools.

1975 The Black Women's Federation (BWF) is formed.
It has similar roots to the Federation of South
African Women but allows only Black membership.

1976 On 16 June, a series of demonstrations and protests led
by Black school children in South Africa against the
Afrikaans Medium Decree, 1974, are violently quashed
when police open fire, killing at least 176 children and
injuring 1,000. The event becomes known as the Soweto
Uprising.[11]

**Gay Aid Identification Development and Enrichment
(GAIDE), founded in Durban, is the first
gay and lesbian organisation to form since the Homosexual Law Reform Fund dissolved in 1969.**

1977 Steve Biko, activist and leader of the grassroots anti-apartheid campaign known as the Black
Consciousness Movement, dies in police custody.

1978 P.W. Botha serves as the last Prime Minister from 1978
to 1984, and the first executive State President from
1984 to 1989.

1979 **Police raid New Mandy's Club, a gay club in Johannesburg. Clientele of the club fight back.[12]**

1982 **The Gay Association of South Africa (GASA) forms.
It adopts a non-militant apolitical stance. In Cape
Town, GASA links up with 6010, an organisation
formed around the same time, thereafter known as
GASA-6010.[13]**

1983 **The group Lesbians in Love and Compromising
Situations (LILACS) is formed at the University of
Cape Town.**

1984 **Simon Nkoli, a member of GASA, founds the Saturday
Group, the first gay organisation geared towards Black
people.**

1985 The Immorality and Prohibition of Mixed Marriages
Amendment Act comes into effect. Among the amendments, it repeals Section 16 of the Immorality Act, 1957,
prohibiting interracial sex, and the Prohibition of Mixed
Marriages Act, 1949.

On 21 March, police in Langa (Uitenhage), Eastern Cape
open fire on a march to mark the 25th anniversary of
the Sharpeville shootings; the reported death toll varies
between 20 and 43.[14]

President P.W. Botha declares a State of Emergency.

Twenty-one other political leaders, including Simon
Nkoli, stand trial at the Delmas Treason Trial, which
continues until 1988.

1986 **Lesbians and Gays Against Oppression (LAGO) is
formed in Cape Town. A key objective is to address gay
rights alongside the anti-apartheid struggle.**

1987 More than 300,000 miners across South Africa go on
strike for better pay and conditions.

**GASA is expelled from the International Lesbian and
Gay Association for refusing to condemn apartheid.
Black people also report feeling excluded.[15]**

1988 The Immorality Amendment Act is amended. Among
the amendments, it prohibits lesbian sex, which had
previously been unregulated by the law.[16]

**Simon Nkoli founds the interracial Gay and Lesbian
Organization of the Witwatersrand (GLOW) in Johannesburg.**

1989 David Goldblatt establishes Market Photo Workshop,
a photography school, gallery and project space in
Johannesburg.

Frederik Willem de Klerk becomes State President.

On 13 September in Cape Town, Archbishop Desmond
Tutu leads one of the biggest anti-apartheid protest
marches to take place in South Africa.

**The AIDS Support and Education Trust (ASET) is
established out of GASA-6010 and is renamed The
Triangle Project in 1996. Today, The Triangle Project
is one of the largest LGBTQI organisations in South
Africa.**

**The Sunday's Women Group is founded in Durban
in the tradition of American lesbian-feminist
consciousness-raising groups of the 1970s.**

1990 In an announcement to parliament, F.W. de Klerk declares the formal end of apartheid. He unbans 33 political organisations. Nelson Mandela and other political prisoners are released from jail.

GLOW organises Africa's first Lesbian and Gay Pride March in Johannesburg.

1990–4 Conflict erupts in KwaZulu-Natal and Pretoria-Witwatersrand-Vereeniging regions variously caused by a 'third force' of police; polarisation between hostels dominated by the Inkatha Freedom Party and ANC-aligned township residents; Zulu nationalists; white supremacists; and police failures to maintain order. As many as 14,000 people die.[17]

1991 Start of multi-party talks. F.W. de Klerk repeals remaining apartheid laws, and international sanctions are lifted.

On 15 February, the government of South Africa and the ANC announce an agreement on terms of the ANC's decision to suspend its armed struggle against apartheid.

1992 **The Association of Bisexuals, Gays and Lesbians (ABIGALE) is formed in the Western Cape. It is explicitly political, with majority Black members.**

Prudence Mabele becomes one of the first Black women in South Africa to publicly share her HIV-positive status.[18]

1993 Chris Hani, leader of the South African Communist Party and chief of staff of uMkhonto we Sizwe, the armed wing of the ANC, is assassinated.

1994 The first democratic elections in South Africa are held. The ANC wins and the presidency of Nelson Mandela begins.

1996 On 10 December, President Nelson Mandela announces the official Constitution of the Republic of South Africa. Chapter 2, section 9 of the Bill of Rights reads: 'The state may not unfairly discriminate directly or indirectly against anyone on one or more grounds, including race, gender, sex, pregnancy, marital status, ethnic or social origin, colour, sexual orientation, age, disability, religion, conscience, belief, culture, language and birth.' South Africa therefore becomes the first country in the world to constitutionally prohibit discrimination based on sexual orientation.

The Truth and Reconciliation Commission holds public hearings chaired by Archbishop Desmond Tutu.

Gay and Lesbian Archives (GALA) is established.

1999 Thabo Mvuyelwa Mbeki becomes president.

2000 The Promotion of Equality and Prevention of Unfair Discrimination Act (or the 'Equality Act', Act No.4 of 2000) prohibits discrimination and harassment on the grounds of age; albinism; birth; colour; culture; disability; ethnic or social origin; gender or gender identity; HIV status; language; nationality; migrant or refugee status; occupation or trade; political affiliation or conviction; race; religion; sex, which includes inter-sex; or sexual orientation.

2002 Muholi co-founds the Forum for the Empowerment of Women (FEW) in Gauteng, a non-profit organisation founded as a space for black lesbian women to meet and organise for opportunities to access healthcare, education, employment and housing.

The remains of Sara Baartman are returned to South Africa and she is buried near her home, the Gamtoos Valley, in the Eastern Cape. Baartman was a South African Khoikhoi woman who was taken from Africa in 1810 to be exhibited in London and other European cities.

South Africa becomes the first country in Africa to allow same-sex couples to adopt children.

2003 Muholi completes a course in advanced photography at the Market Photo Workshop.

Muholi begins work as a photographer and reporter for Behind the Mask, an online magazine devoted to LGBTI issues in Africa.

The Alteration of Sex Description and Sex Status Act (Act No.49 of 2003) provides for the alteration of certain individuals' sex recorded in the population registry under certain circumstances.

The Coalition of African Lesbians (CAL) is formed in Johannesburg.

2004 *Muholi's first solo exhibition, Visual Sexuality: Only Half the Picture, is presented at the Johannesburg Art Gallery. This, along with their inclusion in the group show Is Everybody Comfortable? at Museum Africa, Johannesburg, and as part of a conference at the University of Western Cape entitled Gender & Visuality, garners national media attention for their work.*

South Africa's first lesbian soccer team is launched by FEW. It is named 'The Chosen FEW'.

FEW launches Soweto Pride to be held annually a week before Johannesburg Pride.

2005 Muholi directs the short documentary *Enraged by a Picture*.

The Tollman Awards for the Visual Arts

Around 100,000 gold miners strike, for the first strike in South Africa's key gold sector since 1987.[19]

Jacob Zuma is charged with raping 31-year-old family friend Fezekile Ntsukela Kuzwayo (Khwezi). He is acquitted after trial in 2006.

2006 Muholi begins their *Faces and Phases* series.

Muholi conceptualises Inkanyiso, an organisation dealing with art, activism, media and advocacy.

Only half the picture, Michael Stevenson, Cape Town; Market Photo Workshop, Johannesburg, South Africa

BHP Billiton/Wits University Visual Arts Fellowship

Thami Mnyele Residency, Amsterdam, The Netherlands

Thami Mnyele Fine Arts Award

The Civil Union Act is passed, legally giving gay couples the same rights as heterosexual couples. South Africa becomes the first country in Africa (and the fifth country in the world) to legalise same-sex marriage.

2007 The Criminal Law (Sexual Offences and Related Matters) Amendment Act repeals many of the remaining elements of the 1957 Immorality Act, comprehensively reforming the law on sex offences to make it gender- and orientation-neutral and making 16 the uniform age of consent.

2008 *Manje, Le Case d'Arte, Milan, Italy*

Kgalema Motlanthe becomes president.

A wave of xenophobic attacks spreads across the country.[20]

Free Gender is founded in the Western Cape for lesbians who have faced violence due to their gender or sexuality.

2009 Muholi's mother dies.

Muholi receives their MFA in Documentary Media, Ryerson University, Toronto.

Muholi registers Inkanyiso with the Department of Social Services.

Former Minister of Arts and Culture in South Africa, Lulu Xingwana, is supposed to make a speech at an exhibition titled *Innovative Women* at Constitution Hill, Johannesburg. After seeing Muholi's images, among others, she cancels her speech and has an assistant read a statement saying: 'Our mandate is to promote social cohesion and nation-building. I left the exhibition because it expressed the very opposite of this... It was immoral, offensive and going against nation-building.' This exhibition was organ-

ised to coincide with Women's Day and was supported by the Department of Arts and Culture.

Like a Virgin, CCA Lagos, Nigeria (two-person show alongside Lucy Azubuike)

Jean-Paul Blachère Award, Les Rencontres de Bamako biennial of African photography

Casa Africa Award for best female photographer, Les Rencontres de Bamako biennial of African photography

Fanny Ann Eddy accolade by the International Resource Network in Africa (IRN-Africa)

LGBTI Art & Culture Award

Residency Ida Ely Rubin Artist-in-Residence, Massachusetts Institute of Technology (MIT), USA

Thami Mnyele Residency, Amsterdam, The Netherlands

2009 Jacob Zuma becomes president.

Participant in Muholi's *Faces and Phases* Nkunzi Zandile Nkabinde publishes *Black Bull, Ancestors and Me: My Life as a Lesbian Sangoma*. The book reflects lesbian sangomas claiming their sexual identities more publicly to highlight that their culture/ spirituality has not always been based on heterosexism or gender and sexuality binaries.

2010 The documentary film *Difficult Love*, co-directed by Zanele Muholi and Peter Goldsmid, is released.

Transgender and Intersex Africa, a non-profit organisation advocating for the rights of transgender and intersex persons in South Africa, is founded.

A Gay Pride flag of South Africa is launched in Cape Town.

2011 *Fragments of a New History, Casa Africa, Las Palmas, Spain*

Inkanyiso, Stevenson, Johannesburg, South Africa

What don't you see when you look at me?, Extraspazio, Rome, Italy

The Department of Justice and Constitutional Development establishes a National Task Team to address gender- and sexual orientation-based violence against LGBTI communities.

2012 Muholi's flat in Vredehoek, Cape Town, is broken into and over five years of artworks on twenty hard drives are stolen. The hard drives have never been recovered.

Muholi shoots their first Somnyama Ngonyama portrait: Sthembile, Cape Town, 2012.

Faces and Phases, Oldenburg, Germany; Goethe Institut, Johannesburg, South Africa

Residency Civitella Ranieri, Italy

Miners strike in two locations in Marikana, a platinum-mining community a two-hour drive to the northwest of Johannesburg; 34 are killed, and 78 are injured. The incident is the most lethal use of force by South African security forces against civilians since the end of apartheid. It is widely compared to the Sharpeville Massacre in 1960 and quickly referred to as the Marikana Massacre.[21]

The National House of Traditional Leaders lobbies for gay rights to be removed from the South African Constitution.

The Joburg Pride parade, attended by some 20,000 people, is disrupted by activists from the One in Nine campaign calling for a minute's silence in remembrance of Black lesbian and transgender victims of hate crimes. Joburg Pride is accused of being depoliticised, and One in Nine calls for a boycott of the parade by LGBTI organisations.[22]

Iranti, an organisation advocating for the rights of LGBTI+ persons, with specific focus on lesbian, transgender (including gender-non-conforming) and intersex persons, is established in Johannesburg.

2013 Muholi co-directs *We Live in Fear*, released by Human Rights Watch.

f(o)und, Prince Claus Fund Gallery, Amsterdam, The Netherlands

Contemporary Visual ARTIvist, Palermo Pride; Cagliari Pride, Italy

Mo(u)rning, Walker Street Gallery, Melbourne, Australia

Fine Prize – Emerging Artist, Carnegie International

Prince Claus Award

Feather Award – Feather of the Year

Mbokodo Award – Creative Photography

Index on Censorship – Freedom of Expression Art Award

Campaigner of the Year, Glamour magazine

2014 *Faces and Phases is published by Steidl.*

Faces and Phases, Einsteinhaus, Ulm, Germany; 6th edition; Massimadi Festival, Montreal, Canada; Venice and Trento Pride, Palazzo Trentini, Italy

fo(u)nd, The O.P.E.N., Singapore International Festival of Arts, Singapore

Zanele Muholi: Faces and Phases, Ryerson Image Centre, Toronto, Canada

Zanele Muholi, Williams College Museum of Art, Williamstown, Massachusetts, USA

Residency La Cité Internationale des Arts, Paris, France

The National Intervention Strategy for the LGBTI sector is launched to address sex- and gender-based violence in South Africa.

Lynne Brown becomes the first openly gay person to be appointed to a cabinet post in any African government.

2015 *Zanele Muholi: Vukani/Rise, Open Eye Gallery, Liverpool, UK*

Zanele Muholi: Isibonelo/Evidence, Brooklyn Museum, New York, USA

Residency: Light Work, Syracuse, USA

President Zuma announces land reform plans in an attempt to redistribute land to Black farmers.[23]

Zulu King Goodwill Zwelithini calls for foreigners to 'pack their belongings and go', leading to a wave of xenophobic attacks in Durban; seven foreigners are killed.[24]

2016 *Somnyama Ngonyama, Standard Bank Gallery, Albany Museum, National Arts Festival, Grahamstown, South Africa*

Zanele Muholi: Faces and Phases, North Carolina Museum of Art, Raleigh, USA

Personae, Photography, the Undocument, FotoFocus Biennial, Cincinnati, USA

International Center for Photography Infinity Award for Documentary and Photojournalism

Outstanding International Alumni Award, Ryerson University, Toronto

Residency at Cassilhaus, North Carolina, USA

State of Capture Report details high levels of corruption in the Zuma-led government.[25]

2017 *Homecoming, Durban Art Gallery, Durban, South Africa*

Faces and Phases II, Market Photo Workshop, Johannesburg, South Africa

Somnyama Ngonyama, Autograph, London, UK (touring exhibition)

Zanele Muholi, Stedelijk Museum, Amsterdam, The Netherlands

Faces and Phases, Sewanee University Art Gallery, Tennessee, USA

Mbokodo Award – Visual Art

Chevalier de l'Ordre des Arts et des Lettres

2018 *Somnyama Ngonyama: Hail the Dark Lioness is published by Aperture.*

Zanele Muholi, LUMA Westbau, Zurich, Switzerland

Honorary Fellowship, Royal Photographic Society,

London, UK

Cyril Ramaphosa becomes president.

The Prevention and Combating of Hate Crimes
and Hate Speech Bill (B9-2018) is formally passed
by cabinet.

**South African actress and LGBTQ activist Laverne Cox
became the first openly transgender person to appear on
the cover of any *Cosmopolitan* magazine.**

2019 *Lucie Award for Humanitarian Photography, Lucie
Foundation, New York, USA*

Rees Visionary Award, Amref Health Africa, New York, USA

Kraszna-Krausz Best Photography Book Award

Residency at Isabella Stewart Gardner, Boston, USA

NOTES

Candice Jansen, *The Queer Spectacular: Zanele Muholi and Visual Redress*, pp.18–21

1 'Zanele Muholi in Conversation with Renée Mussai: ARCHIVE OF THE SELF', in Renée Mussai (ed.), *Somnyama Ngonyama, Hail the Dark Lioness*, exh. cat., Autograph ABP, London 2017, p.1.

2 Zanele Muholi (undated), 'South African Queer History: A Critical Reflection', excerpt from *Mapping Our Histories: A Visual History of Black Lesbians in Post-Apartheid South African Law*: http://www.transnational-queer-underground. net/wp-content/uploads/ZaneleMuholi_mom.pdf, p.2.

3 'Zanele Muholi in Conversation with Renée Mussai: ARCHIVE OF THE SELF', p.4.

4 Ibid.

5 Alana Kumbier, *Ephemeral Material: Queering the Archive*, Sacramento, CA 2014, p.159.

6 See Elizabeth Freeman's 'Time Binds: Queer Temporalities, Queer Histories' (2010), quoted in Kumbier, *Ephemeral Material*, p.161.

7 Tina M. Campt, *Listening to Images*, Durham, NC 2017, p.17.

8 Ibid.

9 Ibid [emphasis not added].

10 Ibid.

11 Ibid.

12 Ibid.

13 'Zanele Muholi in Conversation with Renée Mussai: ARCHIVE OF THE SELF', p.6.

14 Ibid.

15 Campt, *Listening to Images*, p.113.

16 Njabulo S. Ndebele, *South African Literature and Culture: Rediscovery of the Ordinary*, Manchester 1994, p.43.

17 Ibid., pp.46–7.

Pamella Dlungwana, *Community and Collectivity / Uphathe umphako - ukhumbul' ekhaya*, pp.40–4

1 One with no roots, no family, no community. Someone who travels the world with no obligation to ancestral ties or heritage.

2 'Carry a meal; remember home.'

3 'We're in this together, we don't sleep, we work.'

Renée Mussai, *Letter III: The Archive Other/wise*, pp.56–61

1 Octavia E. Butler, *Parable of the Sower* (1993), London 2019, p.1.

2 Christina Sharpe, *In the Wake: On Blackness and Being*, Durham, NC, and London 2016, p.13.

3 Saidiya Hartman, *Wayward Lives, Beautiful Experiments: Intimate Histories of Social Upheaval*, New York 2019, p.xv.

4 Walter D. Mignolo and Catherine E. Walsh, *On Decoloniality: Concepts, Analytics, Praxis*, Durham, NC, and London 2018, p.10.

5 Toni Morrison, *Playing in the Dark: Whiteness and the Literary Imagination*, Cambridge, MA 1990, p.46.

6 See also David J. Getsy (ed.), *Queer: Documents of Contemporary Art*, London and Cambridge, MA 2016, p.15.

7 Sharpe, *In the Wake*, pp.106, 108, 109 and 113. Also cited here: Frantz Fanon: 'When we revolt it's not for a particular culture. We revolt simply because, for a variety of reasons, we can no longer breathe.'

8 Hartman, *Wayward Lives, Beautiful Experiments*, p.xiv.

9 Allan Sekula, 'The Body and the Archive', *October*, vol.39 (Winter 1986): 33.

10 W.E.B. Du Bois: *The 1900 Paris Albums*, Autograph, London, 12 September–29 November 2010. Curated by Renée Mussai and Mark Sealy.

11 Rinaldo Walcott, *Queer Returns: Essays on Multiculturalism, Diaspora, and Black Studies*, Ontario 2016.

12 Claudia Rankine, *Citizen: An American Lyric*, London 2014, p.146.

13 This remark infers and is adapted from the inscription on nineteenth-century carte-de-visite portraits of Sojourner Truth: 'I Sell the Shadow to Support the Substance'.

14 Ariella Azoulay, *The Civil Contract of Photography*, New York 2008, p.14.

15 Rankine, *Citizen*, p.28.

16 Azoulay, *The Civil Contract of Photography*, p.17. See also bell hooks, 'The Oppositional Gaze', in *Black Looks: Race and Representation*, Boston 1992.

17 Katherine McKittrick (ed.), *Sylvia Wynter: On Being Human as Praxis*, Durham, NC, and London 2015, pp.31 and 33.

18 Sekula, 'The Body and the Archive', p.4.

19 Morrison, *Playing in the Dark*, p.18.

20 Audre Lorde, 'The Transformation of Silence into Language and Action', in *Sister Outsider: Essays and Speeches*, Berkeley, CA 2007, p.44.

21 For an illuminating discussion on photography's sonic frequencies, see Tina M. Campt, *Listening to Images*, Durham, NC, and London 2017.

22 The three women were subjected to 'corrective rape' and brutally murdered in KwaThema, a township in Gauteng, south-west of Springs on the East Rand. See Zanele Muholi, *Faces and Phases 2006–14*, Göttingen 2014.

23 Hartman, *Wayward Lives, Beautiful Experiments*, p.xv.

Sarah Allen, *Thinking Activism: Zanele Muholi and Queer Photography Histories*, pp.80–5

1 While some academics argue that Western terminology and frameworks are not useful in the African context, Muholi defines their practice as queer, and so the use of the term here seems appropriate. Subject matter, context, audience, reception, consumption and queer readings all contribute to the production of a queer image. The work considered here is made by self-identified queer photographers.

2 Conversation with the artist, 28 January 2020.

3 https://aperture.org/blog/magazine-zanele-muholis-faces-%C2%9D-phases/ Muholi studied for their MFA in Documentary Media at Ryerson University, Toronto. During this time they were exposed to Biren's work and the work of other US-based photographers; they also cite several British photographers among their influences. It is therefore on North America and the UK that this text will focus.

4 Interview between the author and Joan E. Biren, 26 July 2019.

5 Ibid. See JEB, 'Lesbian Photography: Seeing Through Our Own Eyes', *Studies in Visual Communication* 2 (1981): 81–96.

6 See Ruth Morgan and Saskia Wieringa, *Tommy Boys, Lesbian Men and Ancestral Wives*, Johannesburg 2005, for an assessment on the complexities of coming out in South Africa.

7 https://www.questformeaning.org/spiritual-themes/the-transformation-of-silence/ See 'The Transformation of Silence into Action', speech by Audre Lorde, Lesbian and Literature panel, Modern Language Association, 28 December 1977. Republished in Lorde, *Sister Outsider: Essays and Speeches*, Berkeley, CA 1984.

8 JEB, 'Lesbian Photography: Seeing Through Our Own Eyes'.

9 *Fotógrafas Africanas / African Women Photographers*, p.49.

10 See https://aperture.org/blog/magazine-zanele-muholis-faces-%C2%9D-phases/

11 *Fotógrafas Africanas / African Women Photographers*, p.47.

12 Sulter used props which locate the work in the African context of the Egyptian 18th dynasty. In doing so, she wanted to redress the fact that Western cultural histories often begin with Ancient Greece. See Ben Uri, *Looking In: Photographic Portraits by Maud Sulter and Chan-Hyo Bae*, London 2013, pp.10–11.

13 *Somnyama Ngonyama, Hail the Dark Lioness*, New York 2018, p.176.

14 https://www.artnews.com/art-news/artists/lyle-ashton-harris-12262/ The series was made during Harris's study at CalArts, where he noted that he was one of 'just a few peo-

ple of colour in that program', and it was 'a necessity for me to intervene [in] that space' (in Drew Sawyer, *Art After Stonewall*, New York 2019, pp.288–9). See Okwui Enwezor, *Lyle Ashton Harris: Excessive Exposure*, New York 2010, p.19, for further discussion on Harris's broader engagement with the history of whiteface.

15 Maria C. Sanchez and Linda Schlossberg, *Passing: Identity and Interpretation in Sexuality, Race, and Religion*, New York 2001, p.3. See also Allyson Hobbs, *A Chosen Exile: A History of Racial Passing in American Life*, Cambridge, MA 2014, for discussion of history of passing in the specific American context.

16 http://www.artnews.com/2019/04/02/lyle-ashton-harris/

17 Sawyer, *Art After Stonewall*, p.289, and Lyle Ashton Harris, in 'Lyle Ashton Harris and Alex Fialho: Oral history interview transcript', 27–29 March 2017, https://www.aaa.si.edu/collections/interviews/oral-history-interview-lyle-ashton-harris-17456#transcript

18 See Zethu Matebeni, 'Contesting Beauty: Black Lesbians on the Stage', in *Feminist Africa: The Politics of Fashion and Beauty in Africa*, Issue 21, 2016: 31.

19 *Faces and Phases 2006–14*, p.7.

20 Rotimi Fani-Kayode, 'Traces of Ecstasy', *Ten-8*, no.28, 1988: 41.

21 For reference to anthropological photography which Muholi's work can be read as resisting, see, for example, Gustav Theodor Fritsch's work in South Africa in the 1860s or Alfred Martin Duggan-Cronin's documentation on Bantu tribes of South Africa (1928–54).

22 Fani-Kayode's work can also be understood to comment on the position of the African mask as one of the most prominent signifiers of African culture outside Africa, as well as the co-option of the African mask by modernist artists.

23 https://www.stevenson.info/exhibition/1440

Yasufumi Nakamori, *Queering Space through Photography: Zanele Muholi's Colour Portraits*, pp.96–100

1 Zanele Muholi, 'Ngibonile – I have seen', in *Fotógrafas Africanas / African Women Photographers*, pp.44–9.

2 https://art21.org/watch/extended-play/zanele-muholi-mobile-studios-short/ The short video titled *Mobile Studios: Zanele Muholi* shows the ways Muholi interacts with and photographs a participant during their picture-making.

3 Email interview with Zanele Muholi through Sinazo Chiya, 8 December 2019.

4 Interview with Zanele Muholi, 27 January 2020.

5 For example, on my recent visit to Cape Town, I observed that a beautiful beach I stopped by to see a sunset, known as the Bakoven Beach in Cape Town, was filled almost exclusively by white beachgoers.

6 For general discussion, see Jayne M. Rogerson, '"Kicking Sand in the Face of Apartheid": Segregated Beaches in South Africa', *Bulletin of Geography*, Socio-economic Series, no.35, 2017: 93–109.

7 Ibid., pp.103–4.

8 For general discussion, see Jenny Marsden and Tina Smith (eds.), *Kewpie, Daughter of District Six*, Cape Town and Braamfontein 2019.

9 Interview with Zanele Muholi, 10 November 2019.

10 For general discussion, see https://www.constitutionhill.org.za/

Sindiwe Magona, *See Anew: Religion, Marriage and Funerals,*
pp.112–15

1   The term 'traditionalists' must be qualified, as not all
who profess to be traditionalists are bigots, and there are
traditions worth keeping. What is to be condemned is
the practice of bigots hiding under the label 'tradition'.

2   https://mg.co.za/article/2006-11-06-fear-and-violence-still-
rule-gay-township-life

3   http://vmci.org.za/home/

4   Written correspondence with the artist, 5 November
2019.

5   See https://www.youtube.com/watch?v=SqDsEChblrI.
Also https://inkanyiso.org/2013/11/18/2013-nov-9-ayanda-
nhlanhlas-wedding/

6   See https://inkanyiso.org/2014/06/23/2014-june-23-the-
lovely-couple-on-their-anniversary-vacation-in-cape-town/

Sarah Allen, *Another Approach is Possible,* pp.160–3

1   As Pumla Dineo Gqola notes, 'black lesbians' bodies … are
in fact highly visible manifestations of the undesirable'. This
state of hyper-visibility is confirmed by 'the range
of names given to them in various languages, along with the
very unambiguous attacks': *Only Half the Picture,* pp.83–4.

2   *Somnyama Ngonyama, Hail the Dark Lioness,* New York 2018,
p.188.

3   See, for example, Stephen O. Murray and Will Roscoe (eds.),
*Boy-Wives and Female-Husbands: Studies in African Homosexual-
ities,* New York 1998; Signe Arnfred, *Re-thinking Sexualities in
Africa,* Uppsala 2004; Mark Gevisser and
Edwin Cameron, *Defiant Desire: Gay and Lesbian Lives in South
Africa,* Johannesburg 1994. Muholi's work was
used to illustrate the entire publication authored by
Ruth Morgan and Saskia Wieringa, *Tommy Boys, Lesbian Men
and Ancestral Wives,* Johannesburg 2005, and within
the publication by Alleyn Diesel, *Reclaiming the L-Word:
Sappho's Daughters Out in Africa,* Cape Town 2007.

4   See bell hooks, *Black Looks: Race and Representation,*
New York and Abingdon 2015, and Audre Lorde, *The
Black Unicorn,* New York 1978, as quoted in Zanele Muholi,
*Mapping Our Histories: A Visual History of Black Lesbians in
Post-Apartheid South Africa* (completed as part of their MFA
in Documentary Media at Ryerson University in Toronto);
Sindiwe Magona, *Please, Take Photographs,* Cape Town 2009.

5   *Somnyama Ngonyama, Hail the Dark Lioness,* p.196.

Sarah Allen, with Bongani Matabane, Chronology,
   pp.170–5

1   It should be noted that 'anthropologists and Africans
   alike have been almost unanimous in denying the possibility that woman-woman marriages include sex or even
   emotional attachment … few of these denials however
   are based on actual enquiries or observations of sexual
   behaviour': Stephen O. Murray and Will Roscoe (eds.),
   *Boy-Wives and Female-Husbands: Studies in African Homo-
   sexualities,*
   New York 1998, p.262.

2   Text authored by Dr Wayne Dooling, Senior Lecturer
   in the History of Southern Africa, SOAS University of
   London.

3   https://www.sahistory.org.za/article/general-south-
   african-history-timeline-1950s

4   Kim Miller, 'Selective Silence and the Shaping of
   Memory in Post-apartheid Visual Culture: The
   Case of the Monument to the Women of South
   Africa', *South African Historical Journal* 63, no.2 (2011):
   295–317.

5   Kevin Shillington (ed.), *Encyclopaedia of African History,*
   3 vols., New York and Abingdon 2004, p.1394.

6   Winnie Madikizela-Mandela, *491 Days: Prisoner Number
   1323/69,* Athens, OH 2014, p.594.

7   Philip Harrison, *Gay and Lesbian,* Cape Town 2005,
   p.12.

8   Kobus Du Pisani, 'Shifting Sexual Morality? Changing
   Views on Homosexuality in Afrikaner Society During
   the 1960s', *Historia,* 57, no.2 (November 2012): 182–221.

9   Mikki van Zyl, Jeanelle de Gruchy, Sheila Lapinsky,
   Simon Lewin and Graeme Reid, 'The Aversion Project:
   Human rights abuses of gays and lesbians in the South
   African Defence Force by health workers during the
   apartheid era' (1999).

10 https://www.sahistory.org.za/article/forced-removals-
   south-africa#endnote-21

11 https://www.sahistory.org.za/dated-event/soweto-upris-
   ing-leaves-174-blacks-and-two-whites-dead-following-10-
   days-rioting

12 Mark Gevisser and Edwin Cameron, *Defiant Desire: Gay
   and Lesbian Lives in South Africa,* Johannesburg 1994.

13 Jens Rydström, 'Solidarity – With Whom? The International Gay and Lesbian Rights Movement and Apartheid', in Neville Hoad, Karen Martin and Graeme Reid
   (eds.), *Sex and Politics in South Africa,* Cape Town 2005,
   pp.34–49 (p.37).

14 Robert J. Thornton, 'The Shooting at Uitenhage, South
   Africa, 1985: The Context and Interpretation of Violence',
   American Ethnologist 17, no.2 (1990): 217–36 (p.234).

15 M. Mbali, *South African AIDS Activism and Global Health
   Politics,* London 2013, p.55. See also Rydström, 'Solidarity –
   With Whom?', p.39.

16 Immorality Amendment Act (No.2 of 1988), 25 February
   1988. Vol.15. N.p., 1988.

17 *Rise and Fall of Apartheid: Photography and the Bureaucracy of
   Everyday Life,* New York and London 2013, p.468. See also
   Timothy Gibbs, 'Inkatha's Young Militants: Reconsidering
   Political Violence in South Africa', *Africa* 87, no.2 (2017):
   362–86 (p.377).

18 Andrew Green, 'Prudence Mabele', *The Lancet* 390,
   no.10096 (2017): 732.

19 T. Dunbar Moodie, 'Managing the 1987 mine workers' strike',
   Journal of Southern African Studies 35, no.1 (2009): 45–64.

20 https://www.atlanticphilanthropies.org/wp-content/
   uploads/2010/07/4_What_happened_c.pdf, p.3.

21 Peter Alexander, 'Marikana, turning point in South
   African history', *Review of African Political Economy* 40,
   no.138 (2013): 605–19 (p.605).

22 https://sacsis.org.za/site/article/1450

23 http://www.futuredirections.org.au/publication/
   challenges-confronting-south-africa-land-reform/

24 https://www.sahistory.org.za/article/xenophobic-
   violence-democratic-south-africa

25 https://www.sahistory.org.za/sites/default/files/2019-
   05/329756252-state-of-capture-14-october-2016.pdf

SELECTED BIBLIOGRAPHY

MONOGRAPHS

2020 *Zanele Muholi*, London.

2018 *Somnyama Ngonyama, Hail the Dark Lioness,* New York.

2014 *Faces and Phases 2006-14*, Göttingen.

2011 *Zanele Muholi: Fotógrafas Africanas/ African Woman Photographers*, Madrid.

2010 *Faces and Phases*, Munich.

2006 *Only Half the Picture*, Cape Town.

**SELECTED THEMATIC BOOKS
AND EXHIBITION CATALOGUES**

2019 Charlotte Mullins, *A Little Feminist History of Art*, London.

2017 Alex Pilcher, *A Queer Little History of Art*, London.

2015 Brian Wallis, Christopher Phillips and George Baker, *The Order of Things: Photography from the Walther Collection*, Göttingen.

2014 Betti-Sue Hertz, *Public Intimacy: Art and Other Ordinary Acts in South Africa*, San Francisco.

2013 Tamar Garb and Awam Amkpa, *African Photography from the Walther Collection: Distance and Desire – Encounters with the African Archive*, Göttingen.

Kylie Thomas, *Impossible Mourning: HIV/AIDS and Visuality after Apartheid*, Lewisburg.

2011 Corinne Diserens, *Appropriated Landscapes: Contemporary African Photography from the Walther Collection*, Göttingen.

Sylvia Tamale (ed.), *African Sexualities: A Reader*, Cape Town.

What We Talk About When We Talk About Love, Catalogue 61, Cape Town.

2010 Okwui Enwezor and Gabriele Conrath-Scholl, *Events of the Self: Portraiture and Social Identity – Contemporary African Photography from the Walther Collection*, Göttingen.

Rebelle: Art & Feminism 1969–2009, Arnhem.

2009 Christine Eyene and Bisi Silva, *Like a Virgin*, Lagos.

2008 *Disguise: The Art of Attracting and Deflecting Attention*, Catalogue 35, Cape Town.

2005 Ruth Morgan and Saskia Wieringa, *Tommy Boys, Lesbian Men and Ancestral Wives*, Johannesburg.

SELECTED ARTICLES AND REVIEWS

2019 Fayemi Shakur, 'Zanele Muholi Captures Powerful Portraits of South Africa's LGBTQ Community', CNN *Style*, 18 June.

Anne McNeill, 'Zanele Muholi: Somnyama Ngonyama, Hail The Dark Lioness', *Granta*, 21 May.

Raquel Willis, 'Zanele Muholi Forever Changed the Image of Black Queer South Africans', *Out Magazine*, April.

Zuko Komisa, 'Zanele Muholi on Queer Legacy, Pronouns and New Work', *Kaya FM*, March.

2018 Maurice Berger, 'Zanele Muholi: Paying Homage to the History of Black Women', *The New York Times*, 3 December.

Yrsa Daley-Ward, 'Zanele Muholi, a South African Artist Who Uses Self-Portraits as Visual Activism', *The New York Times*, 28 November.

'"I Want to Be Counted in History": Watch How Photographer Zanele Muholi Uses Her Camera to Tell the Stories of Trans Women', *Artnet News*, 28 September.

Imani Roach, 'Zanele Muholi and the Women of the Women's Mobile Museum Talk Portraiture, Self-love and Fighting the Patriarchy', *Artblog*, 18 May.

Susanna D'Aliesio, 'Zanele Muholi's Somnyama Ngonyama – Hail the Dark Lioness', *British Journal of Photography*, 17 April.

Robin Scher, '"They Are History Makers": Artist Zanele Muholi on Her Multifarious Portraits', ART *news*, 18 January.

'Zanele Muholi. Identity: A Photography Special', *Financial Times Weekend Magazine*, 5 January.

2017 Aaron Leaf, 'Zanele Muholi on Queering the Zeitz MOCAA', *Okay Africa*, 11 October.

Renée Mussai, 'Zanele Muholi Selected by Renée Mussai: Somnyama Ngonyama, Hail The Dark Lioness', *Firecracker*, 8 October.

Garreth Van Niekerk, 'Inside The World of Zanele Muholi's Brave Beauties', *Huffington Post South Africa*, 26 September.

Charlotte Jansen, 'The Photographer Challenging the Idea That Being Queer Is "Un-African"', *Vice*, 1 August.

Yelena Keller, 'Photographers Who Have Captured LGBTQ Life in the African Diaspora', *Artsy*, 1 August.

Emine Saner, 'Interview – "I'm scared. But this work needs to be shown": Zanele Muholi's 365 Protest Photographs', *The Guardian*, 14 July.

Elizabeth Coop, 'Why Photographer Zanele Muholi Inflicts Pain on Herself', *Dazed*, 10 July.

2016 Allie Biswas, 'Art in Conversation: Zanele Muholi with Allie Biswas', *The Brooklyn Rail*, November.

'Donna Smith Reflects on a Decade of Faces and Phases', *Creative Feel*, 7 November.

Gontse Mathabathe, 'Voice and Visibility: Zanele Muholi's "Faces and Phases 10"', *Artthrob*, 12 October.

Carl Collison, 'On Ten Years of "Faces and Phases": "We are making history here"', *Mail & Guardian*, 23 September.

Laura Snoad, 'Zanele Muholi's Best Photograph: Out and Proud in South Africa', *The Guardian*, 25 August.

Yonela Mgwali, 'Only Death Would Stop Me', *Forbes Africa*, February/March: 46–47.

Tymon Smith, 'An Important Departure for a Real Conversation: Zanele Muholi's "Somnyama Ngonyama"', *Artthrob*, 29 January.

2015 Oliver Roberts, 'Gaze of our Lives', *Sunday Times*, 6 December: 16.

Javiera Luisina Cadiz Bedini, 'Brave Beauties – Pratt Photography Lecture: Zanele Muholi', *Art Africa*, November: 61–5.

Kwanele Sosibo, 'Zanele Muholi: Hail the Dark Lioness', *Mail & Guardian*, 20 November.

Vuyiswa Xekatwane, 'Conquering Fears of Queerness: Zanele Muholi's Solo Show "Somnyama Ngonyama"', *Between 10 and 5*, 20 November.

Remi Onabanjo, 'Zanele Muholi on her Life's Work Archiving Black South African Lesbian, Gay, and Trans People', *Africa is a Country*, 23 October.

Jenna Wortham, 'Zanele Muholi's Transformations', *The New York Times Magazine*, 8 October: 64–9 and 74.

Neelika Jayawardane, 'Zanele Muholi's Visual Activism "Isibonelo/Evidence" at the Brooklyn Museum', *Africa is a Country*, 6 October.

Laura Robertson, 'A Q&A with...Zanele Muholi, LGBT Photographer', *a-n*, 23 September.

Kathleen Massara, 'Breaking the Silence', *Guernica*, 3 August.

Rena Silverman, 'Same Sex, Love and Hate, in South Africa', *International New York Times*, 8 July.

Jackie Bischof, 'South African Photographer Captures Challenges for LGBT Community, Almost a Decade After Gay Marriage Legalization', *Newsweek*, 30 June.

Julia Friedman, 'A Photographer Documents the Highs and Lows of LGBTQ Life in South Africa', *Hyperallergic*, 30 June.

Martha Schwendener, 'Review: Zanele Muholi, a Visual Activist, Presents "Isibonelo/Evidence"', *International New York Times*, 14 May.

Agustina Zegers, 'God is a Lesbian', *DIS Magazine*, 12 May.

Cristina Ruiz, 'Photography: Zanele Muholi Shoots Down Prejudice', *Financial Times*, 8 May.

Peter 'Souleo' Wright, 'On the "A" w/Souleo: South African Photographer Captures the Pain and Beauty of LGBT Life', *Huffington Post*, 8 May.

Bidisha, 'Pride and Prejudice: How Zanele Muholi Documents South Africa's LGBTI Community', *BBC Online*, 15 April.

Deborah Willis, 'Zanele Muholi Faces and Phases: Conversation with Deborah Willis', *Aperture Magazine*, no.218 (Spring): 58–64.

Yassine Senghor, 'LGBTQIA History Month: Our Heroes – Zanele Muholi', *Regendre*, 13 February.

Sonia Harford, 'South African Artist's Midsumma Exhibition a Visceral Reminder of LGBTI Discrimination', *The Sydney Morning Herald*, 30 January.

2014 Dr Gaëlle Morel, 'Zanele Muholi: Faces and Phases (2006–ongoing)', *Ryerson Image Centre Editions*, n.d.

Deborah Willis, 'Queer', *Aperture*, 2 December.

Alexis Okeowo, 'Photographing a "difficult love" in South Africa', *The New York Times: Lens*, 9 June.

Clarissa Sosin, 'Township Life of LGBTI's: Dying for Justice in Thokoza', *Mail & Guardian*, 23 May.

Hans Ulrich Obrist, 'On Love and its Enemies', *Das Magazin*, March.

Mary Corrigall, 'Sense of Belonging', *The Sunday Independent*, 2 March.

Sarah Wild, 'Desire for Change Unites Post-apartheid Activism', *Mail & Guardian*, 21 February.

Jonathan Cane, 'Zanele Muholi: The Task of Mourning', *Mail & Guardian*, 17 February.

2013 Claire Breukel, 'Unapologetic Zanele Muholi', *Women's Review of Books*, September–October.

Holland Cotter, 'Zanele Muholi: Faces and Phases', *The New York Times*, 21 March.

Glennisha Morgan, 'Zanele Muholi, South African Photographer, Highlights Lesbians, Transgender Women', *The Huffington Post*, 18 March.

2012 Percy Zvomuya, 'Love in a Brutalised world', *Mail & Guardian*, 8 June.

Chika Okeke-Agulu, 'Who Wants to Silence Zanele Muholi?', *The Huffington Post*, 28 May.

Greg Marinovich, 'Love, Sex and the Fear of Small Woman – Zanele Muholi', *The Daily Maverick*, 25 May.

Matt McCann, 'Theft Stalls, but Does Not Stop, a Project', *The New York Times: Lens*, 3 May.

Tanya Olckers, 'Walking with Zanele Muholi', *Alice*, no.4, January–February.

2011 Gabeba Baderoon, 'Gender, Within Gender: Zanele Muholi's Images of Transbeing and Becoming', *Feminist Studies*, vol.37, no.2 (Summer).

Charl Blignaut, 'Love in a Time of Murder', *Sunday Times*, 17 July.

2010 Ziphezinhle Msimango, 'My City – Joburg: Zanele Muholi', *Sunday Times*, 8 August.

Lisa Van Wyk, 'Xingwana: Homophobic Claims "baseless, insulting"', *Mail & Guardian*, 5 March.

Dirk Ludigs, 'Afrikanische Vor-Bilder: Fotos von Zanele Muholi', *L MAG*, 3 March.

'Lulu Xingwana Describes Lesbian Photos as Immoral', *Mail & Guardian*, 3 March.

Jason Warner, '"Homophobic" Arts Minister in Lesbian Arts Photo Furore', *Cape Times*, 3 March.

David Smith, 'South African Minister Describes Lesbian Photos as Immoral', *The Guardian* (UK), 2 March.

2009 Zanele Muholi, 'Ngiyopha: A Photo-biographical Project', 26 October.

2007 Mary Corrigall, 'Fighting Stigmatisation of Lesbianism as Un-African', *The Sunday Independent*, 17 June.

Zanele Muholi, 'Faces and Phases', *Camera Austria*, 100: 64–71.

2006 Kathryn Smith, 'Zanele Muholi at Michael Stevenson Cape Town', *Art South Africa*, vol.04, no.02 (Winter): 75.

Gabi Ngcobo, 'What Do We See When We Look At Us', *Art South Africa*, vol.04, no.03 (Autumn): 49–50.

Hazel Friedman, 'Under The Skin', *Art South Africa*, vol.05, no.02 (Summer): 55.

2004 Nonkululeko Godana, 'Is Anybody Comfortable?', *Thisday*, 6 September, Arts/9.

SELECTED VIDEO INTERVIEWS AND TALKS

2019 'Zanele Muholi discusses visual activism, building archives and photography.' *Paris Photo*. 3 December.

Tribute video for 2019 Lucie Awards Honoree Zanele Muholi for the 'Zanele Muholi on "Somnyama Ngonyama, Hail the Dark Lioness" at Seattle Art Museum'. Seattle Art Museum. 20 September.

'Zanele Muholi Unplugs from the Studio.' Art21 – Extended Play. 29 May.

'Questions of Practice: Photographer Zanele Muholi on Museum Accessibility.' Pew Center for Arts & Heritage. January.

2018 'Questions of Practice: Photographer Zanele Muholi on What it Means To Be a "Visual Activist".' Pew Center for Arts & Heritage. November.

'Zanele Muholi's Visual Activism.' Aperture Foundation. 11 July.

2017 'Artist Talk: Zanele Muholi.' Princeton University Art Museum. 21 December.

'Exhibition Trailer – Zanele Muholi.' Stedelijk Museum. 1 August.

'Zanele Muholi introduces us to their practice and recent projects, on the occasion of the exhibition Art/Afrique – Le nouvel atelier at Fondation Louis Vuitton.' Kadist Paris. 24 July.

2016 'Prologue 1: Zanele Muholi – photographer and visual activist.' The First Supper Symposium. 6 September.

'Albert Gallatin Lecture with Zanele Muholi.' NYU Gallatin. 26 February.

'Lecture in Photography: Zanele Muholi.' Museum of Contemporary Photography, Columbia College, Chicago. 24 February.

'Muholi explains their passion for their work and why they considers themself a "visual activist", on the occasion of receiving the 2016 ICP Infinity Awards for Documentary & Photojournalism.' ICP; Harber Studios. 16 January.

2015 'Zanele Muholi on their journey into photography, on the occasion of their 2015 exhibition at Stevenson Johannesburg, "Somnyama Ngonyama".' We Creatives. 3 December.

'Conversation: Zanele Muholi and Binyavanga Wainaina discuss the current state of arts, literature, education, and LGBTI rights across Africa.' Brooklyn Museum. 5 November.

Zanele Muholi: Bathini.' Stamps School of Art & Design at the University of Michigan. 8 October.

'Zanele Muholi talks about her work during "Vukani/Rise"', for Homotopia TV. 16 September.

'Zanele Muholi: 2015 PEN World Voices Festival Opening Night: The Future is Now.' 6 May.

'Zanele Muholi interview.' The Photographers' Gallery. 17 April.

'Zanele Muholi artist talk with Chris Boot.' LOOK3 Festival of the Photograph. 1 March.

2014 'Artist Talk, Zanele Muholi with Lebo Mashifane.' Yale University Art Gallery. 18 September.

'Zanele Muholi: When do we start talking about intimacy?' Design Indaba. 16 May.

2013 'Zanele Muholi on the Importance of Documenting Human Rights.' The Aspen Institute. 30 June.

'Interview with Zanele Muholi on the occasion of International Film Festival and Forum on Human Rights (FIFDH).' FIFDH; JO Prod. 8 March.

'Carnegie International – In Conversation: Zanele Muholi and Lerato Dumse.' Carnegie Museum of Art. 21 January.

2012 'Zanele Muholi – Fragments of a New History.' Masasam.

LIST OF EXHIBITED WORKS

Measurements are given in centimetres, height before width. Unless stated otherwise the medium is photograph, gelatin silver print on paper. Archival material displayed in the exhibition is not listed. Information is correct at time of publication but subject to change.

Zol • 2002
70 × 51

Bra • 2003
27.5 × 27.5
Purchased with funds provided by Wendy Fisher 2015

Comfort • 2003
48.5 × 60

Dada • 2003
48.5 × 30

ID crisis • 2003
32.3 × 48.5
Purchased with funds provided by Wendy Fisher 2015

Iphondo • 2003
50 × 50

Ordeal • 2003
53.5 × 60
Purchased with funds provided by Wendy Fisher 2015

Sistahs • 2003
38.5 × 25.5

Aftermath • 2004
60 × 39.5
Purchased with funds provided by Wendy Fisher 2015

Case number • 2004
25.5 × 38.5

Hate crime survivor I • 2004
25.4 × 38.5

Enraged by a Picture • 2005
Video
17min

Independent • 2005
Photograph, C-print on paper
52.5 × 70

Isibuko I • 2005
38.5 × 25.5

Isibuko II • 2005
80 × 55.5

Not butch, but my legs are • 2005
41.5 × 60

Period I • 2005
Photograph, C-print on paper
50 × 37.5

Period V • 2005
Photograph, C-print on paper
50 × 37.5

Self • 2005
Photograph, C-print on paper
40 × 35

Status unknown • 2005
Photograph, C-print on paper
22.5 × 30

Triple I • 2005
30 × 40

Triple II • 2005
40 × 50

Triple III • 2005
37.5 × 50

Black Beulah • 2006
Photograph, C-print on paper
76.5 × 100

Busi Sigasa, Braamfontein, Johannesburg • 2006
50.5 × 76.5

Jabu Radebe, Yeoville, Johannesburg • 2006
Photograph, C-print on paper
60 × 60

Martin Machapa • 2006
Photograph, C-print on paper
100 × 76.5

Stanley I • 2006
Photograph, C-print on paper
100 × 69

Too Beulahs • 2006
Photograph, C-print on paper
76.5 × 100

Untitled • 2006
Photograph, C-print on paper
20 × 30

Dikeledi Sibanda, Yeoville, Johannesburg • 2007
76.5 × 50.5

Hompi and Charles Januarie, KwaThema, Springs • 2007
76.5 × 76.5

Katlego Mashiloane and Nosipho Lavuta, Ext. 2, Lakeside, Johannesburg • 2007
Photograph, C-print on paper
76.5 × 76.5

Katlego Mashiloane and Nosipho Lavuta, Ext. 2, Lakeside, Johannesburg • 2007
Photograph, C-print on paper
76.5 × 76.5

Katlego Mashiloane and Nosipho Lavuta, Ext. 2, Lakeside, Johannesburg • 2007
Photograph, C-print on paper
76.5 × 76.5

Katlego Mashiloane and Nosipho Lavuta, Ext. 2, Lakeside, Johannesburg • 2007
Photograph, C-print on paper
76.5 × 76.5

Miss D'vine I • 2007
Photograph, C-print on paper
76.5 × 76.5

Miss D'vine II • 2007
Photograph, C-print on paper
76.5 × 76.5

Nokuthula Dhladhla, Berea, Johannesburg • 2007
76.5 × 50.5

Nosipho Solundwana, Parktown, Johannesburg • 2007
76.5 × 50.5

Nosipho Solundwana II, Parktown, Johannesburg • 2007
76.5 × 50.5

Sindi Shabalala, Parktown, Johannesburg • 2007
76.5 × 50.5

Sosi Molotsane, Yeoville, Johannesburg • 2007
76.5 × 50.5

Tumi Mkhuma, Yeoville, Johannesburg • 2007
76.5 × 50.5

Nkunzi Nkabinde, Braamfontein, Johannesburg • 2008
76.5 × 50.5

Nosizwe Cekiso, Gugulethu, Cape Town • 2008
76.5 × 50.5

Penny Fish, Vredehoek, Cape Town • 2008
76.5 × 50.5

Thandi Mancane Selepe, Alexandra, Johannesburg • 2008
76.5 × 50.5

Lebo Mashifane, District Six, Cape Town • 2009
76.5 × 50.5

Lebo Mashifane II, District Six, Cape Town • 2009
76.5 × 50.5

LiZa I • 2009
76.5 × 50.5

Miss Lesbian I, II, III, IV, V, VI, Amsterdam • 2009
Photograph, C-prints on paper
86.5 × 60.5 each

Sisipho Ndzuzo, Embekweni, Paarl, Cape Town • 2009
76.5 × 50.5

Thabile Mbatha, Vredehoek, Cape Town • 2009
76.5 × 50.5

Bakhambile Skhosana, Natalspruit, Katlehong, Gauteng • 2010
76.5 × 50.5

Des're Higa, Makhaza, Khayelitsha, Cape Town • 2010
76.5 × 50.5

Zanele Muholi and Peter Goldsmid
Difficult Love • 2010
Video, high definition, projection, colour
47min, 33sec

Dorothy Magome, Mafikeng, North West • 2010
76.5 × 50.5

Funeka Soldaat, Makhaza, Khayelitsha, Cape Town • 2010
76.5 × 50.5

Lerato Dumse, KwaThema, Springs, Johannesburg • 2010
76.5 × 50.5

'Makhethi' Sebenzile Ndaba, Constitution Hill, Johannesburg • 2010
76.5 × 50.5

Mbali Pearl Zulu, KwaThema, Springs, Johannesburg • 2010
76.5 × 50.5

Mini Mbatha, Glebelands, Durban • 2010
Photograph, C-print on paper
76.5 × 50.5

Ms Le Sishi I, Glebelands, Durban • 2010
Photograph, C-print on paper
76.5 × 50.5

Muzi Khumalo III, Constitution Hill, Braamfontein, Johannesburg • 2010
Photograph, C-print on paper
76.5 × 50.5

Nhlanhla Esther Mofokeng, Thokoza, Johannesburg • 2010
76.5 × 50.5

Nunu Sigasa, Germiston, Johannesburg • 2010
76.5 × 50.5

Pamella Dlungwana, Woodstock, Cape Town • 2010
76.5 × 50.5

Refilwe Mahlaba, Thokoza, Johannesburg • 2010
76.5 × 50.5

Skye Chirape, Brighton, United Kingdom • 2010
76.5 × 50.5

Thandi Mancane Selepe, Braamfontein, Johannesburg • 2010
76.5 × 50.5

Tumi Mkhuma, Katlehong, Johannesburg • 2010
76.5 × 50.5

Tumi Nkopane, KwaThema, Springs, Johannesburg • 2010
76.5 × 50.5

Zukiswa Gaca, Makhaza, Khayelitsha, Cape Town • 2010
76.5 × 50.5

Debora Dlamini, KwaThema Community Hall, Springs, Johannesburg • 2011
76.5 × 50.5

Des're Higa, Vredehoek, Cape Town • 2011
76.5 × 50.5

Lungile Cleo Dladla, KwaThema Community Hall, Springs, Johannesburg • 2011
76.5 × 50.5

Pam Dlungwana, Vredehoek, Cape Town • 2011
76.5 × 50.5

Phumzile Nkosi, Vosloorus, Johannesburg • 2011
76.5 × 50.5

Sebo Shabalala, Umlazi, Durban • 2011
76.5 × 50.5

Siya Mcuta, Cape Town Station, Cape Town • 2011
76.5 × 50.5

Sunday Francis Mdlankomo, Vosloorus, Johannesburg • 2011
76.5 × 50.5

Tinashe Wakapila, Harare, Zimbabwe • 2011
76.5 × 50.5

Vile Asanda Fanti, Stockholm, Sweden • 2011
76.5 × 50.5

Vuyelwa 'Vuvu' Makubetse, KwaThema Community Hall, Springs, Johannesburg • 2011
76.5 × 50.5

Xana Nyilenda, Newtown, Johannesburg • 2011
76.5 × 50.5

Zanele Muholi, Vredehoek, Cape Town • 2011
76.5 × 50.5

Ayanda Magoloza, Kwanele South, Katlehong, Johannesburg • 2012
76.5 × 50.5

Collen Mfazwe, August House, Johannesburg • 2012
76.5 × 50.5

Karabo Sebetoane, Parktown, Johannesburg • 2012
76.5 × 50.5

Kekeletso Khena, Green Market Square, Cape Town • 2012
76.5 × 50.5

Lesego Thwale, Constitution Hill, Braamfontein, Johannesburg • 2012
76.5 × 50.5

Mpumi Moeti, Kwanele South, Katlehong, Johannesburg • 2012
76.5 × 50.5

Nhlanhla Esther Mofokeng, Katlehong, Johannesburg • 2012
76.5 × 50.5

Phila Mbanjwa, Pietermaritzburg, KwaZulu-Natal • 2012
76.5 × 50.5

Sizile Rongo-Nkosi, Glenwood, Durban • 2012
76.5 × 50.5

Thembela Dick, Vredehoek, Cape Town • 2012
76.5 × 50.5

TK Thembi Khumalo, BB Section Umlazi Township, Durban • 2012
76.5 × 50.5

Ayanda Magoloza, Thokoza Township, Johannesburg • 2013
76.5 × 50.5

Bathini Dambuza, Tembisa, Johannesburg • 2013
76.5 × 50.5

Candice Nkosi, Tsakane, Johannesburg • 2013
76.5 × 51

Lebo Leptie Phume, Daveyton, Johannesburg • 2013
76.5 × 50.5

Lerato Dumse, Parktown, Johannesburg • 2013
76.5 × 50.5

Stesh Gonya, Parktown, Johannesburg • 2013
76.5 × 50.5

Tumi Nkopane, KwaThema, Johannesburg • 2013
76.5 × 50.5

Vuyelwa 'Vuvu' Makubetse, Daveyton, Johannesburg • 2013
76.5 × 50.5

Xana Nyilenda, Los Angeles • 2013
76.5 × 50.5

ZaVa I, Paris • 2013
50.5 × 76.5

ZaVa III, Paris • 2013
50.5 × 76.5

ZaVa IV, Bordeaux • 2013
60 × 60

Charmain Carrol, Gaborone, Botswana • 2014
76.5 × 50.5

Inkanyiso I, Paris • 2014
50 × 33.3

Le Sishi, Parktown, Johannesburg • 2014
76.5 × 51

Lee Siba, Parktown, Johannesburg • 2014
76.5 × 51

Mfana, London • 2014
20 × 13.5

Miss Tee Menu, Parktown, Johannesburg • 2014
76.5 × 51

Nathi Dlamini at the After Tears of Muntu Masombuka's funeral, KwaThema, Springs, Johannesburg • 2014
Photograph, C-print on paper
100 × 67

Nosi 'Ginga' Marumo, Roodepoort, Johannesburg • 2014
76.5 × 50.5

Refiloe Pitso, Daveyton, Johannesburg • 2014
76.5 × 50.5

Sharon 'Shaz' Mthunzi, Daveyton, Johannesburg • 2014
76.5 × 50.5

Sharon 'Shaz' Mthunzi, Daveyton, Johannesburg • 2014
76.5 × 50.5

Somandla, Parktown, Diptych (I) • 2014
50 × 33.3

Somandla, Parktown, Diptych (II) • 2014
50 × 33.3

Somnyama I, Paris • 2014
80 × 53.3

Vukani I, Paris • 2014
80 × 50.8

Yaya Mavundla, Parktown, Johannesburg • 2014
76.5 × 51

Zodwa, Paris • 2014
80 × 48.8

Babhekile II, Oslo • 2015
50 × 37.7

Bester I, Mayotte • 2015
70 × 50.5

Bester IV, Mayotte • 2015
80 × 57.8

Bester V, Mayotte • 2015
50 × 41

Bona, Charlottesville • 2015
80 × 50.6
Purchased with funds provided by the Africa Acquisitions Committee 2017

Bona II, Charlottesville, Virginia • 2015
29 × 50

Futhi Mkhize, Durban • 2015
76.5 × 50.5

Lerato Dumse, Brooklyn, New York • 2015
76.5 × 50.5

Luh Cele I, Umlazi, Durban • 2015
76.5 × 50.5

Luh Cele II, Umlazi, Durban • 2015
76.5 × 50.5

MaGesh Zungu, Brooklyn, New York • 2015
76.5 × 50.5

MaID in Harlem, African Market, 116 St • 2015
50 × 40

Menziwa Biyela, Verulam, Durban, KwaZulu-Natal • 2015
76.5 × 50.5

Nolwazi II, Nuoro, Italy • 2015
60 × 44.5

Pastor Fezeka Royo, Durban • 2015
76.5 × 50.5

Sharon 'Shaz' Mthunzi, Oslo, Norway • 2015
76.5 × 50.5

Sibusiso, Cagliari, Sardinia, Italy • 2015
80 × 56

Somnyama IV, Oslo • 2015
100 × 83
Purchased with funds provided by the Africa Acquisitions Committee 2017

Thabile Mbatha, Maitland, Cape Town • 2015
76.5 × 50.5

Thando II Nuoro, Sardinia, Italy • 2015
80 × 52.6

Thembeka I, New York Up-
state • 2015
49.6 × 38.6
Purchased with funds provided
by the Africa Acquisitions
Committee 2017

Thembekile, Parktown •
2015
79.9 × 61.6
Purchased with funds provided
by the Africa Acquisitions
Committee 2017

Thulani II, Parktown • 2015
50 × 36.2

Tinashe Wakapila, Durban
• 2015
76.5 × 50.5

Vile, Gothenburg, Sweden
• 2015
80 × 66.3

Vile Fanti, Gothenburg, Sweden • 2015
76.5 × 50.5

Basizeni XI, Cassilhaus, North
Carolina • 2016
80 × 60.9

Bathini Dambuza, Parktown,
Johannesburg • 2016
76.5 × 50.5

Bhekezakhe, Parktown •
2016
50 × 35.9

Bhekisisa, Sakouli beach,
Mayotte • 2016
52 × 100

Faniswa, Seapoint, Cape Town
• 2016
80 × 64.7

Fezekile IV, Cincinnati •
2016
50 × 37.8

Fisani, Parktown • 2016
80 × 56.7

Julile I, Parktown, Johannesburg • 2016
65.8 × 100

Karabo Sebetoane, Parktown,
Johannesburg • 2016
76.5 × 50.5

Kwanele, Parktown • 2016
80 × 68.5

Lebo Leptie Phume, KwaTh-
ema, Springs, Johannesburg
• 2016
76.5 × 50.5

Lebo Mashifane, Tsakane,
Johannesburg • 2016
76.5 × 50.5

Luh Cele, Durban • 2016
76.5 × 50.5

Makhethi S Ndaba, Consti-
tution Hill, Johannesburg •
2016
76.5 × 50.5

Mbali Pearl Zulu, KwaThema,
Springs, Johannesburg • 2016
76.5 × 50.5

Namhla at Cassilhaus, Chapel
Hill, North Carolina • 2016
80 × 53.3

Nontuthuzelo Mduba,
Parktown, Johannesburg •
2016
76.5 × 50.5

Ntozabantu VI, Parktown
• 2016
80 × 53.5

Ntozakhe II, Parktown •
2016
100 × 71.8

Phila I, Parktown • 2016
80 × 53.5

Phila Mbanjwa, Pietermaritzburg, KwaZulu-Natal • 2016
76.5 × 50.5

Phindile Madlala, Durban,
KwaZulu-Natal • 2016
76.5 × 50.5

Phumzile Nkosi, Johannes-
burg • 2016
76.5 × 50.5

Sebenzile, Parktown • 2016
Vinyl wallpaper

Senzekile II, Cincinnati •
2016
60 × 42.6

Skye Chirape, Amsterdam
• 2016
76.5 × 50.5

Smangele Mzizi, Constitution
Hill, Johannesburg • 2016
76.5 × 50.5

Sosi Molotsane, Parktown,
Johannesburg • 2016
76.5 × 50.5

Teekay Khumalo, Umlazi
township, Durban • 2016
76.5 × 50.5

Thembela Dick, Parktown,
Johannesburg • 2016
76.5 × 50.5

Thobeka Bhengu, Cincinnati,
United States • 2016
76.5 × 50.5

Thulile II, Umlazi, Durban
• 2016
50 × 41

Viola May, Durban • 2016
76.5 × 50.5

Xiniwe at Cassilhaus, North
Carolina • 2016
80 × 62.2

Zabantu I, Boston • 2016
60 × 56.3

Zamile, KwaThema • 2016
100 × 78

Zanele Muholi, Parktown,
Johannesburg • 2016
76.5 × 50.5

Zhane Mkhize, Durban •
2016
76.5 × 50.5

Ziphelele, Parktown • 2016
60 × 55.8

Bellinda Ndandani, Gu-
gulethu, Cape Town • 2017
76.5 × 50.5

Bester VII, Newington Green,
London • 2017
80 × 56.5

Boitumelo Mnguni, KwaThe-
ma, Johannesburg • 2017
76.5 × 50.5

Christine Madonsela, Daveyton, Gauteng • 2017
76.5 × 50.5

Collen Mfazwe, Daveyton,
Gauteng • 2017
76.5 × 50.5

Enzokuhle Mtolo, Pieter-
maritzburg, KwaZulu-Natal
• 2017
76.5 × 50.5

Hiya, The Square, Cape Town
• 2017
27.8 × 25.6

Khumo Pulumo, Parktown,
Johannesburg • 2017
76.5 × 50.5

Lindelwa Lids Nyiki, New
Brighton, Port Elizabeth •
2017
76.5 × 50.5

Londeka Siba Dlamini, Central, Port Elizabeth • 2017
76.5 × 50.5

Lulamile, Room 107 Day Inn
Hotel, Burlington • 2017
40 × 29.3

MaID, Delaware • 2017
60 × 40

Matseko Mahlaba, KwaTh-
ema, Springs, Johannesburg
• 2017
76.5 × 50.5

Mellisa Mbambo, Durban
South Beach • 2017
Photograph, C-print on paper
100 × 67

Monde Phatlane, Daveyton,
Gauteng • 2017
76.5 × 50.5

Mpho Mtsweni, KwaThema,
Springs, Johannesburg • 2017
76.5 × 50.5

Nomthandazo Mohotlhoane I,
KwaThema, Springs, Johannesburg • 2017
76.5 × 50.5

Nomthetho Vingi, Arcadia,
Port Elizabeth • 2017
76.5 × 50.5

Nonkululeko 'Mercury'
Duma, Pietermaritzburg,
KwaZulu-Natal • 2017
76.5 × 50.5

Pastor Fezeka Royo I, City
Hall, Johannesburg • 2017
76.5 × 50.5

Phumzile Qenge, Daveyton,
Johannesburg • 2017
76.5 × 50.5

Portia Karlsen, Pietermaritzburg, KwaZulu-Natal • 2017
76.5 × 50.5

Progress Selota II, Pretoria
• 2017
76.5 × 51

Pumelela Nqelenga, Pietermaritzburg, KwaZulu-Natal
• 2017
76.5 × 50.5

Thembela Dick II, Cape Town
• 2017
76.5 × 50.5

Thobeka Bhengu, London
• 2017
76.5 × 50.5

Tumi Mkhuma I, Katlehong,
Johannesburg • 2017
76.5 × 50.5

Wamkelwa January, Cape
Town • 2017
76.5 × 50.5

Xoli Ngqeme, Daveyton,
Johannesburg • 2017
76.5 × 50.5

Yaya Mavundla I, Parktown,
Johannesburg • 2017
76.5 × 51

Zandile Malinga, Daveyton,
Gauteng • 2017
76.5 × 50.5

Eva Mofokeng, Braamfontein,
Johannesburg • 2018
Vinyl wallpaper

Indlovukazi Mapule, Durban
• 2018
76.5 × 50.5

Lena, London • 2018
120 × 80

Mellisa Mbambo, Durban •
2018
76.5 × 50.5

Nonhle Kunene, Durban • 2018
76.5 × 50.5

**Palesa Mkhwebane, Daveyton,
Johannesburg** • 2018
76.5 × 50.5

Pastor Z. Zungu, Durban •
2018
76.5 × 50.5

**Roxy Msizi Dlamini, Parktown,
Johannesburg** • 2018
76.5 × 51

Sazi Jali, Durban • 2018
76.5 × 51

Tinashe Wakapila, Durban
• 2018
76.5 × 50.5

Babaza III, Philadelphia • 2019
57 × 46.3

**Bangizwenkosi, The Sails,
Durban** • 2019
60 × 40

**Buhlalu I, The Decks, Cape
Town** • 2019
69 × 51

Buzile, ISGM, Boston • 2019
59.4 × 58.1

Cwazimula, ISGM, Boston
• 2019
60 × 45.7

Khulumani II, ISGM, Boston
• 2019
60 × 45.5

Labo II, Torino, Italy • 2019
60 × 40

Limise II, Germany • 2019
50 × 33.3

Mnyamezeli II, Torino, Italy
• 2019
Vinyl wallpaper

**Owake, X, Sheraton, Brooklyn,
New York** • 2019
60 × 40

Qhamukile, Mauritius • 2019
100 × 66.6

Qiniso, The Sails, Durban •
2019
39.9 × 26

**Thatha II, Sheraton Hotel,
Brooklyn** • 2019
69.3 × 53.5

Viola May, Venice, Italy • 2019
76.5 × 50.5

Vumani II, Boston • 2019
100 × 100

Zazi II, ISGM, Boston
• 2019
60 × 40

Ziphe, Emhlabeni, Zimbabwe
• 2019
60 × 40

Akeeleh Gwala, Durban •
2020
76.5 × 51

Candice Nkosi, Durban •
2020
Vinyl wallpaper

IMAGE CREDITS

All works by Zanele Muholi unless otherwise stated.
© Zanele Muholi, Courtesy of the Artist, Stevenson,
Cape Town/Johannesburg and Yancey Richardson/New York.

p.60 (left) Commissioned by Autograph, London.

p.81 Photograph by Joan E. Biren (JEB), from Joan E. Biren Papers.
© 2020 JEB (Joan E. Biren).

p.83 (right) *Constructs #10* from Constructs, Suite of Four
(#10,#11,#12,#13), 1989. Vintage silver gelatin prints. Overall
dimensions installed: 86 × 197 in. (218.44 × 500.38 cm). *Constructs
#10* paper dimensions: 77½ × 48 in. (196.9 × 121.9 cm). Edition of 3,
2 APs. © Lyle Ashton Harris. Courtesy of the artist and Salon 94,
New York.

p.85 (above) © Rotimi Fani-Kayode, Courtesy Autograph, London.

p.114 C-print. Image size: 20.9 × 31.4. Paper size: 24.6 × 35.

p. 115 (above) C-print. Image size: 33 × 49.5. Paper size: 43 × 59.5.
Edition of 5 + 2 APs.

p.118 © Carrie Mae Weems. Courtesy of the artist and Jack
Shainman Gallery, New York.